Part One
CONSERVATION

To James and Rachel, whose future is in this book

For UK order queries: please contact Bookpoint Ltd, 39 Milton Park, Abingdon, Oxon OX14 4TD. Telephone: (44) 01235 400414, Fax: (44) 01235 400454. Lines are open from 9.00–6.00, Monday to Saturday, with a 24 hour message answering service. Email address: orders@bookpoint.co.uk

For USA & Canada order queries: please contact NTC/Contemporary Publishing, 4255 West Touhy Avenue, Lincolnwood, Illinois 60646–1975, USA. Telephone: (847) 679 5500, Fax: (847) 679 2494.

Long renowned as the authoritative source for self-guided learning – with more than 30 million copies sold worldwide – the *Teach Yourself* series includes over 200 titles in the fields of languages, crafts, hobbies, sports, and other leisure activities.

A catalogue record for this title is available from The British Library.

Library of Congress Catalog Card Number: On file

First published in UK 1999 by Hodder Headline Plc, 338 Euston Road, London, NW1 3BH.

First published in US 1999 by NTC/Contemporary Publishing, 4255 West Touhy Avenue, Lincolnwood (Chicago), Illinois 60646–1975 USA.

The 'Teach Yourself' name and logo are registered trade marks of Hodder & Stoughton Ltd.

Copyright © 1999 Nicholas and Rosalind Foskett

In UK: All rights reserved. No part of this publication may be reproduced or transmitted in any form or by any means, electronic or mechanical, including photocopy, recording, or any information storage and retrieval system, without permission in writing from the publisher or under licence from the Copyright Licensing Agency Limited. Further details of such licences (for reprographic reproduction) may be obtained from the Copyright Licensing Agency Limited, of 90 Tottenham Court Road, London W1P 9HE.

In US: All rights reserved. No part of this book may be reproduced, stored in a retrieval system, or transmitted in any form, or by any means, electronic, mechanical, photocopying, or otherwise, without prior permission of NTC/Contemporary Publishing Company.

Cover photo: The Stock Market
Typeset by Transet Limited, Coventry, England.
Printed in Great Britain for Hodder & Stoughton Educational, a division of Hodder Headline Plc, 338 Euston Road, London NW1 3BH by Cox & Wyman Ltd, Reading, Berkshire.

Impression number	10 9 8 7 6 5 4 3 2 1
Year	2004 2003 2002 2000 1999

CONTENTS

Introduction 1

Part One Conservation 3

1 People, environment and conservation **5**
Conservation and environment 5
People and the environment through history 7
Environment and conservation in the twentieth century 11
Green philosophy and green politics 17
Conservation, greenness and the public 20
Activities 20

2 Conservation, development and the world economy **22**
Introduction 22
What is 'development'? 23
Trade, aid and North–South interdependence 28
Sustainability and sustainable development 34
Environmental economics 36
Green consumerism and the 'greening' of business 41
Summary 46
Activities 47

Part Two Environment and Resources **49**

3 The Earth, ecosystems and natural environments **51**
Introduction 51
Ecology, habitats and ecosystems 52
Food webs, energy transfer and productivity 54
Changing ecosystems 57

Harvesting from ecosystems	61
The world's major biomes	62
The natural environment – a millennium map	70
Summary	70
Taking action	71
Activities	72

4 People, resources and the environment — 73

Introduction	73
Global population	73
Resources	81
Resources, population and development	82
Summary	85
Taking action	86
Activities	86

5 Energy and resources — 87

Patterns of energy use	87
Energy use and conservation issues	90
Energy extraction and resource limits	90
Stretching resources	93
Alternative energy resources	96
Energy use and environmental impact	100
Summary	102
Taking action	103
Activities	104

6 Biodiversity, conservation and natural habitats — 105

Introduction	105
Biodiversity as a conservation issue	106
Conserving ecosystems	108
Strategies for conserving natural habitats	115
Biosphere reserves – case studies	116
Soils, soil conservation and people	119
Summary	122
Taking action	122
Activities	123

7 | Animals, plants and biodiversity — 124
Introduction — 124
Conserving endangered species — 124
Species conservation – the international perspective — 127
Species conservation in action — 129
Conservation issues in farming — 134
Summary — 136
Taking action — 137
Activities — 137

8 | The world's seas and oceans — 138
Introduction — 138
Marine ecosystems — 138
Marine resources — 141
Marine pollution — 146
Managing marine environments — 148
Summary — 150
Taking action — 151
Activities — 151

9 | Atmosphere, weather and climate — 152
Weather, climate and conservation issues — 152
The energy of the atmosphere — 153
Modelling the global climatic system — 154
The role of the oceans — 157
Storms and storm tracks — 158
El Niño and the Southern Oscillation — 161
Major climatic zones — 162
Climate change — 165
Summary — 167
Taking action — 167
Activities — 168

10 | Climate change and human impact — 169
Introduction — 169
Ozone depletion — 170
Carbon dioxide and the greenhouse effect — 174
Summary — 180
Taking action — 181
Activities — 181

11 | Managing environment and resources __ 182
Introduction _____ 182
Uncertainty and the precautionary principle _____ 182
Risk assessment and environmental management _____ 183
Quality standards and environmental management _____ 186
Environmental planning techniques _____ 187
Managing environmental developments – a case study 190
Summary _____ 192
Taking action _____ 193
Activities _____ 193

Part Three Politics, conservation and the law _____ 195

12 | Environmental issues and conservation – international perspectives _____ 197
Introduction _____ 197
Global action for conservation _____ 198
The EU and the environment _____ 206
Conservation, the environment and education _____ 210
Summary _____ 212
Activities _____ 213

13 | Environmental issues and conservation – national and local perspectives _____ 214
Introduction _____ 214
Conservation and environmental protection in the UK 214
Environment and conservation in the USA _____ 220
Environment and conservation in the South – the case of India _____ 222
NGOs, environmental protection and politics _____ 225
Grassroots movements and conservation _____ 227
Local conservation in action _____ 228
The green parties _____ 229
Summary _____ 231
Activities _____ 231

14 Conservation, environment and the future — 232
Introduction — 232
Priorities for action — 232
Political will — 235
Think global, act local — 236
Sustainability and the city — 237
In conclusion — 238

Appendix 1 Contacting conservation groups — 239

Appendix 2 Bibliography — 243

Index — 245

INTRODUCTION

This book has been written to provide a broad introduction to conservation. It is divided into three parts. Part One examines some of the key ideas and concepts in conservation. Part Two focuses on the science of the environment and the processes that need to be understood to be able to undertake conservation in practice. Part Three looks in more detail at some of the recent trends in the politics of conservation by considering national and international examples of environmental practice, policy and law.

1 PEOPLE, ENVIRONMENT AND CONSERVATION

Conservation and environment

Recent decades have seen the growth of interest in, and concern for, the environment. Driven by media coverage of important environmental events, such as the release of radioactivity over large areas of northern Europe by the meltdown of the Chernobyl nuclear reactor in the Ukraine in 1986, or the possible health impacts of increased nitrates in groundwater, there has developed a growing awareness of the potential impact on people's lives and futures. Concerns about an 'environmental crisis' have been raised by scientists from a wide range of disciplines (chemistry, biology, atmospheric science). These concerns have been publicly presented and argued by environmental organizations such as Greenpeace, Friends of the Earth, and the Sierra Club, and have been placed on the agenda of governments in many countries. The global conferences on the environment, from Stockholm in 1972 to Rio de Janeiro in 1992 and Buenos Aires in 1998, have brought together politicians and environmentalists and have raised the profile of environmental issues through debate in the public arena.

Such concerns raise strong arguments for reducing, halting or reversing changes to the environment resulting from human activities. This is the field of **conservation**, which focuses on protecting environments from damaging change. Conservation is not preservation (i.e. it does not imply 'no change'), but instead involves careful management of the Earth's resources. Protecting the **environment** is often interpreted as referring to 'nature', and those parts of people's living space which are natural – rivers, the soil and land, plants, animals and the atmosphere. While concern about this **natural environment** (or **physical environment**) is a key part of conservation, the environment of most people is entirely a human landscape, the product of centuries of human use. Farming landscapes, cities and even many seemingly 'natural' landscapes are simply human creations. While some of these created **human environments** are the very evidence of environmental crises, many are as important a part of people's environment and culture and are as much in need of conservation as entirely natural environments. Conservation of valued buildings, parklands and historical areas of towns and cities is as important, therefore, as the conservation of virgin rainforest.

The word 'conservation' is one which has gone in and out of fashion. During the 1960s and 1970s it was widely used to describe any activities involved in preserving the environment. However, its use began to imply attempts to prevent change and 'fossilize' environments, so the term became less fashionable, and was replaced by phrases such as 'environmental protection' or 'environmental management'. Its use has revived in more recent years, though, as the range of ideas covered by the word conservation has become recognized. Conservation means many things:

> **Protection** Many environments are under threat from human activity. The drainage of wetland areas in many parts of the world, for example, threatens to destroy those environments and the species that live in them or depend on them. Preventing such loss, and attempting to protect that environment is a key aim of conservation.
>
> **Preservation** The needs of future generations, for resources, for an environment that is not harmful to human health, and for an environment that is spiritually and individually stimulating, provide an important reason for conservation. This is the aim of preservation. Preservation does not imply that there should be *no* change in an environment, but that its essential characteristics and the species that live there should survive. A key role, for example, of zoos or nature reserves is the preservation of threatened animal and plant species and their genetic resources (biodiversity). While preservation may be important to maintain the character of landscapes and environments, keeping as wide a range of plants and animals

as potential new sources of materials or drugs may be important for the future of humanity.

Restoration Conservation includes the restoration and repair of environments damaged by people or animals. The work of many local conservation groups in planting woodland, clearing ponds and restocking rivers after pollution incidents are examples of conservation through restoration.

Management The management of the environment involves attempting to allow human use of the environment while minimizing the impact and damage that it may cause. It can include any or all of the ideas of protection, preservation and restoration. An important idea within environmental management is that of **sustainable development**. This idea is examined in more detail in Chapter 2, but refers to the use of the environment while protecting it for the future.

Management, of course, involves trying to deal with competing claims between, for example, those wishing to change an environment and those wishing to preserve it without change. It is, therefore, likely to be a site of conflict between different groups of people with differing aims and views, and brings conservation into the world of politics and decision-making. Conservation is not simply about understanding the science of the environment and using that to protect, preserve and restore habitats and environments. It is also about working with individuals and groups of people at all scales, from local to global, to make decisions and choices that reflect the needs of the environment as well as the needs of people. Conservation is, therefore, a highly political activity involving governments, businesses, environmental groups and the actions of every individual human being. Figure 1.1 shows how conservation relates to science, politics, economics and ethics.

People and the environment through history

People have always used and abused their environment. Early humans were happy to kill wild creatures for food and other resources and to protect the family from danger, and waste was

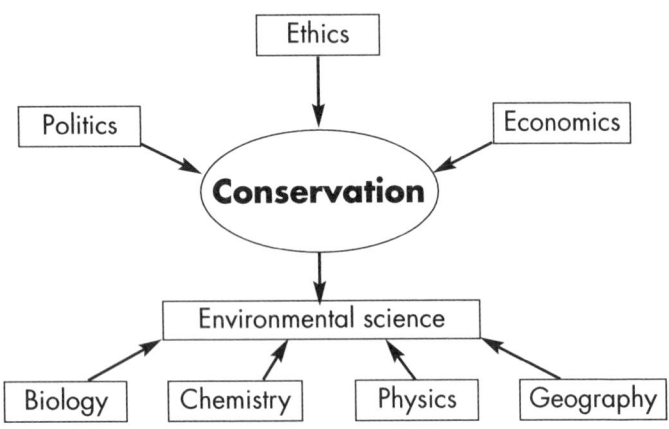

Figure 1.1 Conservation and its links to other disciplines

simply discarded. The impact on the environment was extremely small, however, for the technology available to change the environment was very limited, and the total population of people was very low. At the time of Christ the population of the world was only approximately 50 million, compared to 6 billion by the end of the twentieth century. At the same time the amount of energy consumed by each person for their daily life was only about 5% of that which will be used each day per person in the year 2000. Concern about the environment and the damaging impact of human activity is thus a relatively new idea.

Throughout human history people have had a relationship with **nature**. This has always included a view of nature as providing food, shelter, clothing and other basic resources, but has often extended to a spiritual or 'religious' view of nature. The power of natural forces, and the inability of humans to have much impact upon them, bestowed a mystery and veneration of nature. Nature had (and has) power over the whole of human life and existence. Nature has always been viewed as 'dangerous', and fear of the forces of nature, of wild animals, and of disease are commonly found in writings throughout history. Towns and villages were viewed as places of safety, protected from the 'wilderness' of nature, and the valuing of wild areas for leisure and recreation emerged in the Western world only in the nineteenth century. In many parts of the less developed world such images of the threat of nature are still the dominant view.

Throughout human history in the West four main views of nature's relationship with people can be identified:

Stewardship of nature

This idea develops from the view that the human race is special amongst all living things, placed within nature by God, but with a special responsibility for the care and protection (**stewardship**) of nature. Its roots lie strongly not only in the Jewish and Christian traditions, but in the faiths of Islam, Buddhism and Hinduism. This perspective is well demonstrated by the story of Noah's Ark, with the instruction from God to Noah to save and protect living creatures from the disaster of the flood.

Imperialism over nature

This perspective dominated western ideas of nature in the eighteenth and nineteenth centuries, but has roots that can be traced back to early Christian and Jewish writings. Its main idea is that people can develop the technology to exploit nature and to overcome its threats and challenges. Indeed, Francis Bacon (1561–1621), the founder of modern philosophy, suggested that the conquest of nature is the greatest aspiration humans may have. Such a view underpins much of the attitude to nature of the agricultural and industrial revolutions in the West, and is well summarized in the writings of the British social critic Thomas Carlyle in 1829:

> ... this age of ours ... is the Age of Machinery .... We remove mountains and make seas our highway: nothing can resist us. We war with rude Nature; and ... come off always victorious and loaded with spoils.

Romanticism and nature

Romanticism is associated with art, music, literature and poetry of the late eighteenth and early nineteenth centuries, and has strong themes of the value of nature for itself and its contribution to the quality of human life beyond the mere provision of resources. The poetry of William Wordsworth, the paintings of John Constable, the work of landscape gardeners such as Lancelot 'Capability' Brown, and the music of Ludwig van Beethoven provide a romantic view of the natural world, and project it strongly as amongst the triumphs of God's creation. Nature moves from being perceived as wild, dangerous and threatening to being wild but beautiful and of great importance to the human spirit and existence.

Utilitarianism and nature

The utilitarian view of nature can be traced to the writings of the philosophers John Stuart Mill (1806–73) and Jeremy Bentham (1748–1832). Its key ideas are that infliction of pain or damage on any living thing is inherently wrong, and that life should be about the pursuit of actions that provide the greatest balance of pleasure over pain. This has both a hedonist and a moralist component. Hedonism is the philosophy which sees the pursuit of pleasure as the main purpose of life. In relation to nature it would suggest that sustaining nature, including marvellous landscapes and different species, is important to underpin the pursuit of satisfaction in human life in both material and spiritual terms. The moralist component relates to the protection of life for its own sake. The abolition of the slave trade in the West in the nineteenth century can be linked to such a view. The extension of this view to all living things, however, is an important part of utilitarianism, and the origins of animal welfare and animal rights movements can be traced philosophically back to such a view.

The roots of modern conservation and environmentalism can be identified in each of the perspectives described above, and by the end of the nineteenth century a number of organizations had emerged that began to transfer these philosophies into action on behalf of the natural environment. Zoological societies and scientific societies interested in natural science developed during the nineteenth century, and the world's first national park at Yellowstone in the USA was established in 1872. In the UK, the late nineteenth century saw some of the first environmental legislation and interest groups being established, such as the 1872 Commons and Footpaths Act and the National Trust, an independent society established to protect both landscape and property of historical and cultural value, formed in 1894. The administration of Theodore Roosevelt in the USA (1901–9) might be identified as the first to take a governmental interest in nature and conservation, and the passing of the Newlands Reclamation Act (1902) is an early example of environmental protection legislation in that country.

Environment and conservation in the twentieth century

The twentieth century has seen the growth of interest in conservation amongst both individuals and governments. Four important aspects of this development can be identified.

Government environmental bodies and national legislation

The pace of the growth of environmental concern by government has varied from country to country, but all of the world's nations now have their own environmental bodies and legislation. In the UK, for example, the first statutory body concerned with conservation was the Nature Conservancy (now English Nature), established shortly after World War II, and formal legislation began with the 1949 National Parks and Access to the Countryside Act, which created national parks and nature reserves. By 1968 a separate government Department of the Environment had been established, with responsibility for legislation. In the USA the federal government established the Environmental Protection Agency in 1970, and environmental legislation is promoted at both federal and state level.

Non-governmental organizations (NGOs) and conservation

Early concern about environmental matters and conservation was expressed by groups of individuals setting up organizations, often in the pursuit of a single interest. In the UK, for example, the Royal Society for the Protection of Birds (RSPB) was established in 1904, and in most countries such non-governmental bodies are now numerous, ranging from national organizations to local and community groups. Internationally, four such NGOs have been of particular importance in promoting conservation issues and campaigning for the environment – the Sierra Club (founded in the USA in the 1960s), Greenpeace (founded in Canada in 1970), Friends of the Earth (founded as a splinter group of the Sierra Club in 1970), and the World Wide Fund for Nature, previously the World Wildlife Fund, founded in 1961.

The strategies and tactics used by such NGOs range from education to campaigning, to political lobbying and to direct action. Although direct action is rare, it generates a high media profile and, in some cases, negative public opinion. In 1995 members of Greenpeace took over the redundant oil platform *Brent Spar*, on its way to a dumping site in the North Atlantic, to protest at the potential marine pollution that would result from its disposal in this way. While the publicity persuaded the oil company to produce an alternative plan for disposing of the platform, negative publicity about the accuracy of Greenpeace's claims damaged the organization's image for some time. Direct action by NGOs can also generate strong reaction from governments if the activity seeks to prevent government-supported or funded projects. In 1985, for example, the Greenpeace ship, *Rainbow Warrior*, was sunk in Auckland harbour, New Zealand, by French secret forces to prevent it interfering with nuclear testing in the Pacific by the French government. The negative publicity for the French government and for their nuclear testing programme was substantial.

International co-operation on conservation

International co-operation between governments on environmental issues dates principally from the establishment of the United Nations Organization (UNO, or UN) after World War II. Through the UN, a number of international organizations have been created. These have included organizations specifically charged with environmental matters and those with a broader interest which includes environmental issues. For example, the International

Union for the Conservation of Nature and Natural Resources (IUCN – now the World Conservation Union), established in Switzerland in 1948, and the United Nations Environment Programme (UNEP), have a prime environmental concern, while the Food and Agriculture Organization (FAO), and the World Meteorological Organization (WMO) have wider briefs. Such UN bodies have been important in establishing international conferences on environmental matters such as those in Stockholm (1972) and Rio de Janeiro (1992), and have supported international agreements such as the Montreal Protocol (1987) on reducing carbon dioxide emissions into the atmosphere. The UN, however, is not the only source of international pressure, for many other groups of states have made environmental agreements. As early as 1940 states in the Americas signed the Conservation on Nature Protection and Wildlife Preservation in the American Republics, and since the 1970s the European Union has operated a strong environmental protection strategy built around a series of environmental action programmes.

Benchmark events in conservation

An important driving force in the developments outlined above has been the fact that environmental issues and conservation matters have attained a high public profile during the last half century. A number of events and incidents have brought concerns about the environment into the media, so that both individuals and governments have begun to consider environmental issues as a matter of priority. While each individual's environmental conscience may be been awakened by specific events, a number of major incidents have attracted sufficient attention to be seen as environmental 'benchmark' events. These events have stimulated clear responses by pressure groups, by the public and then by government through the development of legislation or environmental policy. Some of these key events, and the response they generated, are detailed below.

The DDT debate (1962)

Publication of the book *Silent Spring* by Rachel Carson drew attention to the effects of DDT, a pesticide accumulating in the bodies of birds and passing along the food chain from plants to insects and higher animals. It demonstrated the problem of the unintentional side-effects of human interference with natural systems, and raised questions about the effects of 'technological fixes'. Growth of environmental groups during the 1960s and 1970s was in part the result of concern over the unseen impacts of human activities.

The first lunar landing (1969)

The landing of *Apollo* on the moon stimulated a widening interest in space and the cosmos, and provided the first good photographs of Earth from space. This recognition of the enclosed nature of Earth was an important step in understanding the interaction of land, sea, atmosphere and people in a global ecosystem. It gave rise to the idea of 'spaceship Earth' – the view that there is a finite resource base on which we all depend for survival. In addition to demonstrating the 'wholeness' of the Earth as the human environment, the notion of the 'stewardship of nature' as a moral and spiritual responsibility for human beings was one of the strong emotions generated by the space programme.

The 1970s oil crises

The substantial raising of oil prices by the world's oil producers under the auspices of OPEC (the Organization of Petroleum Exporting Countries) on two occasions in the early 1970s drew the attention of the industrialized nations to the limited nature of non-renewable resources and the dependence on those resources for sustaining their standard of living and quality of life. The concepts of sustainable development and the search for alternative energy sources of a more long-term nature were strongly influenced by these events. A number of direct consequences of the oil crises have contributed to environmentalism and conservation.

Firstly, the issue of future resource use was discussed in an important publication in 1974, *The Limits to Growth*, written by an international group known as The Club of Rome (Meadows et al, 1972). This examined trends in resource usage and consumption in comparison with known resources. In particular it considered the relationship between demographic trends (birth rates, death rates and population growth rates) and food supply, industrial production, resource availability and the production of pollutants.

The model produced predicted major global resource issues by the end of the twentieth century. In particular, the likelihood of starvation, economic crisis caused by high resource prices (especially for energy sources such as oil and coal), and the potential for global conflict resulting from this, was emphasized. The team concluded that people still had a chance to strive for more sustainable resource use, but that we needed to act swiftly to increase the chances of success. Although developments in technology and the discovery of new sources of oil meant the predictions have not been fulfilled, the book raised key questions about future resource use.

Secondly, these questions were taken up in a number of international events during the 1970s and 1980s. In 1972 the first UN Conference on the Human Environment was held in Stockholm, at which the importance of international co-operation on environmental protection and the importance of developing sustainable economies was emphasized. In 1980 the World Conservation Strategy was published by the IUCN, which emphasized the importance of maintaining biodiversity and reducing environmental damage to species and their habitats. In 1983 the UN World Commission on Environment and Development (WCED) was established under the chairmanship of Gro Harlem Brundtland, and was charged with identifying ways forward to promote sustainable development. It was the report of the Brundtland Commission (*Our Common Future*) in 1987 which lead ultimately to the Earth Summit in Rio de Janeiro in 1992.

The Bhopal (1984) and Chernobyl (1986) disasters

Major pollution incidents resulting from accidents at industrial sites have raised key questions about the need for environmental protection. Explosions at a chemical factory in Bhopal in India in 1984 caused many deaths and long-term illnesses. Similarly, the meltdown and destruction of the Chernobyl nuclear power station in the Ukraine in the (then) Soviet Union, resulted in 32 immediate deaths, the evacuation of 130,000 people, and large-scale environmental impact. The true death toll from such a major environmental catastrophe will never be known. Large areas around the reactor were left uninhabitable, and the effect of radiation 'fallout' was felt as far away as Scandinavia and the British Isles. In the UK, sales of meat from sheep reared in affected upland pastures continued to be banned in the late 1990s. This disaster emphasized the potential impact of failure in a nuclear power system, and the wide geographical spread of fallout. The international nature of pollution and its lack of respect for international boundaries was clearly emphasized.

Major oil spills

The transport of crude oil by sea using very large tankers (very large crude carriers – VLCCs) has resulted in a number of accidents and major pollution incidents. In 1967 the tanker *Torrey Canyon* was wrecked off the coast of Cornwall, UK, releasing 117,000 tonnes of crude oil into the sea. Large numbers of seabirds and marine animals were killed and the impact on the tourist industry of beach pollution was extensive. In the USA the wreck of the *Exxon Valdez* off the coast of Alaska in 1989 released 10 million gallons of crude oil, leading to the deaths of almost 400,000 birds. The consequence of such disasters has been to raise questions about the legal obligations of business corporations, the development of the 'polluter pays' principle, and has led to calls for greater environmental protection legislation.

Weather extremes of the 1980s and 1990s

Attention has been drawn by the media to many extreme weather events across the world, which, it has been suggested, have in part been the result of human impact on climate. In the UK, for example, a series of weather extremes emphasized the potential impact of climate change. Severe storms in 1987 (The Great Storm of October 15th) and 1990 (the Burns Day Storm of January 24th) preceded a series of years with much warmer and drier weather than normal in the 1990s. In North America the occurrence of extreme hurricane events in the Caribbean and southern USA (for example Hurricane Mitch in 1998) has also raised questions in public debate about whether this was evidence of climate change produced by human impact on the atmosphere – were these the evidence of global warming and the greenhouse effect?

The ozone hole

A thinning of the ozone layer in the atmosphere over Ar first identified in 1979. Ozone (O_3) is an important component of the atmosphere in that it filters out 'harmful' ultraviolet energy from the sun. By the late 1980s the extent of this depletion during the Antarctic spring (September/October) was emphasized, and in 1989 similar depletions were found over the northern hemisphere. The loss has been attributed to chemical reactions between the ozone and chlorofluorocarbons (CFCs) released from the use of aerosol sprays, refrigerants, and other industrial activities. The direct links between industrialization, pollution and large-scale environmental damage appeared to be shown clearly by this discovery, raising fears of the impact of the ozone hole on human health.

The Rio Summit (1992) and beyond

In 1992, the UN Conference on Environment and Development was held in Rio de Janeiro, Brazil. The political leaders of most of the world's nations were present, and a number of significant agreements on the development of environmental policy and conservation strategies were signed, most notably the Rio Declaration and Agenda 21, an agenda for action on the environment and development for the twenty-first century. Follow-up meetings in Kyoto, Japan in 1997 and in Buenos Aires, Argentina in 1998 have emphasized the need for international co-operation on environmental matters, and have raised the profile of key issues within the media.

Green philosophy and green politics

The growth of environmental awareness and concern has been labelled 'environmentalism' by the media and attributed to a so-called 'green movement'. There is regular discussion of the 'greening of government', the 'greening of business' or the growth of 'green politics'. In reality, though, the 'green movement' is highly diverse, with many groups having radically different views about the environment, the steps that should be taken for onservation, and the way that people should relate to their environment. As Brown (1990) has said, 'Environmentalism is a diverse and often deeply divided movement with attitudes that ... are often irreconcilable'.

In broad terms, environmentalism has two main schools of thought – ecocentrism and anthropocentrism. **Ecocentrism** is a view that at all times people must live in accordance with their position as part of the environment, in harmony with nature. It has no confidence in modern technology providing anything more than delays to the destruction of the environment. **Anthropocentrism**, on the other hand, believes in the power and inventiveness of people in overcoming the limits of nature. One element of this view is **technocentrism**, which emphasizes the technological skills and advances of human beings and believes that the environment can be both exploited and conserved by the development of appropriate technology. Using this broad division, a simple classification of 'greenness' can be developed.

Deep green

This viewpoint has developed from the ideas of 'deep ecology' introduced by the Norwegian philosopher and environmentalist Arne Naess. It stresses the need to return to living in harmony with nature and rejects many of the technological developments of the twentieth century. It believes that sustainability is possible only with simple technologies, and that these can be supported only by small self-reliant communities. A key component of these ideas is that of 'green rights', and the recognition of the rights of animals and plants as well as those of humans. It sees humans as a part of nature, not apart from nature. Deep greenness is a strongly ecocentric philosophy.

Shallow green

This perspective is less ecocentric than 'deep greenness', but still emphasizes the importance of working in harmony with nature. The use of 'appropriate and alternative technology' (i.e. simple, environmentally sound technologies such as wind power and organic farming) is emphasized, as is the need to check the environmental effects of every activity people undertake (**eco-**

auditing). Business and commerce is acceptable providing it operates in an environmentally healthy way, but there is a focus on small, community-based organizations and government. It believes that the harmful excesses of people on the environment can be controlled by setting limits on environmental use and penalties for those who flout these limits.

Dry green

'Dry greenness' is a technocentric view which believes that the use of science, and reliance on scientific principles and the understanding of the science of the environment, can enable people to 'manage' the environment and use it sustainably while maintaining a high standard of living. It favours the use of existing political and economic systems with appropriate government regulation to promote environmental well-being and conservation.

'Greenness' is not only a philosophy, though, for environmental issues have become an important part of politics and political debate. The growth of 'green politics' has been a characteristic of the Western democracies since the 1970s, and has had three key strands. Firstly, the establishment of political parties dedicated to environmental matters grew out of 'Die Grunen', an environmentalist party formed in West Germany. Similar parties were founded elsewhere, with variable success in democratic elections – in 1983 the Green Party in West Germany polled more than 5% of the votes in national elections, as did the Green Party in elections to the European parliament in the UK in 1989. Overall, the success of such parties has been limited, though, and their political role has declined in response to the second strand, the 'greening' of traditional political parties. Most traditional parties, whether right wing, left wing or centrist, now profess and seek to demonstrate strong environmental principles in their policies, and have captured the green vote back from the environmental parties.

The third strand is the politics of 'direct action', developed by diverse environmental groups, and often based on single issues. Such **radical environmentalism** has been demonstrated on many occasions, for example:

- anti-nuclear demonstrations (for example, in protest at the establishment of nuclear missiles at the Greenham Common airbase in England during the late 1980s);
- road construction protests, such as the actions of those protesting against the building of the Newbury by-pass road in the UK, finally opened in 1998;
- protests and direct action against the building of the Narita airport in Japan (1966–78);
- the activities of animal rights campaigners.

Such political action is linked most strongly to groups with strongly ecocentric philosophies.

Conservation, greenness and the public

Concern for the environment and an interest in conservation amongst the public has grown substantially since 1960 in the West and continues to grow in less developed countries too. A MORI poll in 1995 in the UK suggested that 90% of people made their consumer choices with some consideration of environmental issues, 60% undertook some recycling of household materials, 25% were actively interested in environmental issues in the media, and 5% were active in environmental activities. In the USA over 50% of people support the aims of the environmental movement. However, Down (1984) has shown that interest in and concern for the environment depends on the occurrence of important environmental incidents, and wanes when there is no 'headline environmental news' or when economic concerns are at a high level. Environmentalism can be thought of as a fashion philosophy. Developing wider understanding of environmental issues is, therefore, an important part of the environmental educational policies proposed by, for example, Agenda 21 and the EU.

ACTIVITIES

1 Identify an environmental issue in the media that is attracting national interest (for example, a pollution incident or a road construction project). Collect as much information as you can and try to identify:

  a What is happening and why.

  b Which groups of people have an interest in the event, what their different viewpoints are, and why they have these views.

  c What is being proposed to mitigate against environmental damage arising from the event.

2 Do the task outlined in Activity 1, but this time for an issue which is of interest only locally, perhaps recorded in your local newspaper.

3 Use your local telephone book to identify the conservation and environmental groups in your locality. Contact them for information on their activities, and try to identify why they operate as they do and what they are seeking to achieve.

2 CONSERVATION, DEVELOPMENT AND THE WORLD ECONOMY

Introduction

The growth of concern about conservation issues over recent decades has become entwined with questions about 'development', both in the more wealthy countries of the West, known as **developed countries (DCs)** or **more developed countries (MDCs)**, and in the poorer countries of the world known as **less developed countries (LDCs)**. This is because environmental problems are often a by-product of economic growth. In MDCs, for example, the development of industry and transport has used natural resources prolifically and produced damaging air and water pollution. As economies have grown, so the amount of resources used and the pollution produced have increased.

As LDCs seek to expand their economies there is a risk of similar environmental problems arising. It is not just economic *growth* that can lead to environmental problems, though. While low levels of economic development may mean that communities are living in harmony with their environment, as shown by some of the native tribes living in the rainforests of the Amazon basin in Brazil, poverty, especially when combined with population growth, can lead to over-exploitation of fragile environments. Soil erosion and tree loss in some parts of LDCs may be the result of growing populations taking marginal land into farming, or clearing woodlands for firewood.

Aspiring to an improvement in quality of life, however, is a universal human view. If such improvements demand increased economic development then pressures on the environment will also increase unless that development is managed carefully. Indeed, some conservation groups argue that no economic development is possible without environmental damage resulting. This chapter examines the link between environment and development, and the issues that their connection raises.

What is 'development'?

Development has traditionally been taken to mean *economic* development – increasing the amount of wealth that a country produces. This is achieved by expanding production from agriculture, industry or service activities, and engaging in trade with other countries. One of the most common measurements of development is **gross national product per capita (GNP per capita)**. This is the total value of all the goods, products and services produced by a country in one year, divided by its population. Table 2.1 shows the GNP per capita for a number of countries. The gap in wealth between the richest and poorest nations is very large, with GNP per capita in the wealthiest countries almost 100 times greater than that in the poorest nations. One of the main aims of development for most countries is to increase their GNP per capita.

GNP per capita, however, is not the only **development indicator** that can be used, for many other aspects of the economy or society tell us something of development. Indicators showing aspects of health (such as life expectancy, hunger, disease, and the number of hospitals and doctors) may be used, as may education indicators such as the proportion of the population educated to primary or secondary levels, and levels of literacy. Other economic indicators include the proportion of the population employed in agriculture, industry or services. Examples of some of these other indicators are also shown in Table 2.1. Many of these, of course, simply reflect the wealth of a country and its impact on the lives of its people. The wealthier a country is, the more it can spend on health care and education, for example. However, these indicators also stress that development is not just about increasing wealth – it is also about improving the **quality of life** of individuals and societies.

The importance of quality of life has been emphasized by an alternative view of what development means. **Human needs-centred development** is an idea, first proposed by Dudley Seers in

Table 2.1 Indicators of 'development' – some global contrasts in the mid-1990s

Country	GNP per capita ($)	Life expectancy (years)	Literacy rate at age 15 (%)	Infant mortality rate (deaths/1000 live births)
UK	18060	75	99	9
USA	24740	78	99	9
Australia	14400	76	99	8
India	320	56	34	100
China	360	70	81	43
Sweden	23750	77	99	6
Saudi Arabia	7050	62	50	72
Bangladesh	220	56	37	120

1969, which sees development for most people as being increasing satisfaction with a variety of human needs. Seers identified eight 'conditions' for human needs-centred development to be occurring:

1. low levels of poverty;
2. low levels of unemployment;
3. relative equality amongst people in society;
4. democracy in political life;
5. true national independence;
6. good literacy and educational levels;
7. relatively equal status for women and their participation in all aspects of society;
8. sustainability to meet future needs.

To take this into account a useful indicator of development, the **Physical Quality of Life Index (PQLI)**, has been developed. This combines three indicators of quality of life for each country to give a broader picture of development from the point of view of people living in that country. The three indicators are:
- *life expectancy*, which is the average age to which a new-born child can expect to live. In MDCs this is typically 75–80 years, while in the poorest countries it is as low as 40 years;
- *infant mortality*, which is the number of children per thousand born who die in the first year of life. In wealthy countries this is as low as seven or eight per thousand, while in some LDCs this figure is as high as 150 per thousand;
- *the literacy rate*, which is the percentage of the population able to read. This ranges from almost 100% in some countries to less than 30%, particularly for women in the least developed states.

To calculate PQLI, each of these measurements is calculated so that a value of 100 is the best value amongst all countries, and a value of zero is the worst. Each country's score is then calculated for each indicator on such a scale. The three scores are added together then divided by three for each country, to give a final score out of 100. Most of the rich industrialized countries have a PQLI of over 90, while many of the least developed countries fall below 30. A score of 77 is generally regarded as the basic minimum level of human need. This is achieved by some LDCs (e.g. Argentina), and approached quite closely by others (e.g. Brazil and China), but many have much lower scores.

Which countries are the most and least developed? The UN Human Development Report of 1994 distinguishes five groups of countries according to their level of development, each of which comprises one-fifth of the world's population:
1. The (**MDCs**). These comprise the richest fifth of the world's countries, including, for example, the USA, the UK, Australia, New Zealand and Japan, who between them have 85% of the total world GNP and 85% of world trade.

2 The **oil-exporting countries**. The wealth of these countries is based mainly on the export of oil, and their wealth has been created mainly in the last 50 years. This group includes countries such as Saudi Arabia, Kuwait and Libya, and many have a GNP per capita equivalent to that of the MDCs.
3 The **newly industrialized countries (NICs)**. These are countries whose economic growth has been very rapid as a result of recent industrial and trade development. This group includes the so-called 'tiger economies' of Singapore, Taiwan and South Korea, whose growth in the last 20 years has been amongst the fastest in the world.
4 The **debtor countries**. These are countries which have borrowed large sums of money from the MDCs and have, therefore, accumulated large international debts. These countries are handicapped from further development by the burden of repaying their debts to the MDCs. This group includes countries such as Mexico, Brazil and Ghana.
5 The **LDCs**. These are the countries with the lowest GNP per capita. This group comprises 35 countries who between them have only 1.4% of the world's GNP, less than 1% of world trade, but 20% of global population. Most of the least developed countries are found in Africa, and include Chad, Malawi and Madagascar.

This description of countries according to their level of development is only one of many which are used. In the 1950s the term '**Third World**' came into use, originally meaning countries that were neither Western and wealthy, such as the USA and the UK (the First World) nor lead by communist/socialist political regimes, such as those in eastern Europe and the Soviet Union (the Second World). Because most of such countries were less economically developed, however, the term soon came to be used for all LDCs, irrespective of their political system. In 1980 the **Brandt Report**, produced by an international commission on world trade and development chaired by Willy Brandt, introduced yet another set of

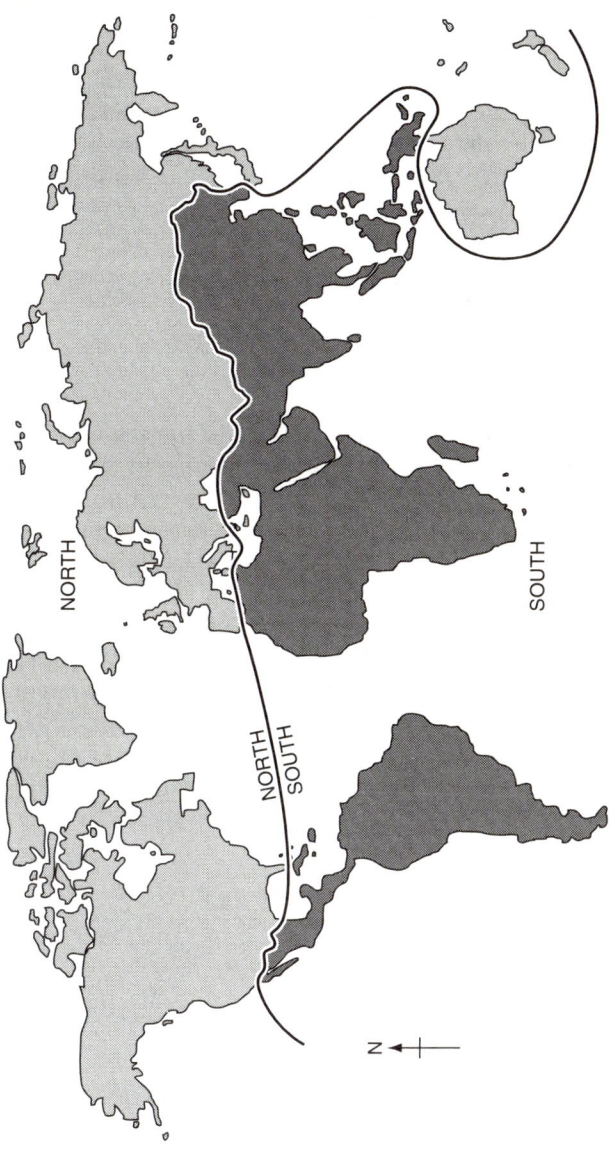

Figure 2.1 The North–South divide

terms, distinguishing the countries of **the North** from those of **the South**. The North comprises countries with advanced and developed economies, while the South comprises the world's less advanced countries. This **North–South divide** was clearly expressed in the map produced by the Brandt Report (Figure 2.1). It is important to note that, despite their geographical position, Australia and New Zealand are included in the North because they are economically developed countries.

Trade, aid and North–South interdependence

Interdependence

The 1980 Brandt Report (*North–South: A Programme for Survival*) was important in drawing the world's attention to the way in which the countries of North and South are simply part of an **interdependent** world economy. Trade between countries provides a stimulus to economic growth, and decisions and actions in North or South will impact on the rest of the world economy. Two-thirds of world trade involves the countries of the North, and it is through trade with the countries of the North that many LDCs seek to expand their wealth and income. The Brandt Report emphasized, therefore, that the countries of the North play a critical role in supporting the countries of the South in achieving development and improvements in the quality of life. In particular, government policies on trade and on aid to LDCs were shown to be critical in supporting world development.

There have, traditionally, been two approaches to stimulating development and quality of life improvements in LDCs – **trade** and **aid**.

Development and trade

The pursuit of development by trade amongst LDCs has been an important feature of the world economy in the last century. Much of this development through trade has taken place since the end of World War II, and has been shaped by the **The Bretton Woods Agreement (1944)**. This agreement, signed at Bretton Woods, New

Hampshire, USA by 44 of the world's major trading nations, established four important international organizations:

- The **United Nations**;
- The **World Bank** (properly known as the International Bank for Reconstruction and Redevelopment), whose responsibility is to provide long-term finance for investment by countries;
- The **International Monetary Fund (IMF)**, whose responsibility is to provide short-term assistance to countries in economic difficulties;
- The **General Agreement on Trade and Tariffs (GATT)**, with a responsibility for regulating world trade.

These organizations have provided systems to support economic development around the world, but are largely 'controlled' by the developed countries with the greatest political and economic power. This imbalance was further emphasized by the establishment of the Organisation for Economic Cooperation and Development (OECD) by 25 of the world's strongest trading nations, within which a further concentration of economic power is found in the **Group of Eight (G8)** – USA, Germany, the UK, Canada, France, Russia, Italy and Japan – which is strongly influential in shaping the world economy and trade.

Against this world trade and development framework, a number of different approaches have been taken to pursuing economic development through trade, and many countries have tried to use a combination of these.

The sale of primary products to MDCs

Primary products are goods or materials produced directly from natural resources, such as timber, minerals and foodstuffs. For example, Zambia, in southern Africa, uses its huge resources of copper to generate income from sales to industries in MDCs, Many of the countries of the Caribbean and Central America have economies based on the sale of bananas to the developed world. Dependence on the sale of primary goods, however, can provide problems for LDCs.

Firstly, dependence on selling agricultural products makes countries highly dependent on the vagaries of the weather. Floods, hurricanes and droughts can destroy crops and severely affect the economy. The impact of Hurricane Mitch on the banana crops of Guatemala in 1998, for example, destroyed an important part of the national economy.

Secondly, competition between LDCs keeps the prices low, and the control MDCs have over trade also pushes prices down. As a result, the real price of most primary products has declined over recent decades, even though the price of the goods manufactured from them has gone up. The price of tea, for example, fell by over 50% from 1950 to 1990, leading to reductions in income to tea-growing countries. Only where producers can join together to raise or maintain prices can this be resisted, as in the case of the Organization of Petroleum Exporting Countries (OPEC), which has traditionally managed to maintain fairly high prices for oil. By the late 1990s, however, even the strength of OPEC could not prevent oil prices falling to levels not seen for 30 years.

Economic development through the sale of primary products can have important environmental effects. In order to compete in the market, countries may be forced to exploit their raw materials and agricultural products at very low costs, or without managing the natural environment with care. In many of the countries of Southeast Asia, for example, the clearance of tropical forests for the sale of timber to MDCs has resulted in a number of environmental problems, including soil erosion, loss of animal and plant species, and changes to streamflow and local climate. In parts of Brazil and Venezuela, forest has been cleared for pasture land to graze cattle to supply beef to Europe and North America, and has produced similar environmental consequences.

The development of heavy industry

The economic growth of Europe and North America was built on the heavy industries of iron and steel making and engineering. Some countries have sought economic growth by following a similar path. The countries of eastern Europe (Poland and former Eastern Germany, for example) chose to use their reserves of brown coal to fuel a heavy industrial base. However, the high sulphur content of the coal and the lack of environmental controls resulted in severe environmental pollution to rivers, the atmosphere and damage to the land. Air pollution, producing acid rain, caused forest damage in neighbouring countries, and dealing with the impact of such pollution became a major challenge for governments in these countries during the 1990s.

The development of a consumer goods industry

A third approach to economic growth has been through developing consumer goods industries to export products to MDCs. From an early base making cheap plastic and electrical goods and textiles, many countries, such as Taiwan and South Korea, have grown to become major manufacturers of electronic goods, cars and higher value consumer goods such as jewellery. Until the late 1990s the economy of South Korea, for example, had grown at a rate of more than 5% per year for nearly three decades. While some of these industries are relatively clean, many use materials made by heavy industry, which in turn may cause substantial pollution problems. The air and river pollution in major cities in the newly industrialized countries (Taipei in Taiwan, and Seoul in South Korea, for example) provides a major environmental problem.

Development through tourism

The tourist industry is one of the world's major employers, and the growth of 'long haul' tourism has been rapid in the last two decades. Many LDCs have seen tourism as an important source of income, and as a way of diversifying their economies away from primary products. As a result they have encouraged tourists for beach holidays (for example, in the West Indies), holidays visiting historical and cultural sites (for example, Aztec sites throughout Mexico), or tourism involving viewing spectacular landscapes or wildlife (for example, in the game reserves of East Africa).

Although the income generated is important to national and local economies, a number of environmental issues arise from increasing tourism. Firstly, the construction of holiday resorts on the coast may both damage sensitive environments and lead to increased levels of pollution from sewage disposal. In southern Turkey, for example, concern over the loss of the breeding grounds of the Mediterranean turtle because of tourist development caused substantial objection from environmental groups. Secondly, the encouragement of large numbers of tourists into a small number of important sites ('tourist honeypots') may cause damage to the very sites the visitors have come to see. In Nepal, the impact of 'trekking' tourists on the sites they stay in has caused considerable concern about soil erosion and pollution.

Dependence on tourism is just as unstable as dependence on exports, for it can be badly affected by political instability in a country or the economic circumstances in the MDCs from where the tourists come. The tourist industry in The Gambia, in West Africa, was severely damaged as a result of a military coup in 1994–5, and is only now recovering.

The problem of international 'debt'

To find the initial finance to set up an industrial base or to pay for improvements in agriculture or infrastructure (roads, water supply, etc.), many LDCs have borrowed money from the developed world nations. Some of this is provided directly by governments, either from one country to another (**bilateral loans**), or through international organizations such as The World Bank providing finance from many member states (**multilateral loans**). Some is provided directly by banks and financial organizations in the developed world. Changes in the world economy, failure of the loans to generate enough growth in the borrower country, increasing interest rates in MDCs or the misuse of the loans in the LDCs have resulted, however, in many countries failing to repay their loans. The burden of debt has become very large for some countries, with Mexico, Brazil and Argentina having debts amounting to almost 75% of their annual GNP. Brazil borrowed large sums during the 1970s to fund a period of rapid economic growth. The effect of rises in oil prices, increases in interest rates and economic recession in the developed world and the restriction of access to some Western markets such as the EU through taxes and tariffs has caused the debt to grow rapidly. By the mid-1990s Brazil's debt was nearly $150 billion. Paying back the loans and the interest on them has become a major international issue. 'Servicing' the loans can use much of the wealth generated by the economy, resulting in little benefit to the country and its people. From an environmental and conservation perspective this means that pressure to use natural resources increases and there is less money to pay for environmental protection and conservation.

Many of the world's development NGOs have been campaigning for large international debts to be cancelled by MDCs, to break the debt problem. While this would allow countries to channel future wealth into real development, and would enable some environmental protection to take place, many Western governments believe it would be very damaging to world finance systems for such debts to be unpaid, and would encourage other countries to borrow money with no intention of repaying it.

The impact of debt on the environment has been recognized through '**Debt for Nature**' swaps. These involve a country having some of its debt cancelled and some additional finance provided at low rates of interest, as long as that funding is used for environmental protection and conservation. Such swaps have as yet not been widespread, and have lead only to the cancellation of US $1 billion of debt globally, mostly in the countries of Latin America.

Development through 'aid'

'Aid' is the provision of assistance to LDCs either as non-repayable grants or as 'soft' loans with very low rates of interest (if any), and is usually in the form of finance and technical assistance (for example through the work of engineers, health workers or teachers). Most is provided by **Official Development Assistance** (**ODA**) through governments and international agencies, but much is provided by NGOs and charitable organizations. The UN has set a target for MDCs to use 0.7% of their GNP for ODA, but few countries reach that target. Globally, Saudi Arabia is the most generous provider of ODA, using 4% of its GNP for this purpose, but the average amongst OECD countries is only 0.4%.

There are strong arguments both for and against 'aid' to assist development. Its benefits are that:
- aid stimulates development at low cost to LDCs;
- aid is an expression of the moral obligations of MDCs to assist LDCs;

- by stimulating growth in LDCs, aid can have direct trade benefits to MDCs;
- aid directed through NGOs and charities can be focused on those people and projects where it can have most impact;
- aid is a form of recognition that many of the problems stem from colonial exploitation of resources in LDCs by MDCs.

However, aid also has a number of disadvantages, which opponents of the aid system use:

- aid often does not reach those most in need;
- aid makes countries dependent on MDCs and removes the drive to 'self-help';
- aid is often misused by corrupt or inefficient governments;
- aid is often tied to the purchase of high-technology goods and equipment from MDCs.

All of the arguments used for and against aid are true to some extent and its value depends on how it is used in each specific situation. From a conservation point of view, aid may be beneficial or harmful. It is often an efficient source of development assistance targeted on local projects supporting community activities to manage environmental problems – for example, in tackling issues of soil erosion from overgrazing in the Sahel countries of Burkina Faso and Niger. However, where it is used for large projects such as dam construction (for example, in the construction of the Pergau Dam in Malaysia – using British aid), it may be seen to be environmentally harmful.

Sustainability and sustainable development

Increasing quality of life through economic development is a clear goal of every national government on Earth. Concern about the impact of such growth on the environment, however, is one of the major issues that economic development raises. Is there a way of both conserving the environment and achieving improvements in people's standard of living and quality of life? Are policies which limit growth for the sake of the environment realistic, when some countries are condemned to poverty through inequalities of growth that have persisted for decades?

In 1984 the UN established the WCED, under the chairmanship of Gro Harlem Brundtland from Norway, to consider ways of combining development with long-term environmental strategies. In their report, entitled *Our Common Future*, published in 1987, they emphasized the importance of the idea of **sustainable development**.

The Brundtland Commission defined sustainable development as:

> Development which meets the needs of the present without compromising the ability of future generations to meet their own needs.

While this appears at first sight to be a straightforward idea, there are many very significant implications of moving towards sustainable development. Sustainable development requires that economic decisions are taken with reference to environmental issues and the principles of ecology, and that each society must live within the limits that its environment imposes on it. This does not mean that sustainable development is about 'no growth', but that each society must recognize the limits to growth which are necessary. In particular, only growth that does not deplete environmental resources at a rate faster than the environment can replenish itself can be sustained. This raises critical challenges to politicians and governments to move the culture in all aspects of the economy and trade towards emphasising sustainability. The Brundtland Commission, for example, indicated that the pursuit of sustainable development would require:

- a political system that involves effective participation by all citizens;
- a system of agriculture, mining and industry that has an obligation to preserve the environment and biodiversity;
- an international system of trade and finance that fosters sustainability;
- an emphasis on social justice which addresses poverty.

A common misunderstanding about sustainability and sustainable development is that it is 'anti-industry' and 'anti-business', for it seeks to limit economic growth. However, the 1984 World Industry Conference on Environmental Management (WICEM) demonstrated that this was not the case by stressing two important issues:

1. Although business may be the cause of many environmental problems, the abilities and creativity of business means that it will also play a key part in generating workable technical and economic solutions to many environmental problems.
2. The environment 'business' is in itself an important part of the whole business world, and many commercial opportunities will arise from conservation and environmental constraints, for example in developing 'environmentally friendly' goods or providing services to environmental management.

The idea of sustainable development has become central to discussions of environment and development, and underpinned the agreements at the Rio Earth Summit in 1992 and the development of many national policies for development that emerged in the 1990s. The pursuit of sustainable development and its achievements so far are considered in Chapters 12 and 13.

Environmental economics

The establishment of sustainable development requires governments, politicians and business to re-examine the ways in which they look at the operations of trade, production and the economy. In particular they need to build consideration of environmental factors into economic and accounting models, and to apply the principles of **environmental economics**. Environmental economics stresses the fact that the economy operates by extracting natural resources from the environment, processing them into more useful and valuable products and distributing them for use, but that at each stage it must dispose of large amounts of waste. The economy, therefore, is underpinned by the operation of ecological systems. While the whole field of environmental economics is beyond the scope of this book, a number of important principles can be identified:

- monetary appraisal methods;
- the Constant Natural Assets Rule; and
- the use of economic instruments.

Monetary appraisal methods

Classical economics gives no value to most environmental 'goods', such as clean air, clean water and beautiful landscapes. The cost of the loss of such environmental 'goods', or damage to them, is not built into the accounting systems used to calculate the price that should be charged for goods. Seeking to calculate the price or value of such goods in known as monetary appraisal.

Firstly, there are the direct costs or values within the system. For example, plans to develop an area of land for planting for forestry will include monetary calculations of the income that might be expected from the project through, for example, selling the timber, selling venison from deer in the forest, selling shooting rights in the forest or income produced from visitors coming to the forest for recreation. Set against this will be the costs of establishing and managing the forest such as the purchase of the land, the cost of employees, the charges for borrowing money to establish the project and the cost of buying-in expertise from foresters, landscape designers, etc. For each of these, calculations are fairly simple. In addition some indirect costs and benefits to society as a whole can be calculated for the project – for example, the savings on imported timber, or the benefits of providing jobs in a rural area.

Secondly, there are also many indirect 'non-market' factors, which are not usually allocated a price but which should be included in the costing model. These include:

- the 'value' of a new woodland wildlife habitat;
- the 'value' of increasing biodiversity in the area;
- the 'value' of stabilizing the soil against soil erosion;
- the 'value' of providing shelter to surrounding farmland by the trees;
- the 'cost' of losing a grassland habitat and its species;

- the 'cost' of increasing the acidity of the soil by planting conifers;
- the 'value' or 'cost' of changing the landscape scene from grassland to woodland.

Thirdly, there are so-called 'non-use' values: the value (cost) which needs to be added in for retaining the environment in its natural state – i.e. untouched. This may be because of its beauty or wilderness value.

Environmental economists have sought ways to evaluate the 'monetary value' of such items which might otherwise be valued as 'free', and a number of approaches can be described here:

Opportunity costs

These calculate the value that must be foregone in order to retain something of environmental value rather than use it for another purpose. For example, the cost of planting a recreational forest can include the cost of *not* using the land for arable farming.

Dose–response methods

These can be used to calculate the likely cost of pollution from a development. It is possible to measure the reduction in yields in crops or fish, for example, from different levels of pollution, and to use this as a model. In other situations this model can be used to estimate the cost of different levels of pollution output from a proposed new factory.

Contingent valuation methods

These involve asking people to say what they would be willing to pay, in theory, for the preservation of an environmental benefit (e.g. a beautiful landscape), or what compensation they would be willing to accept for its loss.

Hedonic pricing methods

These involve calculating how house prices differ according to how much of an environmental 'good' they have access to. For example, houses with views of broad-leaved trees have higher values than identical houses which do not.

The Constant Natural Assets Rule

The traditional way of deciding whether projects should be allowed to take place is the use of **cost–benefit analysis (CBA)**. This measures the costs of a project and the value of the benefits and, if the benefits outweigh the costs, the project will be allowed. However, traditional approaches to CBA do not include a sustainability element (i.e. any inclusion of the need to ensure that environmental resources will not be lost in the process). New approaches to CBA suggest that the **Constant Natural Assets Rule (CNA)** should be applied, which involves including in the calculation the cost of passing on to future generations a stock of natural assets (an **environmental capital bequest**) no smaller than exists at present. For example, building a road across a wildlife site must include the cost of creating a replacement elsewhere, such as reclaiming an area of waste land as a new habitat reserve. Similarly, clearing a forest for timber must include the cost of replanting a similar area of woodland. Although, in principle, this is a worthy objective, ensuring that the quality of the replacement is as high as the original environment is difficult to assess, and it is easy to be wise after the event!

The use of economic instruments

The methods described above are ways of trying to build in some measure of the cost and value of the environment or of environmental damage. A more direct approach, however, is to use direct economic measures to either charge a cost to individuals or organizations causing environmental damage or reduce charges for those taking actions that do not damage the environment. Several methods are currently in use or being considered by governments.

Emission charges

This approach includes charging businesses according to the amount or volume of waste they produce and its environmental impact – the so-called 'polluter pays' principle. In the UK a charge is made on waste material disposed of in landfill sites to encourage reduction in waste or increase in recycling of goods.

Product charges

Product charges are taxes levied on goods that have a high environmental cost, and are used to try to reduce the amount of that product being bought. An example proposed in a number of countries is the idea of a carbon tax (see Chapter 4), in which a tax on fossil fuel consumption would be passed on to consumers as higher prices.

Fiscal (tax) incentives

This approach allows individuals or companies taking action to protect the environment to have a reduced tax burden. Examples would include giving allowances for installing 'cleaner technologies' in a manufacturing company, or, as in the UK, imposing lower taxes on lead-free fuel or on cars with smaller engines.

Pollution fines

Fines are imposed on those breaching pollution levels. Most of the world's nations use such measures to penalize companies causing pollution incidents.

Tradeable emission permits

To reduced the amount and level of pollutants, governments can allow such pollution by companies only where they are given a 'permit' or 'licence'. Such permits indicate the limits of pollution that may be generated. No business could produce such pollutants without a government licence, but the permits would be tradeable between companies. Discussion of developing such tradeable permits at an international level in relation to carbon dioxide and greenhouse gas emissions have been an important element of recent world climate conferences. In this way, countries seeking to develop more polluting industries would need to purchase a permit on the open market from a country with a reducing level of atmospheric pollution.

Green consumerism and the 'greening' of business

Becoming 'green'

How far has concern for the environment and conservation developed in society? We can consider this by looking at how the attitudes and behaviours of people and business has changed, and whether 'green' issues affect the ways they make decisions, live their lives, and operate their businesses. Becoming 'green' is not a simple process, but a number of features of 'being green' can be identified:

- developing a concern for the well-being of people in other countries and cultures;
- developing a concern for the well-being of future generations;
- developing a concern for the environment, and seeing the environment as an important component of human well-being;
- seeking to use sustainable approaches in all aspects of economic life;
- developing a concern about equity and fairness in societies around the world;
- supporting open participatory political systems and government;
- shifting away from an emphasis on consumption towards concern for conservation;
- emphasizing the importance of 'quality of life' rather than simply 'standard of living'.

Public understanding of conservation

An important part of the greening of business and industry is the changing attitude of consumers to environmental matters. Public interest in the environment varies from year to year, increasing when a significant environmental issue has been covered in the media and decreasing when economic and (un)employment issues are more prominent. The peak of interest in the 1970s resulting from the impact of the OPEC oil crisis was followed in the 1980s by a general decline in interest as the gloomy environmental forecasts of the 1970s failed to occur and as global economic recession became established. The late 1980s and early 1990s saw a re-emergence of environmental interest as a result of:

- environmental disasters such as forest fires in Southeast Asia and the impact of famine in Ethiopia;
- international debate about the environment through, for example, the 1992 Earth Summit;
- the involvement of high-profile personalities in environmental matters – for example, the singer Sting's concern for environmental impacts on native peoples in Brazil, and Bob Geldof's 'Band Aid' charity to ease famine in Ethiopia.

Overall, though, over this period there has been a steady increase in the concern for green issues amongst the public. In the UK, a Gallup poll in 1982 showed that 50% of the population believed that environmental protection was more important than tackling economic problems, while a similar poll by MORI in 1989 suggested this figure had increased to over 60%. By the mid-1990s membership of environmental groups in the UK exceeded 5 million people, or nearly 10% of the population. Growth in public interest in the environment is important, for individuals push society towards pro-environment actions in two ways:

1. As *consumers* they make day-to-day decisions about purchasing products.
2. As *citizens* they participate in political processes in making choices in elections or actively engaging in politics, in community activities, and in the operation and management of the businesses and public organizations for which they work. The decisions of large corporations, for example, result from the decisions and choices of individuals who are directors, managers and shareholders in those companies.

Green consumerism

Four types of 'green consumer' have been identified in the marketing world:

- *Green activists.* These represent some 5–15% of the population in MDCs, and are those who are active supporters of environmental organizations.
- *Green thinkers.* This group includes the green activists but also those who will usually actively make choices of products and services to 'help the environment'. It includes about 30% of the population in most MDCs.
- *Green consumer base.* This represents 45–60% of the population and includes people who have changed their consumption patterns to reflect concerns about environmental matters.
- *Generally concerned.* This represents 90% of the population and includes all those who express some concern about environmental issues.

'Green consumers' are not a single group of people, therefore, and vary in how and why they make consumer decisions. Research in the USA by Mintel suggests that, overall, 50% of consumers are willing to change the brands of goods they buy to choose more 'environmentally-friendly' products, and 20% are willing to pay higher prices (typically up to 7% more) to ensure the products they buy are 'green'. Other 'green' approaches, though, are used by consumers, including the following:

- Buying second-hand goods or extending the life of consumer goods.
- Consumer boycotts, in which goods deemed unacceptable are not purchased. The boycotting of some companies selling baby milk in protest at their alleged policies of promoting the sales of formula infant feeds in LDCs, for example, was a high-profile consumer campaign.
- Direct consumer protest, including campaigning against businesses perceived as operating policies and practices that are damaging to the environment. The protests in the UK in the mid-1990s against the export of live animals to Europe for slaughter included protesting at companies and at port installations involved in the trade.
- Recycling goods and packaging.

Surveys of business have shown that companies recognize that 'green' decision-making has become important in the market place, and that companies must respond to the pressure of green consumerism.

The 'greening of business'

Concern for the environment in the business community is not new. In 1971 the international computer business IBM developed a formal corporate environmental policy, and by the late 1970s the Blue Angel 'eco-labelling' scheme had been introduced in West Germany. In 1984 the first World Industry Conference on Environmental Management (WICEM I) was held, which stimulated the development of the 'Business Charter for Sustainable Development' drafted by the International Chamber of Commerce (ICC) and launched at WICEM II in Rotterdam in 1991. Most of the world's major corporations and national chambers of commerce are now signatories of this charter, which includes agreements to:

- recognize environmental management as one of the highest priorities for companies;
- integrate environmental policies into every business;
- improve company environmental performance;
- educate and train employees in environmental management;
- adopt the 'precautionary principle' in the development and manufacture of products – i.e. act with caution and proceed only when research into possible negative consequences on the environment has been completed;
- be open to public questioning about environmental performance.

By 1992 almost all companies in Germany had developed a corporate environmental policy, but in other countries of Europe this was less widespread (50% in Holland and 20% in the UK). By the end of the 1990s, however, most companies in the UK have undertaken some form of environmental audit, and in the USA almost half of new products launched have a 'green' component in their marketing.

CONSERVATION, DEVELOPMENT AND THE WORLD ECONOMY

Business is experiencing three main pressures to 'go green'. Firstly, the direct influence of government through environmental protection legislation and the use of financial measures provides a legal obligation to develop environmental policies. Secondly, the influence of 'stakeholders' is very important, with pressure to change coming from customers, trading partners, the community, employees, investors, insurers, the media and environmental pressure groups. Thirdly, there are direct business benefits of developing environmental concern, which include:

- improving the efficiency of use of energy and raw materials reduces costs in the long term;
- reducing waste reduces the costs of waste disposal;
- improved company image enhances sales;
- access to the growing market for 'green' products, estimated to be worth $200 billion globally by the year 2000;
- improved staff commitment to the company;
- cheaper finance and insurance because of the reduced risk of litigation for environmental damage.

By the mid-1990s general surveys of business markets showed that companies with strong 'environmental policies' underpinned by effective conservation practice and environmental management were generally increasing their market share and making higher profits than businesses that were less 'green'. A survey by the finance company James Capel, for example, showed that of the top 1000 companies the 14 'most green' out-performed their competitors by an average of 31% in profits.

A concern often raised by environmental groups, however, is that the 'greening' of business is simply a cynical attempt to gain competitive advantage, rather than a real and permanent shift in business attitudes. In particular, they fear that economic priorities will always outweigh environmental concerns, and that during times of recession or economic pressure companies will simply revert to traditional ways of operating. Peattie (1992) has distinguished different types of green organization:

- 'green looking' organizations;
- organizations with 'green products';

- organizations with 'green marketing';
- organizations with 'green processes and policies';
- green organizations, which have embedded the key principles of the ICC Charter into their operation.

Only with the last two of these organizations is persistence of green operations almost certain under external economic pressures.

Summary

Conservation and the protection of the environment cannot be considered without including issues of economic growth, poverty, social development and human rights, so that development and environment are intertwined ideas. As it is the economic systems that operate around the world which generate most environmental issues, conservation is dependent on identifying what changes can be made to those systems to minimize environmental impacts. Pressure to integrate economic and environmental policies has come both through international government activities, such as the Brundtland Commission, and through changes in the attitudes of individual people as consumers and citizens. This, in turn, affects the ways in which businesses can operate and in which political choices are made.

Concern about conservation and development raises issues of social and moral responsibility, both for individuals and for business and political organizations. It is possible to identify a number of trends in relation to such responsibilities that the green movement of the last two decades has promoted:

1. An increase in the concern of organizations to openly address moral and ethical issues.
2. A shift from a sole concern with 'profit maximization' to a concern with 'quality of life'.
3. Sustainable development is a central aspect of international policy and is based on three ideas:
   - *environment* – the environment is not 'a free good';
   - *equity* – differences in quality of life between North and South are key global issues and must be addressed;
   - *futurity* – all current human activities must include consideration of the future,

emphasizing long-term sustainability rather than short-term gains.
4 A recognition that business and industry is simply part of the community and must reflect the ethical and moral values of that society.
5 Globalization means that such ethical and moral responsibilities for individuals, businesses and other organizations extend to the international arena.

The second part of this book examines the components of the global environmental system and considers how people have impacted on them and are seeking to manage them as resources for the future.

ACTIVITIES

1 In your own home, identify those products that come originally from the less developed world (for example tea, coffee, tropical timber such as mahogany, electronic goods). How much of your current lifestyle appears to be dependent on international trade between MDCs and LDCs?

2 For one of the products you identified in Activity 1, make contact with both the retail company from which you purchased it (the shop or supermarket) and the company that imports or manufactures it in your own country. Ask each organization to identify how it applies 'green' principles to its trade in that product, and how it addresses environmental issues.

3 Choose a less developed country which interests you. Try to draw up a profile of that country's economy and the environmental and development issues that it faces. Possible sources of information include yearbooks, atlases, encyclopedias, websites, NGOs, national embassies or consulates, UN data books (held in most libraries). How closely are the environmental and development issues linked?

4 Consider how far the ways in which you buy products match the following purchasing principles for sustainability:
   a Buy only what you need.

b Buy quality, to avoid frequent replacement.
c Buy local, to reduce transport and the use of preservatives.
d Buy in bulk to reduce packaging and reduce purchase journeys.
e Buy for energy efficiency, for example using low-energy light bulbs.
f Buy for simplicity, by avoiding goods that do more than you need or which are unnecessarily decorated.
g Buy recycled or recyclable products.
h Avoid disposable goods.
i Choose environmentally-friendly goods, such as non-aerosol cleaners.
j Minimize packaging.

Part Two
ENVIRONMENT AND RESOURCES

3 THE EARTH, ECOSYSTEMS AND NATURAL ENVIRONMENTS

Introduction

The space flights of the 1960s and the landing of people on the Moon in 1969 gave the first views of the Earth from space. After centuries of geographical exploration and discovery it was possible to see the Earth as a whole, and the view emphasized that the Earth is a small, self-contained world in space. With the exception of light from the sun, and the occasional meteorite impact, the Earth is self-sustaining, and all life on the planet must survive using the resources within, on the surface of, or in the atmosphere above, it.

As far as we can tell, what makes the Earth unique is that it supports 'life' and living things. The first creation of life, some 3 billion years ago, and its evolution and survival since then, is the result of natural processes at work involving energy from the Sun (and from within the Earth), minerals and water. These processes maintain life and enable it to change over time. Living things, in turn, interact with each other and with their environment, causing further changes to the character and distribution of life. Overall, therefore, the Earth supports a complex 'web' of natural processes and life that provides the environment in which human beings survive.

So complex and sophisticated is the 'web' that some scientists and philosophers have developed the idea of the Earth as a single living thing, which controls and keeps in balance all life on the planet – not through conscious, intelligent or divine thought, but through the processes at work in the environments it creates. This view of the Earth, developed by James Lovelock, is known as the **Gaia Hypothesis**, named after the Greek goddess of the Earth. This hypothesis emphasizes that people are simply part of the Earth system, are subject to its rules and operating laws, and will survive long-term only by living in harmony with those natural systems.

This chapter describes some of the key processes, the environments they produce and the impact of people on those environments.

Ecology, habitats and ecosystems

The study of living things and their environments is the science of **ecology**, a word first used by the German scientist Haeckel in 1869, but a field of study that became important in science from the 1930s onwards. Ecology emphasizes that plants and animals not only live within a particular environment but are also affected by the environment and, in turn, may cause changes in that environment.

The environment within which a plant or animal species lives is called its **habitat**, and is made up of both living and non-living parts, or components. The habitat of a freshwater fish such as a pike, for example, comprises the lake in which it lives – the water, the minerals in the water, the gases in the water such as oxygen, the rocks and minerals of the lake bed and banks – and the other living things in the lake, ranging from weed to rushes to single-celled diatoms, other fish, lake insects and birds that live on the fish.

The living and non-living components of such a habitat continuously interact with each other. To help to understand these interactions the idea of an **ecosystem** has been established by scientists. An ecosystem comprises the plants, animals and non-living components that exist together in a particular location, together with the processes that operate in that environment. In the case of the pike and its lake, the lake ecosystem would comprise the pike's habitat together with all the processes supporting and affecting life in the lake, such as respiration, reproduction, the flow of water into and out of the lake, rainfall and temperature, and the feeding of fish on insects and weed. Ecosystems can be of any size – a small puddle is just as much an ecosystem as is a forest or a lake; on a much larger scale, the whole of the Mediterranean Sea is an ecosystem, as is the whole of the tropical rainforest of Brazil. Figure 3.1 illustrates the idea of an ecosystem, using a pond as an example.

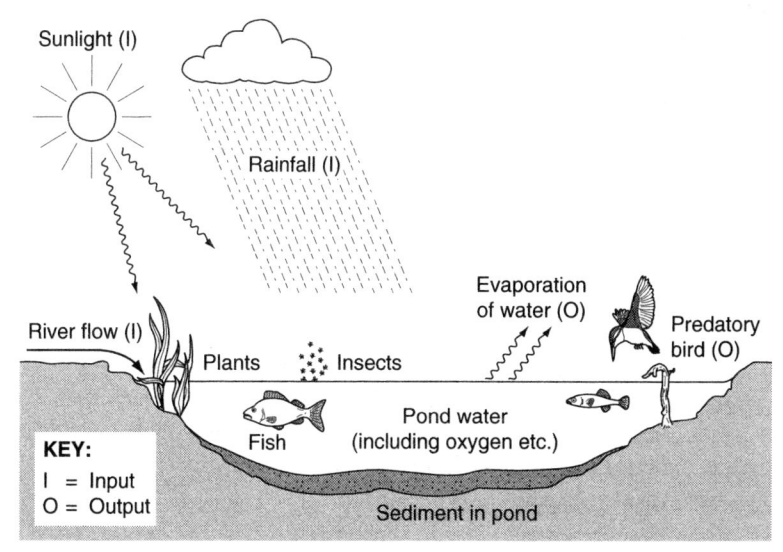

THE EARTH, ECOSYSTEMS AND NATURAL ENVIRONMENTS 53

Figure 3.1 A pond ecosystem

Looking at an environment as a **system** (in this case called an ecosystem), means that we look at it in terms of inputs, processes and outputs. In the case of the lake, the **inputs** are water from rainfall and from streams flowing into the lake, the minerals the water carries, sunlight, and oxygen and carbon dioxide from the air above the pond. **Outputs** from the system will include the flow of water and minerals from the lake, evaporation of water from the lake surface, and the removal of living things by feeding animals and birds. The **processes** in the lake include the following:

- **Photosynthesis** This is the process by which green plants take in carbon dioxide and water and, using sunlight, produce new plant material. In this way plants increase the amount of living material, or **biomass**, of which they are made.
- **Respiration** This is the process by which plants and animals break down sugars, using oxygen, to produce energy for their life processes and for growth. Carbon

dioxide is given off into the surrounding air or water as a result.
- **Predation** This is the process by which animals feed off plants or other animals to obtain 'food' to provide them with energy to live.
- **Reproduction** This is the production of the next generation of the species, by either sexual reproduction or asexual reproduction.
- **Production of waste materials** Waste materials are produced by the processes of photosynthesis and respiration and may be solid, such as animal faeces, liquid, or gas such as carbon dioxide or methane.
- **Decay of dead material** Once living things have died their remains are broken down by bacteria, fungi and other living things. This process is call **decomposition**.
- **Movement** Within an ecosystem animal life will be involved in movement, but the ecosystem's input and output processes will involve movement too, such as the flow of water into a lake, carrying with it mineral and minerals dissolved in the water.

Food webs, energy transfer and productivity

The plants within the ecosystem survive through photosynthesis and respiration, while the animal species survive either by eating plant materials (in which case the animals are called **herbivores**) or by eating other animals (in which case they are called **carnivores**). Figure 3.2 shows a simple **food chain** in an area of heathland, in

Heather → Rabbit → Fox

Figure 3.2 A simple heathland food chain

THE EARTH, ECOSYSTEMS AND NATURAL ENVIRONMENTS 55

which heather is grazed by rabbits, which in turn are killed and eaten by a fox.

In practice the feeding relationships in an ecosystem are much more complex, forming a **food web** rather than a food chain, for most animal species feed off more than one type of plant or animal, and some are **omnivores**, (i.e. they can eat either plants or animals). Figure 3.3 shows a food web in a woodland ecosystem in the UK.

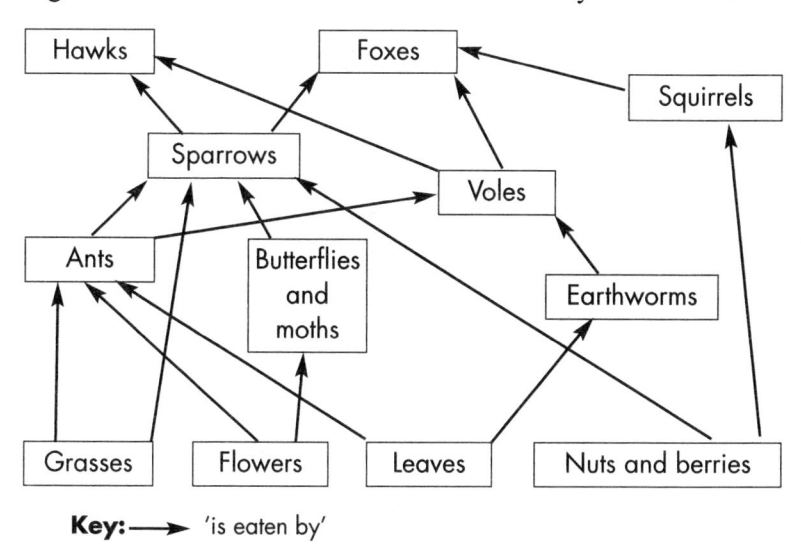

Key: ⟶ 'is eaten by'

Figure 3.3 A woodland food web in the UK

A food chain is the route tracing the energy from sunlight that is trapped by green plants then passed to herbivores and on the carnivores, and finally to the **top carnivores**, the animals which may eat other carnivores and are the top of the food chain. At each stage of this process some of the original energy is either used for the processes of life (movement, reproduction, feeding) or is simply lost by waste. At each stage, or **trophic level**, therefore, there is less energy available to support living things. For example, of the sunlight reaching the surface of a lake only about 1% is captured by green plants during photosynthesis, and only 0.4% of this captured energy will reach the pike at the top of the food chain. At each trophic level there will be less biomass produced, although this may be distributed between large numbers of small creatures or a small number of large creatures. This pattern can be shown through **ecological pyramid** diagrams, examples of which are shown in Figures 3.4a & b.

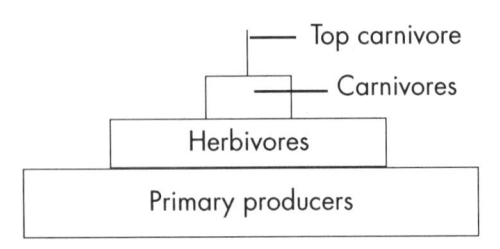

Figure 3.4a   An ecological pyramid of numbers for the pond

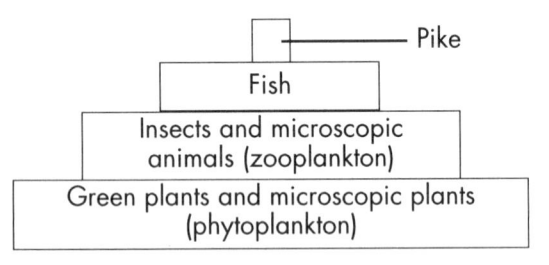

Figure 3.4b   An ecological pyramid of biomass for the pond

The amount of life and living matter that an ecosystem can support varies from place to place on the Earth's surface. Ecosystems on the warmest parts of the Earth's surface have larger energy inputs, and areas where either the underlying rock or water flowing into the ecosystem is rich in nutrients provide greater potential for green plants to grow rapidly. Where high temperatures, high annual rainfall and nutrient-rich waters or soil combine, the highest levels of **productivity** will occur. **Net primary productivity (NPP)** is the amount of energy that an ecosystem accumulates in the plant biomass in every square metre of land surface each year, and is usually measured in $g/m^2/$ year (grams per square metre per year).

The most productive natural ecosystems are tropical rainforests, with an average NPP of 2200g/m^2/year, and swamps and marshland, with an average NPP of 2000g/m^2/year. An average deciduous forest in western Europe or North America will have an NPP of about 1200g/m^2/year, while arid tropical deserts will have an NPP of typically only 90g/m^2/year. Ecosystems with the highest productivity are important for they provide most of the world's 'new plant growth' each year, and because they can support a greater number of plant and animal species and a greater density of plants and animals.

The processes within ecosystems are in detail more complex than described here, and for a more detailed explanation the reader is referred to *Ecology*, by John Cloudsley-Thompson in the Hodder and Stoughton 'Teach Yourself Popular Science' series.

Changing ecosystems

Conservation requires a detailed understanding of the processes that operate in ecosystems, for we need to understand the effect that human activities might have on them, and how people might best manage individual ecosystems for the future. In addition to the day-to-day processes supporting life, described in the previous sections, ecosystems can (and do) change over time, through either natural processes of development or through the interference of external factors such as human interference.

Competition and predator–prey relationships

If we examine any long-established ecosystem we find that every animal or plant in that system has a unique role and pattern of life, with a clear relationship with the other plants and animals in the system. This unique role is known as an **ecological niche**. In the lake we looked at earlier, for example, the pike fills the ecological niche as the top carnivore. The number of pike that the lake can support will depend on the numbers of each other living thing in the lake. A warm summer might cause an increase in plant growth, leading in turn to increased food availability throughout the lake. As a result there may be more food for young pike, more of which will survive. If the number of smaller fish were reduced by, for example, a cold winter or the arrival of a heron, the food supply for the pike would be reduced, competition between pike would cause the weakest not to survive, and the numbers would fall. There is, therefore, a very close link between the number of predators and the numbers of prey in any ecosystem.

This idea is important in ecosystem management, for if human action either removes or adds a species to an ecosystem it will cause significant change. Removing species of animals, either directly for food or indirectly through the effects of pollution, will reduce the availability of prey for top carnivores. Adding a new species will cause competition between that species and the animals currently occupying the niche the new species would naturally fill. Over time only one of those species will survive. Examples of this latter process include the introduction of cats by settlers to the islands of the South Atlantic; the cat soon became the top carnivore.

Small-scale changes in an ecosystem produce effects elsewhere in the system through **feedback mechanisms**. For example, a warm, wet year in which woodland trees produce many berries and fruits will allow birds and insects that feed on them to thrive. Adults will be healthier and produce more offspring, more of which will survive. However, the increased numbers of animals will not be able to survive the next winter when competition for food will be greater, so the numbers will fall for the following year. Such changes that 'switch themselves off' are known as **negative feedback** changes and will result in no long-term changes to the ecosystem. If a change produces other changes which lead to permanent effects, however, the change is described as **positive feedback**. For example, introducing into an ecosystem a new species which takes over a niche from an existing species, or fills a vacant niche, will produce a permanent change. A clear example of this is the introduction of the grey squirrel into England and Wales, which, through competition, replaced the native red squirrel in woodland ecosystems.

Ecological succession and climax

An important natural process in ecosystems is that of **ecological succession**. **Primary succession** occurs when a new environment is formed (perhaps a new volcanic island emerging from the sea, or land left dry by a fall in sea level). Over time this land is colonized, firstly by algae and mosses (which help to break down the rock to form soil), and then perhaps by grasses, shrubs and, finally, trees. As the plants colonize the area, so animals will be attracted in to feed off the plants – insects at first, then birds and small mammals and, finally, carnivores and larger animals. Eventually a fully established ecosystem will be in place, the exact 'character' of which will be determined by the environmental conditions such as climate, rock type or the amount of water available. Such a community is known as a **climax community**. Once established, such an ecosystem may remain in a steady state over a long period of time if the environmental conditions do not change. The ecosystem will adjust to minor changes in any of the inputs, outputs or processes (for example, fluctuations in weather leading to a dry year, or an especially wet summer), and the ecosystem is described as being in a state of **dynamic equilibrium**. However, should any of the components of the ecosystem be changed permanently, then the system itself will change.

Without the intervention of human beings, large areas of the Earth's surface would be covered by natural climax communities, and in many areas these would be ecosystems which are the result of the climate. Such **climatic climax communities** include tropical rainforest, which would naturally cover large areas of the tropical parts of the globe; coniferous forest (known as taiga), which would cloak most of the cold temperate parts of the world across Canada, Scandinavia and Russia; and tundra, in some of the coldest ice-free areas of land. An atlas map of **natural vegetation** shows the theoretical patterns of such extensive ecosystems, or **biomes**.

Secondary succession occurs when a climax community is forced to change because the environmental conditions change. Some of these changes may be natural, such as variations in climate over many centuries or the impact of natural fire or storm damage; others, however, may be the result of human intervention or management.

Human intervention in succession

Today, few areas of the globe are natural climax communities, for most are the result of human intervention. Farming landscapes, parklands, deforested uplands and plantations may all appear 'natural', but are simply ecosystems that are produced and managed by people. In parts of the Highlands of Scotland, for example, the natural vegetation of woodland was removed during the Middle Ages, and the ecosystem found there today is heather moorland. Such an ecosystem is the product of centuries of human intervention by burning and clearing to maintain the heather to support moorland bird life. The ecosystem is sustained only by human management and is not, therefore, a natural climax community. Such an ecosystem is known as a **plagioclimax community**. If the human intervention stopped the ecosystem would develop through succession into a natural climax community.

Despite being the product of human management many such ecosystems are seen by conservationists as important to protect. In the UK the traditional lowland landscapes of small fields with extensive hedgerows are the result of centuries of land enclosure for farming. Many environmental groups wish to prevent the clearance of hedgerows, partly because of the wide range of animal and bird life they support and partly because they regard them as an important part of the cultural landscape of England. Other examples of conserving plagioclimax communities in the UK include protecting:

- the Norfolk Broads, a network of lakes and waterways created by peat digging in the Middle Ages;
- the grassland of the chalk downlands of southern England (for example, the South Downs), an ecosystem rich in insect life and wild flowers produced by patterns of sheep grazing over the centuries;
- the New Forest of Hampshire and Dorset – an area of open deciduous woodland and heaths, produced by over a thousand years of careful management for hunting and timber production. It is a human-produced ecosystem, but is strongly protected by detailed management plans and regulations.

Protection of such landscapes can raise important moral questions for conservationists. While these landscapes are valued by people, they are in many ways no more 'natural' than a city scene. Are they, therefore, deserving of the same protection as the world's natural biomes, such as tropical rainforest? Such a question can provoke strong views on both sides, particularly where conservation uses large resources of money and time.

Harvesting from ecosystems

Understanding the natural processes at work in ecosystems enables us to manage them in such a way that they can provide resources without damaging the long-term survival of the system. In principle it is possible to calculate for any species in any ecosystem the **maximum sustainable yield (msy)**. This is the number or amount of the species that can be removed each year for consumption without damaging long-term sustainability.

If some specimens of an animal are removed from an environment each year for food or resources (for example, deer from a woodland), this increases the food supply available for the remaining animals of that species. They are therefore healthier, and will have more young that survive. Over time, this will result in the species numbers increasing back to the level where they are in balance with the food supply. If the extra numbers generated each year are also removed though, this will represent a **yield** which can be taken each year indefinitely – providing the right balance of age and gender is maintained in the remaining population. The maximum amount that can be taken is the msy.

There are two problems with this model. The first is that there are very few examples of enough being known about a species, its numbers and its natural population change to enable an accurate msy to be calculated. Secondly, msy is dependent on careful management of the catch or yield, and this is very difficult to do, even under highly controlled conditions. Where demand for a species or a product from a species is high, and exceeds the level that can be maintained by calculating msy, there is a danger that the species will be hunted to extinction. The rarer it becomes, the more expensive it becomes, and the more incentive there is for illegal hunting – to the point where the species may disappear. While msy provides a useful model for future research, therefore, until the science has been perfected, it is important that precaution is used in calculating yields and catches from natural ecosystems.

The world's major biomes

The final section of this chapter examines each of the world's ecosystems and describes their characteristics and the main conservation pressures that they are experiencing. Figure 3.5 shows a map of the distribution that these biomes would have without human intervention – it does not, of course, show the real distribution of these ecosystems today.

Forests

Forests are the natural cover for much of the Earth's land surface; as recently as 1700, some 60% of the land was forested. Today the figure is 30%, and the loss of the world's forest resources is one of the major conservation challenges. As part of the global ecosystem, forests play a major role in the cycling of carbon, oxygen and nitrogen, and so are important parts of the global climate system. They also house much of the Earth's variety of plant and animal species, and so maintain the planet's ecological diversity. They are also an economic resource, however: forests provide firewood, building materials, food and export products such as timber, and are vital to the social and economic well-being of many countries, in both the developed and the less developed world. Most wood consumption, however, is by the countries of the North in the form of paper and timber for construction. Pressure to conserve forest resources has to be balanced, therefore, by economic demands, and this raises many conservation and development issues.

The word 'forest' describes many different ecosystems. No two areas of forest are identical, and botanists have developed many classification systems. In simple terms it is possible to divide forests into three groups:

- tropical broadleaved forests;
- temperate deciduous forests;
- coniferous forests.

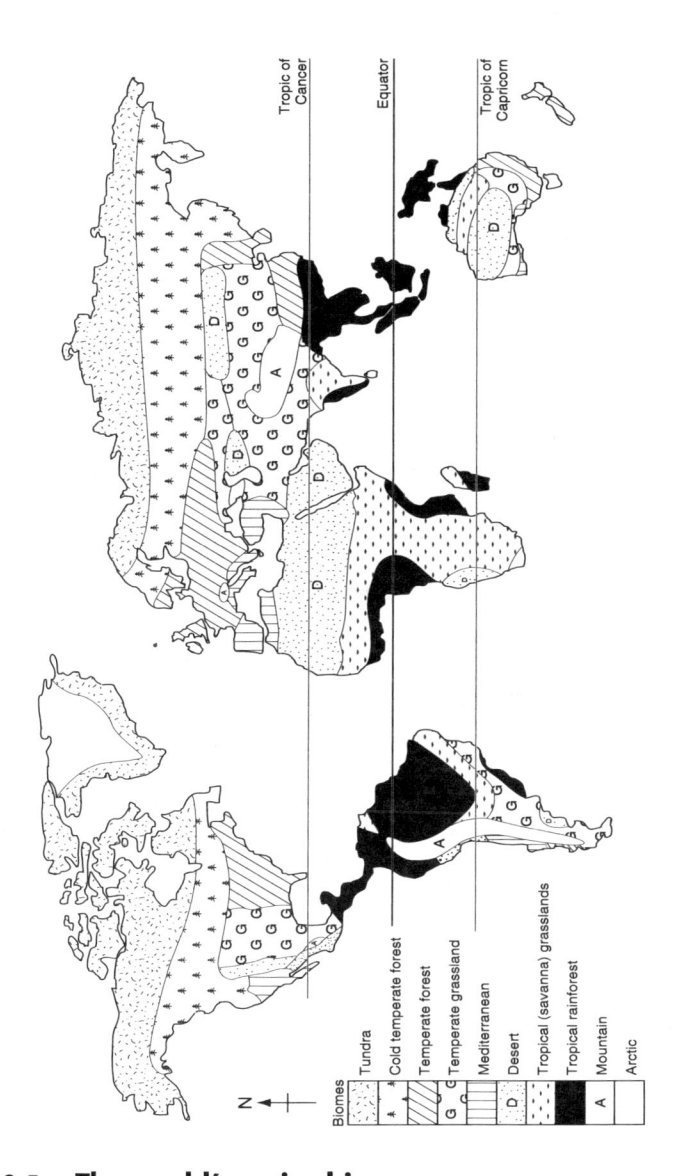

THE EARTH, ECOSYSTEMS AND NATURAL ENVIRONMENTS 63

Figure 3.5   The world's major biomes

Tropical broadleaved forests

This group includes the sub-types of tropical rainforest, tropical deciduous forest and monsoon forest, and is found in locations up to 5° north or south of the equator. It is fast-growing, dense and evergreen as a result of high temperatures (25–35°C) and high rainfall (1500–3500 mm per annum) for much of the year. With up to 30 tree species and 30 animal species per hectare, such forest is rich in biodiversity. Typically, three levels or layers can be identified in such forest: the *ground layer* is dark, with little cover except for decaying material such as fallen trees; the *middle layer* of trees provides the habitat of most animal species; the *canopy layer* is exposed to full sunlight, and is 'home' to a range of bird and insect species.

The main environmental and conservation issues in the tropical broadleaved forests result from rapid clearance for logging and farming. This has significant impact on local, and possibly global, climate, as well as reducing biodiversity. Problems of soil erosion and loss of fertility in soil also result from forest clearance.

Temperate deciduous forest

Such forest is characterized by its seasonal growth. It is found in locations between 30° and 55° north and south of the equator, where rainfall is sufficient for tree growth (750–1500 mm per year). It includes Mediterranean forest and the typical mixed deciduous forest of Europe and North America. Temperatures of 10–25°C and a growing season of 4–10 months make its rate of growth and its productivity less than that of tropical forest. Typically it has 5–10 plant and animal species per hectare; common tree species include beech, elm, oak, maple, aspen, birch and hickory. Ground-living flowering plants and shrubs thrive early in the growing season when the tree canopy is absent before the trees come into leaf.

The principal environmental issues relating to the temperate deciduous forests also relate to forest clearance, although the areas left untouched after centuries of exploitation are now small. Replacement by single-species coniferous plantations, which changes the nature and appearance and diversity of the forests, is an important issue in many European countries that conservation and environmental groups have objected to.

Temperate coniferous forest

This forest, also known as **boreal forest** or **taiga**, is found at high latitudes (55–80°) and also at high altitudes on mountains nearer to the equator, where the altitude produces climatic conditions similar to those in high latitudes. Large areas of Scandinavia, Russia and Canada are clothed in coniferous forest of this type. It survives in areas with lower temperatures (−15 to +15°C) and with lower precipitation (250–1000 mm per annum) than deciduous forest, and mainly comprises evergreen coniferous species such as firs and pines. Productivity and growth rates are low in the short growing season, and such forests contain relatively few species of plants and animals (2–5 per hectare).

The key environmental issues in temperate coniferous forests relate to industrial pollution damage and the need to ensure that harvested timber is replaced by replanting.

Grasslands

The world's natural grasslands are found in two main locations, in the savanna grasslands of the tropics and in the prairie or steppe grasslands of the temperate zone. Some 20% of the Earth's surface would naturally be covered by grassland, but the real area of grass is now much larger than that because many areas of woodland and forest have been cleared to create grasslands. The grasslands are of great importance in the history of the human species, for the earliest human fossils suggest that 'early man' was a grassland dweller – and most of the world's important grain crops (rice, wheat and maize) are simply varieties of grass selected as food crops.

Tropical grasslands

The tropical grasslands lie between the dense tropical forests at the equator and the hot deserts at the tropics, between latitudes 5° and 20° north and south. In Africa they are usually called **savannas**; in South America they are called the **llanos** (in Venezuela) and the **campos** (in Brazil). At their edges they merge gradually into desert or forest – near the tropical forests they may be quite wooded, especially in river valleys, while near the deserts the density of grass will be much less. Tropical grasslands occur where temperatures are high (typically 25–30°C throughout the year) but where the rainfall is not sufficient to support trees and forests – typically where there are marked wet and dry seasons with annual precipitation of 250–1000 mm. Grasses flourish in the wet periods, but are also able to survive lengthy periods without rain.

The tropical grasslands support a wide range of animals, each of which occupies a unique ecological niche in a particular part of the grassland environment. In Africa, zebra and wildebeest are herbivores in open grassland, while elephants and giraffe will graze in bush and wooded savanna. The carnivores of the tropical grasslands of Africa include lion, leopard and cheetah.

The major conservation issues in the tropical grasslands are caused by the spread of farming as a result of population growth in tropical countries. Loss of the grassland habitat reduces the number and range of plant and animal species, and can produce conflict between farmers and wildlife. The pressure to conserve the 'big game' of the savannas has lead to the establishment of many nature reserves, which support an important tourist industry in countries such as Kenya and Tanzania. The protection of threatened species such as elephant and rhino, often killed illegally for their valuable ivory (elephant) and horn (rhino), is an important conservation issue in such regions. Nature reserves can themselves cause environmental problems, however, because of the increased numbers of protected species, and because of the impact of large numbers of tourists in a small number of 'honeypot' sites. Protection of the elephant in the South Luangwa National Park in Zambia, for example, has been so successful that elephant culling is now an annual event.

Temperate grasslands

The temperate grasslands occur in the mid-latitudes (40–60° north and south of the equator), usually in the centre of the continents at some distance from the sea. Here the low winter temperatures (0 to −10°C) prevent deciduous tree growth, and the rainfall at this distance from the sea is insufficient to support vegetation other than grassland. The **plains** and **prairies** of North America, the **steppes** of central Asia and the **pampas** of Argentina are the classical temperate grasslands.

As with the tropical grasslands, the temperature grasslands have been used for farming, particularly for cattle ranching and for growing grain. This has reduced the area of natural grassland very substantially, and has, when not managed carefully, produced problems of large-scale soil erosion. Ploughing the land for crops, or leaving soil as fallow land, leaves the soil exposed to wind and water erosion. Ranching can cause a similar problem, if overstocking leads to trampling and the destruction of the grass cover. In the Great Plains of the USA, poor land management and increased mechanisation in the 1930s resulted in severe soil erosion, made famous as The American Dust Bowl and graphically described in John Steinbeck's novel *The Grapes of Wrath*.

Mediterranean ecosystems

Lying between the Sahara desert of North Africa and the deciduous woodlands of western Europe is the Mediterranean Basin. Around the shores of the Mediterranean Sea lie southern Spain and France, Italy, Greece and Israel, with distinctive ecosystems that reflect the climate of hot, dry summers and mild, wetter winters. The natural vegetation of the Mediterranean region is scrub, grass and small trees and bushes that can survive the intense heat of summer. Olive trees, citrus fruit trees (such as orange and lemon) and cork oak are common in slightly wetter areas, in a type of vegetation known as **maquis**. Many of the plants are strongly aromatic, such as lavender and thyme. Where the soils are drier or limestone rock means there is little surface water the scrub is thinner, with few (if any) trees and patches of bare rock – this pattern of vegetation is known as **garrigue**. Mediterranean ecosystems are also found elsewhere in the world where similar climatic conditions are found, such as California (where the maquis vegetation is known as **chaparral**), South Africa and South-western Australia.

The major environmental issues in the Mediterranean areas have arisen from their growing populations and from their attraction for tourism – many of the world's major tourist destinations are in Mediterranean climate areas. In particular, the risks of fire, started accidentally by people, and the high demand for water for drinking and waste disposal in an arid area can create important environmental problems.

The world's deserts

The popular image of a desert is of the tropical hot deserts with images of camels, sand and an oasis. Deserts, though, are simply areas of very low rainfall, and it is important to distinguish cold deserts and hot deserts.

Hot deserts

The world's hot deserts are found in a belt around the lines of the Tropics of Cancer and Capricorn, mainly on the western side of the continents. Their names are very familiar – the Sahara and Namib (Kalahari) Deserts of Africa, the Arabian Desert, the deserts of the South-western USA, the Atacama Desert of Chile, and the Great Australian Desert. High temperatures throughout the year, with maxima of up to 50°C, and very low rainfall, means that desert vegetation is sparse. Only drought-tolerant plants, such as acacia and baobab trees in Africa and cactus in the Americas, can survive, and flowering and plant reproduction occurs only in the brief periods when water is available after rain. Animals, too, are few, and are adapted to desert life, perhaps by using little water (camels) or by being active only at night (nocturnal animals such as the fenec fox).

In the hot deserts the major conservation issues occur as a result of the extraction of mineral resources or from the demand for water. The demand for water means that construction of reservoirs and pumping of water from underground sources are frequently undertaken. In Egypt, for example, the construction of Lake Nasser and the Aswan Dam drowned parts of the Nile valley, causing loss of farmland and the destruction of many archaeological sites.

Mining for minerals such as iron ore and copper can scar the landscape and create pollution risks from the dumping of waste materials. Oil extraction is an important economic activity in the desert areas of North Africa and the Persian Gulf, and leakages during extraction or spillage during transport create significant pollution risks. At the end of the Gulf War in 1990, the burning of Kuwait's oilwells by the Iraqis caused very substantial land and air pollution.

Cold deserts

The cold deserts are those parts of the world where temperatures are so low in winter or the land is so far from the sea that rainfall is very low. Large areas of central Asia, such as the Gobi Desert of Mongolia and Western China are cold deserts, but we can also include most of Antarctica in this category. Vegetation is sparse or absent, and few animals survive in the demanding environmental conditions. As with the hot deserts, the major environmental threats come from exploitation for minerals and natural resources.

The tundra

Between the coniferous forests of high latitudes and the ice-covered polar regions lie the **tundra** areas. The tundra ecosystem comprises mosses, lichens and grasses, with occasional dwarf trees such as willow and birch, which can survive the extremely low winter temperatures and can reproduce during the short summers. The animals of the tundra, such as caribou, reindeer, arctic fox and polar bears, must tolerate the same conditions. The herds of reindeer and caribou, for example, migrate through the year to find the best grazing and to avoid the worst weather conditions.

The main environmental threats to the tundra are the effects of mineral exploitation, for human population is low. The extraction of oil on the North Slope of Alaska, for example, has increased the environmental risk of pollution, both from oil spillage and from the creation of new towns with their problems of waste disposal.

Marine ecosystems

The biomes described above are all land-based ecosystems, but two-thirds of the Earth's surface is covered by sea. Much less is known about marine ecosystems, but they are extremely varied in their nature. The coastal waters of estuaries and mangrove swamps, for example, have very high levels of productivity because of the nutrients carried into them from land, and they support very diverse and rich ecosystems. However, their closeness to land makes them very vulnerable to pollution and damage from human activities. The ecosystems of the continental shelves and deep oceans are much more remote from human impact, but appear to be less rich and productive. Chapter 8 examines the nature of marine ecosystems in more detail and looks at the major conservation issues they face.

The natural environment – a millennium map

The impact of human activity on the world's ecosystems has reduced the area of natural biomes very substantially. Only in the largest biomes most remote from centres of population or with few obvious economic resources are there areas largely untouched by people, as in parts of the Amazon Rainforest or the Sahara Desert. Even there, though, it is possible to measure the presence of pollution carried by the world's weather systems. A map of the natural biomes in the year 2000 (a millennium map) would be very different from that shown in Figure 3.5, and would show a smaller area each year that the map was drawn: The Amazon forest reduced in size by 10% in the 1980s and by a further 7–8% during the 1990s, for example. An important question for conservation, therefore, is whether the millennium map represents a minimum state that we must seek to preserve – at present only political and economic decisions will dictate whether that view is possible.

Summary

The science of the links between plants, animals and their environment is ecology. Understanding the processes at work in ecosystems is essential if people are to reduce the impact of their actions on the environment and if we are to be able to manage the environment for sustainability. Issues associated with the management of plagioclimax communities are important ones, as is understanding the yield of each environment that can be taken to provide resources. Each of the world's major ecosystems, or biomes, has distinctive conservation threats which need to be understood if we are to minimize or prevent the negative effects of population growth, demand for resources and the problems of pollution damage.

Taking action

In each chapter in this second part of the book we shall consider some of the actions that individuals might take in support of conservation, locally or at a larger (or even global) scale.

Contributing to conservation through extending our understanding of ecosystems might include:

1 Supporting, practically or financially, the work of one of the conservation charities undertaking research on how ecosystems work. In the UK, most naturalists' trusts have local nature reserves where they map and record the species found and observe the processes at work in the ecosystem. At a larger scale, organizations such as the RSPB and WWF sponsor research into tropical ecosystems through charitable donations. Organizations such as Earthwatch operate holidays for tourists to contribute to research in ecosystems around the globe.

2 Lobbying governments to provide research funding to scientists working on ecological research through, for example the Natural Environment Research Council (NERC) in the UK.

ACTIVITIES

1 Visit a local nature reserve. From the information provided on display boards and in leaflets try to identify:

   a as many of the green plants that make up the bottom of the ecological pyramid;

   b the insects, animals and birds that are the herbivores in the ecosystem;

   c the animals that are the carnivores in the ecosystem;

   d the top carnivores.

2 For a local ecosystem (perhaps the nature reserve in Activity 1), identify the main human threats to it. Is the ecosystem a climate climax community or is it a plagioclimax community? If it is the latter, how has it been produced by human activity?

3 Choose one of the main biomes that particularly interests you. Using encyclopedias, library information books, CD-ROMS or the Internet, find out the main human threats to the survival of that ecosystem.

4 | PEOPLE, RESOURCES AND THE ENVIRONMENT

Introduction

Environmental issues are caused by the use or misuse of the natural environment by humans or by changes in the environment which make it more difficult for human existence. People need to use the resources of the environment for their basic needs of food and shelter but as they seek to improve their standard of living they make more and more demands upon the environment. The MDCs use many more resources per person than do the LDCs, and are responsible for most of the resource use around the globe. Therefore, while it is easy to blame environmental issues on a rapidly growing world population, it is the rapid and unequal use of resources rather than population growth itself which is the real problem. This chapter looks at both population growth and resources to identify the main conservation issues.

Global population

Population growth

The world's population at the end of the twentieth century is approximately 6.5 billion. This is ten times larger than in 1700, and nearly four times larger than in 1900. It is growing at an accelerating rate, increasing at a rate of 100 million every year and the United National Population Fund (UNFPA) predicts that by 2025 world population will be 8.5 billion. By 2050 it may be as high as 10.5 billion.

But why is population growth occurring and why is it accelerating? Population growth occurs when the number of births each year exceeds the number of deaths. In most countries of the world the

birth rate (the number of births per year per thousand of the population) exceeds the **death rate** (the number of deaths per year per thousand of the population). In traditional societies birth and death rates were kept approximately in balance – although families had large numbers of children, life expectancy was short because many would die young from disease, inadequate nutrition and poor health care. Population growth by natural increase was, therefore, very slow.

However, advances in medical care and understanding of disease transmission have led to improvements in the treatment of disease, basic hygiene and sanitation. The great child killers of cholera, diarrhoea and smallpox have largely disappeared from the MDCs through the availability of clean water, vaccines and drugs for treatment of disease. In the LDCs, although child death is still much more common than in the MDCs, deaths from such causes are reducing rapidly. In addition, developments in health care and diet have extended life expectancy significantly. In England, for example, life expectancy increased from 45 in 1800 to approximately 78 years in 1999, and similar trends are occurring in the LDCs.

In the MDCs lowering of birth rates and death rates, and increases in life expectancy, happened as a result of the agricultural and industrial developments of the seventeenth to twentieth centuries. Figure 4.1 shows the pattern of change that occurred, and how death rates declined before birth rates due to improvements in health care and sanitation. Eventually, MDC societies adjusted to increased survival rates and people chose to have fewer children. As a result birth rates declined to fall into line with death rates. However, during the period when death rates had fallen but birth rates were still high, a period of rapid population growth occurred. This pattern of change is known as the **demographic transition**, and is the period during which countries moved from a position with high birth and high death rates to one with low birth and death rates via a period of rapid population growth. Today population growth in most MDCs is low – less than 0.5%.

In the LDCs the fall in death rates has occurred much more recently and much more quickly than it did in the MDCs, as health care and

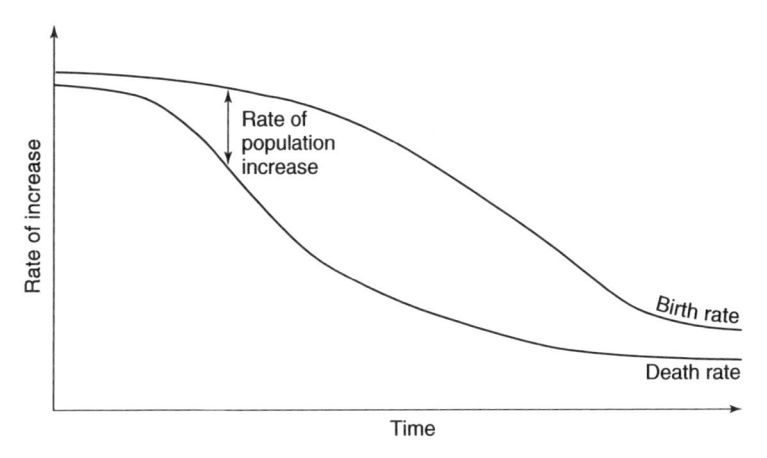

Figure 4.1 Birth rate and death rate changes in MDCs – the demographic transition

hygiene improve. In many countries, however, birth rates have not yet started to fall to follow death rates. As a result annual population growth is rapid, averaging 2% across all LDCs and as high as 3–4% in some. Although such figures sound small, a 2% growth rate leads to a doubling of population in 35 years and a 3% growth rate leads to population doubling in 23 years.

Predictions of future population, either for the world as a whole or for a single country, are based on extending the historical pattern of change (i.e. already known) into the future. Figure 4.2 shows in outline how world population has changed through history, and makes two suggestions for how it might change in the future. Continued accelerating growth (Line A on the graph) is thought by population scientists to be unlikely because of changing attitudes to family size around the world. Such a J-shaped graph of **exponential growth** would create major conservation issues and environmental and political problems. More likely is the flattening out of growth (Line B), producing an S-shaped graph of **sigmoid growth**. The difficulty with this, however, is in judging exactly when the growth might slow down. For the world as a whole the UN has calculated that growth will start to slow during the second half of the twenty-first century, producing a stable world population of about 11.5 billion by the year 2150.

A major issue in the LDCs is the proportion of the population under 15 years of age. For example, in most African countries this age group is by far the most numerous. Even if the fertility of the population fell to replacement level overnight, there would still be many decades of rapid growth as these children reach reproductive maturity.

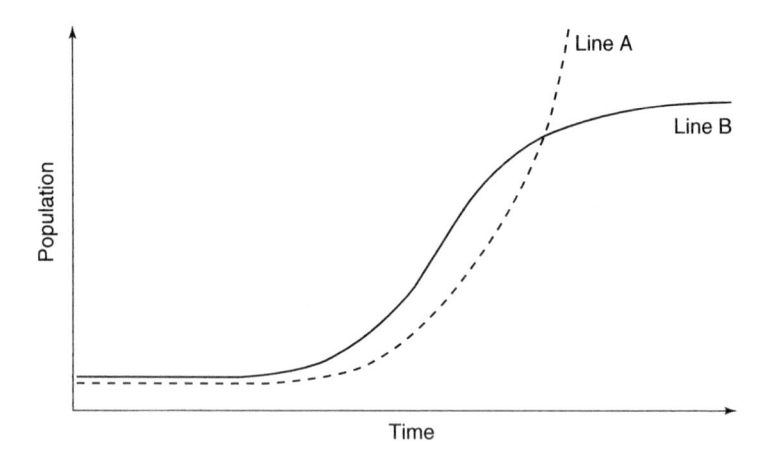

Figure 4.2   Predicting world population growth

Population patterns

The world's population is concentrated in the parts of the globe where the climate and the availability of resources have enabled agriculture to develop or industry to be established. The highest population densities are found in the world's great cities such as Hong Kong and Mexico City; over half the world's people live in cities. Overall, though, the major concentrations of people are in Western Europe, North America, South Asia (India, Pakistan and Bangladesh), China, and South-east Asia. Figure 4.3 shows the world distribution of population.

PEOPLE, RESOURCES AND THE ENVIRONMENT

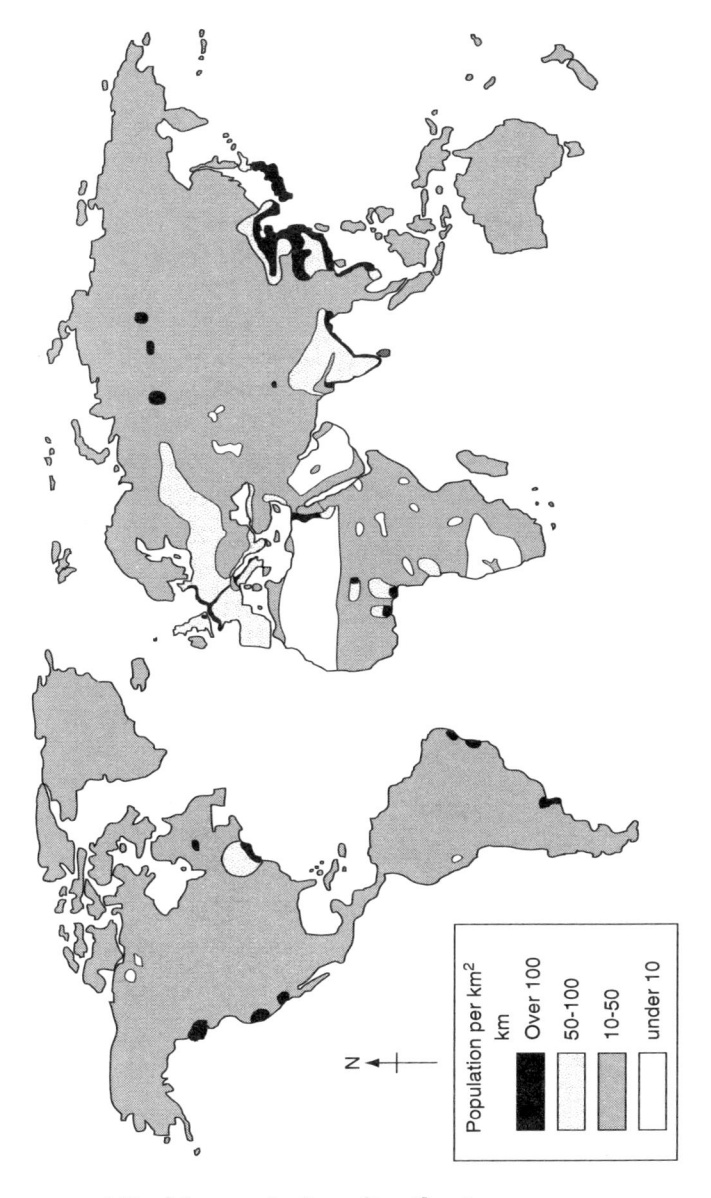

Figure 4.3 World population distribution

A number of aspects of this population distribution are important in understanding environmental and conservation issues:

- Two-thirds of the world's population lives in Asia, with a quarter of the population living in China.
- Population growth is fastest in LDCs, which means that the poorer countries have an increasing proportion of the world's population. In 1950 67% of the world's people lived in the countries of the South. By the year 2000 this figure increased to 80%.
- The fastest population growth rates are in Africa (average 2.5%), which is the continent with the lowest average GNP per capita, the most rural population, and the most severe problems of poverty and food supply.
- Great variations in population growth rates can occur within continents, within countries and even within cities. Data for whole countries hides the variations between the most affluent members of society and the very poorest. In many LDCs the richest amongst the population have birth and death rates similar to those living in the MDCs. In South Africa, for example, the contrast in population characteristics (the **demographic characteristics**) between the white inhabitants of Johannesburg and the black inhabitants of the city's townships such as Soweto is very marked. In contrast, some poor rural areas of MDCs have population growth patterns similar to those in the poorest LDCs.
- The proportion of the world's population living in cities is increasing. High concentrations of people in urban areas can create substantial environmental problems of water supply, waste disposal, pollution from traffic and industry – and, where many of the city dwellers live in poverty, the problems of disease and unemployment. The environmental and conservation issues in urban areas are amongst the most pressing facing humanity.

Limiting population growth

With modern methods of family planning and contraception, the technology is available to slow down population growth in most parts of the world. Most governments and many charities working in LDCs have family planning programmes that seek to encourage the use of contraception and the choice of having a small family. Making family planning available is not enough, however, for there are many political, economic and social barriers to be overcome before parents will start to choose to limit their family size.

Availability and cost of family planning

In the poorest LDCs the cost of providing family planning, and ensuring its continued availability (especially in rural areas) is a major problem. It is in such areas that the role of NGOs and charities may be especially important in providing low-cost access to family planning.

Economic benefits of large families

The traditional view that children are an important guarantor of future income for the family encourages large families, and is hard to change. In most countries there is no state support for the elderly, ill, or infirm, so the role falls entirely to the family group. Large numbers of children provide important social security. The choice to have smaller families often follows from a period of economic growth, with its improved economic security for individuals, in such countries.

Religious constraints

The perspective of religious groups which may be opposed to the use of family planning methods is a barrier to reducing population growth, particularly amongst the Catholic countries of Latin America.

Status and role issues

Views of the role and status of women and men in different cultures may be important constraints on change. In many cultures the role of women is seen as being chiefly to bear children, while the status of men may be dependent on the number of children they have.

Similarly, views of the value of male and female children may affect the number of children parents choose to have. The 'single child' policy in China, for example, is handicapped by the perceived higher status of boys, and the desire of most parents to have a son.

Education issues

A key factor in change is the level of education available, and in particular the education of women. Where the rate of participation of girls in education is higher, there is evidence that they start having children at a later age and have fewer children in total. This may reflect the role of women in choosing family size, and in influencing health care and the economic aspirations of families. Many NGOs and governments working on developing family planning policies now focus their attention on providing primary school education for girls as a priority.

India provides a good example of the problems of seeking to limit population growth in LDCs. Its population in 1990 stood at 853 million, with a growth rate of 2.1%. By the end of the decade it is predicted to be nearly 950 million. Population control has long been regarded as important by Indian governments, and the first family planning clinics were opened in the 1920s. Today there are some 50,000 family planning clinics. Active steps taken to promote family planning have included:

- raising the legal age of marriage from 15 to 18 for women and from 18 to 21 for men;
- the use of publicity campaigns to promote family planning;
- seeking to increase the participation of girls in primary and secondary education;
- inclusion of family planning issues in both school and public education programmes.

By the end of the 1990s some 20% of the population are believed to use family planning methods, and there is some evidence of declining birth rates, particularly amongst the most affluent and the best-educated sectors of society. There are still many barriers, though, to increasing the spread of family planning – poverty, limited education and attitudes to the role of women in Hindu society mean that high birth rates still prevail amongst the poorest sectors of society.

Worldwide, reducing population growth is clearly a major target if many environmental and resource issues are to be avoided. However, reducing population growth can generate its own problems: in particular, it results in an ageing population. The present 'average age' is 35 in the MDCs and 25 in the LDCs, but this is predicted to rise to 50 in both groups of countries by the time a globally stable population is reached. The effects of this can be to reduce the numbers in the most economically active age groups and place the burden of supporting older citizens on a smaller and smaller group. Providing the income to support old age will become a major challenge for governments and individuals around the world in the twenty-first century.

Resources

Resources are simply anything that may be used by people to support their economic or social way of life. We tend to think of resources in terms of raw materials extracted from nature – such as timber, iron ore, wool or agricultural products – but these are what we call **primary resources**. In addition people make use of **secondary resources** – such as manufactured goods or processed foodstuffs – and **tertiary resources**, which are the skills, talents and knowledge of people, and resources such as money (capital), labour and time.

Primary resources are usually themselves divided into **renewable** and **non-renewable resources**. Renewable resources (sometimes known as **flow resources**) are resources which are neither consumed nor destroyed while they are being used, or which can be replaced over a short timescale. Examples of renewable resources include air and water, together with agricultural crops and timber, which, if carefully managed, can be replaced relatively quickly. Non-renewable resources (sometimes know as **stock resources**) are destroyed in use and cannot be replaced by natural processes that operate on a human timescale. Examples include energy sources such as coal and oil; although they are being formed in nature, the speed of this process is very slow – in effect, for human beings they are not being replaced.

Tertiary resources are becoming increasingly important to developing a sustainable society, particularly those which relate to creativity and knowledge. Improvements in the efficiency with which primary resources are used, or ways of reducing the impact of human activity on the environment depend on the innovation skills of people. These in turn are the product of effective, universal education systems. Most governments recognize the importance of education and are seeking to provide education for all at primary and secondary level, and to increase the numbers in higher education. An important conservation issue, therefore, is the development of education, particularly amongst those groups worldwide who participate in education less than others. In the LDCs the issues are mainly education of girls and increasing the provision of secondary education. In the MDCs the importance of **lifelong learning** is an increasing governmental priority.

Resources, population and development

While population growth increases demand for resources and, ultimately, is a problem for the environment and for conservation, it is too simple to link actual population size with environmental problems. Population becomes a problem when there are insufficient resources, so that a low population density in an area with few resources may be more of a problem than a high population density in an area with many resources.

The rate of use of resources is very strongly linked to the level of economic development of a country. The MDCs use more resources per head than the LDCs – in broad terms 20% of the world's population (mainly in MDCs) uses 80% of the resources, while the other 80% of the world's population uses 20% of the resources. While MDCs may portray the world's environmental problems as basically a population problem in the countries of the South, the LDCs may portray it rather as a consumption problem in the countries of the North.

The level of development of a country is not determined by the amount of resources it has available, for many countries (especially in the LDCs) have large amounts of untapped natural resources and very large human resources that they have as yet been unable to make full use of. Limits to development are the result of many factors in LDCs other than resource availability, which include:

- **Poverty** The 'vicious cycle of poverty' means that those who have fewest resources and wealth are most likely to be affected by ill-health, which reduces their capacity to work and so condemns them to further poverty.
- **Health and disease** Low levels of health are a major limit to development and can take large amounts of resource from governments to overcome.
- **Education** Education is one of the key ways in which the human resource of a country can be developed, but in many LDCs levels of education for most people are very low.
- **Social constraints** Many aspects of social organization can limit economic development. These might include strict class and caste systems, attitudes to the role of women in society, and the importance of the extended family.
- **Lack of capital** This is a major limitation, which prevents countries developing their resources.
- **Military expenditure** High levels of expenditure on the military will reduce the amount of finance available to support resource development.

The link between population, resources and development is described in Ackerman's model of Population/Resource Regions (1959). He identifies five types of region with different characteristics:

- *Type A – United States-type regions.* These regions have high levels of technology and low levels of population relative to the resources they possess. Examples include the USA, Canada and Australia.

- *Type B – European-type regions.* These areas have high levels of technology, but have high levels of population relative to the resources they possess. Examples would include the UK, Germany and Spain.
- *Type C – Egyptian-type regions.* These regions have low levels of technology but high levels of population for the resources they possess. Examples would include most of the countries of the Sahel region of Africa, such as Ethiopia, Burkina Faso and Niger.
- *Type D – Brazilian-type regions.* These regions have low levels of technology, but also low levels of population for the resources they have. Examples would include Brazil, Venezuela and Saudi Arabia.
- *Type E – Arctic–desert-type regions.* These areas have very low populations and few available resources.

The most advanced of the types is the United States-type where development is not impeded by technology, population or resources, while the most disadvantaged type is the Egyptian-type, which is impeded by problems in all three factors.

Most of the world's LDCs are of the Egyptian-type, and are close to the point at which they may be using their resources to the limits of their current potential. This creates strong risks of both environmental problems and related human and social problems.

The link between resources and population has long been a focus of scientific interest. In 1798 Thomas Malthus, an economist and clergyman, wrote his *Essay on Population*, which predicted that the size of the human population would be limited by the natural resources available. He believed that, while population numbers increase in a geometric pattern (1, 2, 4, 8, 16...), food supply can increase only in an arithmetic pattern (1, 2, 3, 4, 5, 6...). Ultimately, therefore, starvation and disease will cause the human population to stop growing when it reaches the limits imposed by resources. However, Malthus's ideas have only been demonstrated to work in animal populations under controlled conditions, and his worst predictions for humanity have never really occurred. This is because improvements in farming and food technology, and in other technology using natural resources, have meant that food production has kept pace with population growth.

Malthus's ideas have re-emerged as fashionable in the last 30 years, as Neo-Malthusianism. This suggests (see Chapter 13) that the human race has reached the limits to growth of resource use, so that future population growth will prove as devastating as Malthus predicted. We might expect that the first evidence of such limits to growth would appear in the Egyptian-type population resource areas that Zelinsky identified, yet there is little evidence that such disastrous scenarios are about to develop.

More recently, the concept of sustainability has brought the balance between resources, technology and population into sharp focus. Sustainability has been described by the general equation:

$$S = \frac{R \times T}{P}$$

where: S is sustainability; R is the amount and availability of resources; T is the amount and availability of appropriate technology; P is population.

This shows clearly that there is a direct relationship between sustainability and resources and technology – sustainability increases as the resources and technology increase. However, there is an inverse relationship between sustainability and population – sustainability is less achievable when population size or growth rate increases.

Summary

Population growth and its impact on the use of the world's resources is perhaps the most important conservation issue that exists. The relationship between population size and environmental issues is complex, though, for it is the amount of resources used per head in comparison to the amount available that is the key influence on the scale of environmental impact. World population will continue to grow over the next century, but will probably stabilize by the middle of the 22nd century. The major challenge for humanity is to ensure that at that point it can sustain the provision for resources to give a satisfactory quality of life for 11 billion people.

Taking action

1 Most of the environmental and development charities support family planning programmes in their work in LDCs. Providing financial or practical support for their work can help to promote family planning.

2 A key focus is on the role of education in changing cultural attitudes to family size, and in particular the role of women. Supporting educational charities working in LDCs can help with this development.

3 Resource consumption in the North is a greater conservation issue than population growth in the South. Reducing personal consumption, or focusing on resources from sustainable sources, can help to reduce high consumption levels in the North.

ACTIVITIES

1 Approach one of the population charities such as Population Concern, and identify the range of activities they are undertaking in the LDCs and MDCs.

2 Choose a sample of countries that interest you, including one MDC (e.g. the UK), one LDC (e.g. India), one OPEC country (e.g. Kuwait), one Debtor country (e.g. Mexico), and one Newly Industrializing Country (e.g. Taiwan). Using data from Population Concern, or from the website of one of the population charities or the government of the country itself, try to identify the differences between them in terms of birth rates, death rates, life expectancy, etc. What population policies and strategies does each country have?

5 ENERGY AND RESOURCES

Patterns of energy use

Every activity human beings undertake involves using energy. For the basic activities of life, such as walking and breathing, that energy is provided by the human body from the food we consume (**metabolism**). The average amount of energy used each day in this way is about 2000 kilocalories (kcal) for women and about 2500 kcal for men. For those undertaking very demanding physical activities (for example, a job as a building worker or by playing sport) this may increase to 4500 kcal per day.

From the earliest days of human history, people have used other sources of energy to supplement energy from food. In prehistory this was limited to energy from the burning of wood, for heat, or of flowing water for transport, but by the Middle Ages the use of energy to make clothing, farming implements or weapons, and the use of animal power for transport, increased the total amount of energy used per person. By the end of the twentieth century technology has changed the lifestyles of all human beings so that energy consumption per head has increased enormously. An individual in North America or Western Europe consumes energy **directly** through, for example, the heating and lighting of their home, in running labour-saving devices such as washing machines and dishwashers, for communications through television and telephone, and for transport, often by car. In addition they use much more energy **indirectly** – for example, in the food they eat through the high inputs of fertilizer into farming, the manufacture of the food packaging, the energy required to deliver the food from farm to supermarket to home, the energy used to manufacture the microwave cooker or oven and the refrigerator, and the disposal of packaging and waste material. The average amount of energy used per person across the world is 87 GJ/year (1 gigajoule (GJ) is 1000 million joules), but this figures hides large contrasts between consumption in North America and Japan of 286 GJ/year and consumption in India, Pakistan and Bangladesh of 17 GJ/year. Across the world, therefore, each person consumes energy equivalent to the work of 240 people each day, and in the developed countries it is as if each individual has 788 people working for them continuously.

Where does this energy come from? In the developed world much of it is used as electricity, but electricity is itself made by burning fuels such as oil, natural gas or coal. The heat from burning these fuels in power stations is used to produce steam, which drives turbines, which produce electricity. In LDCs, although electricity is important, much energy is also obtained directly from fuelwood or water power. The original sources of energy (coal, oil, gas, wood, etc.) are known as **primary energy sources**, while electricity is a **secondary energy source**.

By the end of the twentieth century people were using energy each year equivalent to 1.5 billion tonnes of coal – four times more than was used in 1950 and 25 times more than in 1800. Most of the energy used (77%) comes from non-renewable resources such as coal and oil, with the energy obtained from these fossil fuels each year having taken Nature one million years to make. A further 5% of energy was being obtained from nuclear power and only 18% was coming from renewable energy sources such as wood, animal waste, crop residues, water power, solar power or wind. Of the non-renewable resources, most energy (41%) is obtained from oil, with coal (35%) and natural gas (24%) providing the remainder.

Figure 5.1 shows how this primary energy is used across the world. This makes clear the importance of electricity as a source of energy for use, and also indicates how much we use for transport, for domestic use as fuel and for use in industry. The energy generated as electricity is, of course, then used by industry and domestic users, too.

The use of energy is not evenly spread, for most of the world's energy is used by the MDCs. North America, for example, has only 4% of the world's population but consumes a quarter of all energy,

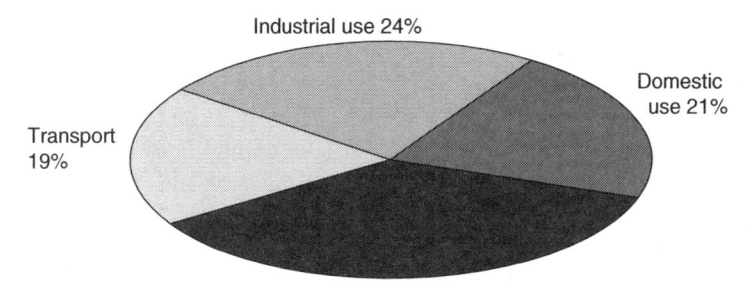

Industrial use 24%
Domestic use 21%
Transport 19%
Electricity generation 36%

Figure 5.1 World primary energy use

whereas China, with a quarter of the world's population, consumes only 3% of its energy. Table 5.1 shows the differences in energy use around the globe.

Table 5.1 Patterns of energy use

Area	Energy use (GJ/capita/year)
World	87
North America, Japan and Oceania	286
Western Europe	151
Africa	25
Eastern Europe (including Russia)	197
Middle East	36
Latin America	52
China	24
South Asia	17

The data for the amount of energy used shows huge differences between regions, but hides variations in the forms of energy used. In the high-energy-use regions most of the energy comes from fossil fuels, whereas in the low-energy-use regions fuelwood and other renewable energy sources such as plant material (biomass) are much more important. In southern Asia, for example, fuelwood that provides the same energy as 150 million tonnes of oil (150 mtoe, or million tonnes oil equivalent) is consumed each year. Such patterns of energy use result from differences in levels of economic development and standard of living between regions – indeed, the amount of energy used per person is sometimes used as an indicator of a country's economic development.

Energy use and conservation issues

The use of energy raises many conservation issues both at a global scale, for individual countries and regions, and for individual citizens. Amongst the most important of these are:

- What reserves of non-renewable energy resources remain?
- What steps can be taken to extend the life of non-renewable energy resources?
- What alternative renewable energy sources exist, and how can they be most effectively used and developed?
- What is the environmental impact of the use of each source of energy?
- How can we meet increasing demand for energy without significant environmental impact?
- What can be done to minimize these environmental impacts?

These questions will be investigated in the sections that follow.

Energy extraction and resource limits

The world's economy is driven mainly by the energy we gain from fossil fuels. The industrial revolution of the eighteenth and nineteenth centuries in the West was founded on the burning of coal, and the twentieth century has seen coal overtaken by oil and natural gas as the main fuel sources. Although reserves of all three of these fossil fuels are still enormous, a clear concern is that there are, ultimately, limits to the amount of these fuels available. Identifying what resources exist for each fuel, and looking at ways in which their use can be reduced or made more efficient, are important conservation issues. Managing existing reserves is also a major political question, for controlling large reserves of energy sources such as oil can provide major political influence to such supplier nations – for example, 75% of the Earth's oil reserves belong to just 15 nations.

Case study – coal extraction

Coal comes in a variety of forms – from low-quality, high-sulphur brown coals to high-energy coals such as anthracite. Each has its own particular uses, and reserves of each type are differently distributed. Overall, though, the reserves of coal would provide supplies for 220 years if we continue to consume them at our current rate. The traditional coal mining regions of western Europe and the eastern USA have declined in importance as reserves have been exhausted and the cost of mining has increased, and most supplies are now obtained from central and western USA, Russia and China, where mining is technically easier and is also cheaper. Competition from oil, which is easier to transport and cheaper to obtain, has reduced coal's share of the world energy market. Coal also has a major impact on the environment, both in its use (see below) and in its mining. The risks to miners from underground working are significant even in modern mines, and particularly in mines in the less-developed world. More importantly, though, the impact of low-cost **opencast mining**, in which coal is removed from just below the ground surface, is enormous in terms of both its effect on the landscape and the cost of restoring the land. Both underground and open-cast mines also risk pollution of the local environment with waste materials.

Case study – the oil industry

The oil industry is the symbol of economic growth in the twentieth century, and has provided for much of that time a relatively cheap and easily accessible source of fossil fuel. Substantial rises in the price of oil in the early 1970s, however, which were imposed by OPEC, reminded both the developed and the less developed world of its dependence on oil. Throughout its history it has been estimated that the reserves of oil would last only 40 years, but new discoveries have kept this figure constant. Estimates by geologists, however, suggest that the 'ultimately recoverable oil resources' were originally about 300 billion tonnes. Ninety billion tonnes have been used so far, 120 billion tonnes are known in identified reserves, and a further 90 billion tonnes are estimated as remaining to be discovered. However, these figures are constantly changing, for three reasons:

1 The amount of oil that exploration companies 'bother' to find is driven by the price of oil. If oil is plentiful and cheap, there is no strong incentive to go out and find new reserves.

2 The amount of oil normally extracted from an oilfield is about 35% – the rest is too expensive to recover. However, if the price of oil increases it becomes economical to recover more from an oilfield.

3 Vast quantities of oil are potentially available, not from traditional oilfields but from rocks such as oilshales or tar sands. Under present circumstances such sources are not worth exploiting economically, but they may become so in the future.

The environmental impact of oil extraction is often regarded as being less than that of coal, but the environmental damage from accident is potentially larger. While some impact may occur as a result of seepage of oil from wells, the biggest risk comes during transport by pipeline or tanker. The impact, for example, of the wreck of the *Exxon Valdez* off the coast of Alaska in 1985 was huge, with significant loss of animal and plant life and permanent damage to the marine ecosystem in the locality. Smaller oil-spills are quite common in the world's major shipping lanes.

Case study – fuelwood in the less developed world

One-third of the world's population relies on wood as a major source of fuel. Half of the wood cut each year around the world is used as fuel, and almost all of this is in the developing world. Although wood is a renewable resource, population pressures in some parts of the world have reduced access to reliable supplies. The removal of trees to meet demand has a number of effects:

- the cost of fuelwood in the cities of the less developed world increases;
- the land cleared of woodland is more prone to soil erosion;
- those who cannot obtain or afford fuelwood use animal dung as an alternative; this reduces an important source of fertilizer to soil and can reduce crop yields;
- a cycle of disease, malnutrition and poverty can become established;
- trees are an important store of water, and without them an area can become more arid.

Nepal provides an example of the impact of fuelwood shortage, for 90% of the country's energy needs comes from wood. The average amount of fuelwood used per person per year is 600 kg, and as the population grew from 5 million in 1953 to 16 million in 1999 so fuelwood has become scarce and forests have been thinned and cleared. Prices in the cities such as Kathmandu have increased rapidly, and in some villages the weekly supply of firewood now takes two days to gather instead of one hour a few years ago. At present, the forests of Nepal produce only 80 kg of timber per person from regrowth.

Stretching resources

To conserve the reserves of energy, an important first step is to look at ways of making the known resources stretch further – to be more efficient in their use. There are several approaches to this:

Increasing efficiency of energy conversion

Most of the energy in fossil fuels is not used when they are burned because the process of **energy conversion** is inefficient. Of the energy in each tonne of coal or oil, only 30% is available as energy if it is converted to electricity. Most of this energy is then used during the transmission of electricity from the power station to the consumer or in the final electrical device. Traditional electric light bulbs provide less than 1% of the energy in the fuel burned to generate the electricity that lights them. Conservation of fossil fuels can be assisted by making this process more efficient – for example, technological improvements in the use of fossil fuels, such as the development of **pressurized fluidized-bed combustion** of coal, can increase efficiency from 30% to 42%. In addition, trying to make use of the heat generated (which is how most of the energy is wasted) for local heating systems can reduce the wastage of energy. Such **combined heat and power (CHP)** schemes, or **cogeneration**, have been developed in many housing estates in European cities such as Paris and Berlin.

Reducing energy consumption

It is in reducing energy consumption that the actions of individuals can be important. Making homes more energy efficient through better insulation, the use of double glazing and draught-proofing, and the building of new homes with smaller windows facing the directions of sunlight receipt are encouraged in many Western countries. Houses built to modern insulation standards use only 25% of the energy of older houses.

A second major approach is the discouragement of private transport, which uses 20% of the world's energy consumption, and the encouragement of more fuel-efficient vehicle engines. An average family in North America or Western Europe, for example, consumes 5 tonnes of oil each year for its private transport needs, compared with only 3.3 tonnes for its electricity needs.

A third approach is through the recycling of waste products, which reduces the demand for energy to manufacture goods from virgin raw materials. Waste materials are also being used to generate power, either using waste as fuel in power stations or by tapping the heat generated from the bacterial decay of waste in rubbish tips and landfill sites. Every 3 kg of waste has the energy content of 1 kg of coal, and the UK government has estimated that landfill sites could provide energy equivalent to the burning of one million tonnes of coal each year.

Governments in some Western countries have tried to encourage such increased efficiency by the use of taxation. In the EU, for example, value added tax (VAT) is added to electricity charges. In the UK the government provides grants for insulation of older houses and has introduced more demanding building regulations which have encouraged energy saving. A second approach is the use of **demand-side management (DSM)**, in which electricity companies are required to sell energy-efficient products such as low-energy light bulbs and roof insulation. Such policies are important in the USA, where a 1992 report suggested that DSM had reduced energy demand in states such as California by as much as 5%. A strategy considered in the EU has been that of a **carbon/energy tax**. This tax would be applied to the burning of fuels containing carbon, and would aim to reduce the use of such fuels and encourage development of alternative energy sources. Opponents of the tax include the less developed EU countries, who feel that it would slow down economic growth by taxing industry, and transport experts, who believe that increasing fuel prices, even by a large amount, will have very little effect on the amount of fuel used.

Fuelwood efficiency

Stretching the efficiency of fuelwood use in the less developed world depends on two main approaches – managing the forests to produce more wood, and reducing the demand for wood. **Tree farms** have been developed in some countries, using fast-growing species such as eucalyptus or pine, but these have often not been successful because they do not belong to the community. In **social** or **community forestry** community fuelwood plantations are managed by the whole village, and these have had more impact on increasing fuelwood supplies. Reducing demand for fuelwood involves developing alternatives, such as windmills or water power schemes, to produce electricity. Alternatively, developing more efficient cooking stoves can reduce fuelwood consumption by 30–50%. In Sri Lanka, for example, such stoves have been developed through a joint project between the UK-based Intermediate Technology Group and the Sri Lanka National Electricity Board.

Alternative energy resources

Most of the energy used around the globe is obtained from non-renewable resources. An important way of sustaining the resources we have is to use more energy from sustainable and renewable sources such as wind power, wave power and direct solar energy. While most of these alternatives have been used to a small degree throughout history, and have been developed more widely in recent years, they still contribute very little to our energy supply.

Solar power

Solar power is the use of the Sun's energy either to heat water directly or to generate electricity through solar electric cells. The sun provides 15,000 times more energy each day than humankind uses, so provides a huge potential energy source. In tropical and sub-tropical areas, such as California or The Gambia, solar power schemes make an important contribution to power generation. For example, in the Mojave Desert, California, a solar energy farm of 600,000 mirrors covers 400 hectares of land and generates 275 MW of power; in The Gambia, solar panels are used to generate the power to pump water from boreholes to provide irrigation for horticultural crop production.

Wind power

Wind power involves constructing windmills either to use the power directly, as in traditional grain mills, or to generate electricity from turbines. In windy countries, such as the UK, wind power has great potential and 'wind farms' have been constructed in western Scotland, west Wales and in Cornwall. In the LDCs, small windmills could be used to provide energy for villages in remote locations.

Geothermal power

Heat from deep within the Earth can be obtained by pumping cold water to great depths and returning it charged with heat, or simply by using naturally occurring hot water sources, particularly in volcanic areas such as Iceland. Smaller local schemes have been developed in the UK, for example in the city of Southampton, where hot water is used to provide space heating in city centre buildings.

Hydropower

Water power has traditionally been used for turning mills, but can be used on a large scale to generate electricity by using falling water to turn turbines. Such **hydro-electric power (HEP)** provides 23% of the world's electricity and in some countries, such as Norway, over 95%. The construction of large dams to store the water may be seen by some as environmentally damaging, and is expensive, but once constructed such dams can generate substantial amounts of low-cost electricity. In the USA, for example, many of the major rivers (for example, the Colorado River) have a series of HEP stations along them. The use of small, local HEP stations rather than large schemes offers great potential for less developed countries, and in China over 80,000 mini-hydro plants have been installed. In Nepal some 600 mini-hydro plants have been built as one attempt to offset fuelwood shortages.

Ocean power

The oceans can provide sustainable energy in a number of ways. The daily movements of the tide (**tidal power**) can be used to generate electricity by storing incoming tidal water behind a dam, and releasing it through turbines at low tide, as at La Rance tidal power station in northern France. Concerns about the impact on the landscape and the local ecosystems of building large dams (**barrages**) across estuaries, however, have been a major objection to proposals for such schemes, for example across the estuary of the River Severn or at Morecambe Bay in the UK. **Wave power** involves the placement of barrages offshore to generate electricity from the movement of waves. **Ocean thermal exchange conversion (OTEC)** uses the temperature differences between warm surface water and cold deep ocean water to generate electricity, and could be used to produce drinking water as a by-product. Trial developments have been undertaken in Taiwan. A fourth, but as yet unexploited, potential energy source from the oceans is to pass large-scale **ocean current movements** through generating devices.

Nuclear power

The use of nuclear power is a by-product of the weapons industry of the 1950s, and almost 500 plants worldwide now provide 16% of the world's electricity. At present all are **nuclear fission** stations, in which the splitting of atoms in controlled nuclear reactions generates heat, which is used to heat water to steam to drive generators. The raw material is uranium, which is a non-renewable resource, but which is used in only small quantities so that its supply is sustainable long into the future. **Nuclear fusion** processes, in which electricity is generated by reactions where atomic particles are forced to combine, has potential for very efficient energy production, but the technology has proved difficult to refine. Nuclear power has become important in countries with limited fossil fuels, and provides, for example, 70% of electricity in France and 25% in Japan. While the potential for further power stations is large, however, there are many environmental concerns about their development. These include the following.

Safety issues

Explosions at Chernobyl in the Ukraine (1986) and at Three-Mile Island in the USA (1979) have raised concerns about the huge impact of a nuclear power station 'disaster'. In addition, there are concerns about the health risks to those living close to such stations from long-term exposure to slightly increased levels of radioactivity, and of the risks to power station workers from small-scale handling accidents.

Waste disposal issues

Spent fuel from nuclear power stations has to be processed to make it less dangerous and then stored while its radioactivity declines (this takes thousands of years). Concerns about the transport of waste to reprocessing plants such as that at Sellafield in Cumbria, UK, and about the risk of leakage from stores, have been a focus of campaigns by environmental groups.

Cost

The cost of generating power from nuclear stations is lower than from most other fuel sources. However, anti-nuclear environmentalists have protested that this hides the real but hidden costs of health damage, the cost of waste disposal and the huge costs of dealing with the power station after it has reached the end of its useful life (**decommissioning**).

Nuclear arms

Nuclear power technology provides countries with the potential for developing nuclear weapons. Concerns over this misuse of technology in countries such as Iraq, Pakistan and Cuba have raised questions about the future of nuclear power.

Power from biomass

The most traditional source of energy is the burning of plant material. The threat to fuelwood resources described above has pushed the development of alternative plant sources and the use of biomass plantations where plants are grown for use as fuel. Fast-growing species such as eucalyptus can be used efficiently for power stations, but an important alternative is to use appropriate crops to make ethanol, which can be used as a petrol substitute for cars. In Brazil 25% of cars run on pure ethanol, made from sugar cane, cassava and maize, and all fuel contains 20% ethanol from such sources. In Europe and North America **biodiesel** has been developed by combining rapeseed oil with methanol; it is a useful alternative to diesel, and can be used in standard diesel engines – three tonnes of rape plant yields one tonne of biodiesel.

The development of alternative energy sources is complicated by the cost of developing the technology, and by the concerns about the environmental impact of, for example, large areas of wind farms or solar panels, in the landscape. As fossil fuels become more expensive, though, the economics of developing alternatives become more attractive to governments and to business.

Energy use and environmental impact

Energy conservation doesn't simply refer to maintaining future supplies for a growing population. The use of energy and the burning of fuels has a major environmental impact, principally through the pollutants that are produced as by-products. In addition, the sites of fuel extraction and power generation (coal mines, oil fields, wind farms, power stations) are an environmental concern because of their **visual impact** – the effect they have on the landscape. In many countries new proposals for developments of this sort require an **environmental impact assessment (EIA)** to be undertaken as part of the planning process (see Chapter 11). Here we shall look at two of the issues linked to pollution.

Power generation and the burning of fossil fuels

The burning of fossil fuels in power stations produces a wide range of waste products that are released to the atmosphere. These are mainly sulphur dioxide (SO_2), carbon dioxide (CO_2) and various oxides of nitrogen (NOx), which can be linked directly to a number of important environmental threats.

Contribution to the greenhouse effect

The greenhouse effect (see Chapter 10) is the process in which pollutants cause heat to build up in the atmosphere, leading to rises in global temperature. Carbon dioxide and the nitrogen oxides are major contributors to this process, and about two-thirds of the 7 billion tonnes of CO_2 that are added to the atmosphere each year come from the burning of fossil fuels.

Acidification

Sulphur dioxide and the nitrogen oxides from fossil fuels react with water in the atmosphere to produce acids that are returned to the Earth's surface in rain, mist and snow. The term **acid rain** covers a wide range of substances, but together they are responsible for large-scale environmental impact. In industrial areas and in areas downwind from such regions acid rain has been responsible for damage to forests and loss of trees, acidification of lakes and destruction of aquatic species, damage to buildings through acid erosion, and adverse effects on human health. Areas particularly badly affected are Scandinavia (with pollution from Western Europe), north-east USA and eastern Canada, and eastern Europe, the Ukraine, Belarus and Russia. In the latter region the major problem is the burning of brown coal (lignite), which has a high sulphur content, in power stations. The extent of damage varies according to how acid the soil and rocks in a particular location are naturally, but the scale of damage in some areas is large. More than 65% of the trees in the UK and more than 50% of the trees in Germany and the Netherlands show signs of damage by acid rain, and in Sweden some 20,000 lakes are acidified, 20% of which can no longer support fish. Pollution by acid rain is a good example of pollution crossing international boundaries, which raises important political and legal issues. In Norway, for example, over 90% of the sulphur pollution producing acid rain comes from other countries. Similar problems occur in North America, where the main sources of sulphur dioxide are the industrial regions of the north-eastern USA. Transport of acid rain into Canada from such sources is inevitable – and when this combines with sulphur dioxide from the world's largest single source (the copper and nickel smelting plants at Sudbury, Ontario), the effect on eastern Canada is large.

Some technological developments can reduce the emission of these pollutants into the atmosphere from power stations, and use of 'cleaner' fossil fuels (gas rather than coal, for example) is also helpful in reducing emissions. In addition, international action to reduce the impact of acid rain has begun – this is examined in more detail in Chapter 10.

Low-level ozone pollution

Ozone (O_3) is usually best known in the context of the development of the so-called 'ozone holes' in the upper levels of the atmosphere. Near the Earth's surface, ozone is produced as a pollutant as a result of the effect of sunlight on gases such as nitrogen oxides. Ozone increases breathing disorders and asthma and is now regarded as an important health issue, particularly in cities. Ozone pollution in Mexico City, for example, has lead to the city government banning the use of certain types of vehicle when levels are high.

Transport and pollution

Transport and the burning of, mainly, oil and petrol, is an important source of pollution in the atmosphere. Vehicles consume one-third of the oil produced around the world, and approximately 15–20% of all CO_2 produced comes from **tailpipe emissions** – the combustion of each litre of petrol produces about 2.5 kg of CO_2.

In some LDCs the proportion of atmospheric pollution from transport is even higher: in India, for example, 85% of carbon monoxide and over 90% of nitrogen oxides come from transport rather than industry. Other pollutants also come from the burning of petrol, including lead, which is added to petrol to improve combustion. Lead from petrol has a serious impact on health, and other chemicals in petrol, such as formaldehyde and benzene, can be cancer-inducing (**carcinogenic**).

Increases in fuel efficiency in cars, reduction in the use of lead in petrol, and use of catalytic convertors (which 'scrub' the waste gases and produce cleaner exhaust) can all contribute to reducing the pollution from vehicles, but the growth of vehicle use often simply cancels out the gains from this. Some states have introduced strong legislation to tailpipe emissions. In California, for example, the maximum permitted level of emissions from cars is being reduced each year until the year 2010, and the introduction of **low-emission vehicles (LEVs)** and **zero-emission vehicles (ZEVs)** is being encouraged. The Federal government in the USA has also made a commitment to reduced emission through the 1989 Clean Air Act.

Summary

As the world's population and standards of living grow, the demand for energy increases. Most of the energy used in the developed world comes from the burning of non-renewable fossil fuels. This raises important questions about how long these resources will last and what alternative renewable or sustainable energy sources might be developed. There are also concerns about the environmental impact of burning coal, oil and natural gas in power stations, factories and as fuel for vehicles, and about the effects on human health. Conservation of fossil fuels is, therefore, an important global issue.

It is not only the developed countries that have energy problems. Half the world's population depends on fuelwood for heat and light, and conserving supplies of this sustainable resource is an important issue. Secondly, aspirations for economic growth push such countries to generate electricity from fossil fuels, thereby contributing to global pollution.

Energy is also an important political issue. The power that comes with owning large energy resources gives some countries considerable influence in the world, and access to oil and coal can be important in international affairs. The Kuwait War of 1990 was partly the result of Iraq's ambitions to take over the oil fields of Kuwait, and the West's determination to keep them in the hands of a friendly power. Trying to reduce energy use is also an issue for developing countries, who see this as a strategy by the West to limit their economic growth.

Taking action

A key question in conservation is about what individuals might do to help global issues. Contributing to conservation of energy might include:

1 Reducing household electricity use by switching off lights, turning down thermostats, using appliances more sparingly, insulating the roof and walls of the house, double glazing, and using energy-efficient light bulbs.

2 Reducing household waste by recycling materials and composting food waste.

3 Reducing consumption of fuel by buying a more fuel-efficient car, sharing car travel to work, or using public transport or bicycles wherever possible.

ACTIVITIES

1 In your home or place of work identify all the ways in which energy is used. This is known as undertaking an **energy audit**. For each use of energy try to identify ways of reducing the amount of energy used. For example, could electric light bulbs be replaced with energy-efficient light bulbs? Could more of the food be bought fresh to reduce the amount of packaging needed? Could children cycle to school instead of going by car?

2 Use your local newspaper, or a national paper, to produce a file of environmental issues linked to energy use – for example, oil pollution incidents, or advertisements for solar panels.

3 Contact your local authority, and identify what support they can give to homes or businesses trying to reduce energy use.

6 BIODIVERSITY, CONSERVATION AND NATURAL HABITATS

Introduction

It is easy to believe that the great age of discovery has long since passed. Few corners of the Earth have not been visited by humans, and with satellite images the mapping of much of the Earth's land surface is well under way. Globalization of communications and of the world economy leaves few parts of the world out of the reach of almost instant contact.

Although we know the basic map of the globe, however, there is much still to be discovered about the ecosystems of the Earth. Scientists have recorded about 1.4 million species of organism, of which 750,000 are insects, 250,000 are plants, 75,000 are fungi and 44,000 are vertebrates. But this is only a small part of the whole picture, for it has been estimated that there are about 10 million species in total. We know of less than 20% of freshwater species, 5% of fungi and 1% of marine organisms.

Despite our limited knowledge, though, we *are* aware that species are being lost at a very rapid rate. Some of the species becoming extinct are well known – the dodo, which disappeared in the eighteenth century, and the passenger pigeon lost from the skies of North America in the nineteenth century, for example. These are only the tip of the iceberg, however, for it has been estimated that between 50 and 100 species are being lost per day, and over the next 30 years some 20–25% of global plant species may become extinct.

Loss of natural ecosystems is as significant as the loss of species. Of the world's major biomes, few areas remain as climatic climax communities due to the impact of human activity. In 1700 some 60% of the Earth's land surface was covered by forest, including tropical and temperate forests. By the early twentieth century this had declined to about 45% and at the end of the millennium only some 30% of land is forested by climatic climax forest.

With the decline in 'natural' environments and the decline in species numbers, an important environmental issue that is now of great concern is that of conserving biodiversity. Biodiversity refers to the variety of living things, from viruses to the blue whale and the giant redwood tree, and there is a widely held view that we need to preserve biodiversity as an important part of conservation. Its importance has been recognized in two important international agreements:

The World Conservation Strategy (WCS)

This was developed jointly by the UN Environment Programme, the Worldwide Fund for Nature and the International Union for the Conservation of Nature. It was published in 1980, and updated in 1990. The objectives of the WCS are to:

- maintain essential ecological processes and systems such as soil, forests and freshwater systems;
- preserve genetic diversity for breeding by preventing extinction of species; and
- ensure the sustainable use of species and ecosystems.

The UN Framework Convention on Biodiversity

Signed at the 1992 Rio Earth Summit, this committed its 150 signatory countries to taking action to preserve biodiversity by protecting plants and animals and ensuring future access to the genetic material of as wide a range of organisms as possible.

But why is biodiversity important?

Biodiversity as a conservation issue

The potential loss of individual species and whole ecosystems is of concern for a number of scientific, ethical, social and political reasons.

Firstly, plants and animals are the basis of almost all food and medicine and a large number of industrial products. This raises issues of both present and future needs. At present we are dependent on a very small number of individual species – for example, 75% of all food is based on just eight crops (wheat, rice, maize, potato, barley, sweet potato, cassava, soya beans), and 95% of global food supply comes from only 30 different plants. Many of these have been selectively bred to produce high-yielding varieties. The concern is that this makes humanity very susceptible to the impact of plant disease. To provide for diversity if such disease should occur it is important to maintain as wide a range of alternative species and varieties of species as possible. By reducing the gene pool for any species by the extinction of varieties and strains, the possibility of future breeding to develop new characteristics or to overcome disease is lost. In Europe, for example, there is concern that most of the 150 species of cattle are under threat of extinction, yet they provide a huge gene pool for potential breeding and improvement of stock.

In terms of future need, there is great concern that many important medicinal and food discoveries remain to be made, but extinctions may mean that we lose species before we know their value or even know of their existence. There are many examples of species that have seemed unimportant but have then become the basis of an essential pharmaceutical or food product – for example:

- The rosy periwinkle, a forest plant found in Madagascar, was discovered to be the basis of two extremely valuable drugs to treat childhood leukemia.
- The bat *Eonycteris spelaea*, found in caves in Malaysia, was heading towards extinction because of the destruction of its cave and swamp habitat. However, it was discovered to be the principal species responsible for pollinating the durian fruit tree, whose production is worth US $200 million per year to the Malaysian economy.

We cannot know, therefore, what the real cost of the extinction of a particular species may be. It is argued that care needs to be taken to maintain *all* biodiversity, but especially to be able to identify what have become know as the Earth's **'hot-spots'**. Hot spots are the locations which are especially rich in the range and number of species, for it is believed that 20% of the Earth's species are found on only 0.5% of the land area.

Secondly, there are moral concerns about the decline in biodiversity. Many environmental philosophies and religious faiths place emphasis on respecting and valuing all living organisms, and place specific responsibility on people for the 'stewardship' of such resources. Linked to this moral issue is the aesthetic point that loss of species impoverishes human existence and the value of the environment to the human spirit.

Protection of biodiversity has two important elements – the protection of ecosystems and the protection of endangered species. Ecosystem issues will be examined here, while issues of species conservation will be examined in the next chapter.

Conserving ecosystems

Each of the world's major ecosystems (identified in Chapter 3) faces a range of threats and issues that affect its future. Here we shall examine two specific examples, the world's tropical forests and the world's wetlands, to identify the causes, nature, effects and possible ways of dealing with conservation issues.

Conservation issues in the tropical forests

The issues of the tropical forests have made their way into the headlines and have become the focus of much research by environmental scientists. The issues relate to the clearance of the climatic climax ecosystem and its replacement by a human-produced and maintained ecosystem, or plagioclimax community.

How fast are the forests being cleared? Figures are difficult to obtain and there is little information on how much forest there is or was, since many forest areas have never been mapped. However, it is estimated that some 900 million hectares of tropical broadleaved forest (equivalent to the area of the USA) remain out of an original total of about 1600 million hectares – or about 60% of the original total. Forest loss continues apace, and authorities suggest that forest is being cleared today at a rate of about 20 million hectares per year (equivalent to the area of a football pitch every minute!) The clearance of forests is the result of a number of pressures:

- ■ *Demand for tropical hardwoods.* The hardwoods of the tropical forests are a major source of timber. Consumption by Western industrial countries of timber such as teak has increased tenfold since the 1950s.
- ■ *Population pressure.* Tropical broadleaved forests are found in countries with high population growth rates. As populations continue to grow, the pressure on land to provide food is increasing. The easiest method for governments to increase food supply is to extend agriculture into previously unused land. In Indonesia, for example, government policy has, since 1949, encouraged farmers to transmigrate from densely populated areas such as Java to less populated islands such as Kalimantan and Sulawesi, where development of new farms involves clearing forest.
- ■ *Economic pressure on LDCs.* All tropical countries are seeking to improve their economic well-being, and one of the easiest ways to do this is to sell primary products (minerals, timber, food) to MDCs. The value of timber and forest product exports to the tropical countries who sell them is US $30,000 million per year, so there is a strong economic incentive for logging contracts to be sold.
- ■ *The firewood issue.* Most areas of tropical forest are very sparsely populated, but in tropical areas where population density is high much of the loss of forest margins is from the use of timber for firewood. Half the world's population uses wood for energy, and half the timber cut in the world is used as firewood. Nearly a quarter of the loss of tropical forest can be attributed to this cause.

The consequences of the clearance of tropical forests raise many issues for those interested in environmental protection and conservation. While it is recognized that much environmental damage is being caused, the economic necessities of everyday life in many tropical countries challenge governments to resist demands from environmental groups. A number of important environmental issues can be identified, however:

- *Climatic impacts.* The tropical forests are very important in the global climate system because the natural respiration processes of trees absorb large amounts of CO_2 and produce large amounts of oxygen. As the area of forest is reduced, so an important way in which CO_2 is used is lost. With the growing production of CO_2 a major cause of global warming, loss of tropical forest may be an important contributor to the greenhouse effect.
- *Loss of biodiversity.* Tropical forests have a rich variety of plant and animal life, although many species have not yet been identified or named. Loss of the forest means loss of the species within it. This is an important issue both in terms of the richness of the human environment and in relation to the loss of potential important resources. Many pharmaceuticals are derived from tropical forest plants, and the loss of species may deprive people of important future developments in this area.
- *Soil and nutrient loss.* Removal of the forest cover lays soil bare to erosion, which may make the land unusable for agriculture, and may also lead to flooding downstream by increasing the 'load' of rivers. Estimates suggest that deforestation in the Himalayas leads to the loss of 6 billion tonnes of soil each year into the river system that feeds the River Ganges in Northern India. In addition, much of the nutrient store in tropical forests is held not in the soil but in the rich vegetation. When trees are removed the nutrients are lost too, leaving a poor, infertile soil which may be unusable for agriculture.
- *Increased aridity.* The forests are an important store of atmospheric moisture. There are serious concerns that the removal of forests on a large scale will increase the risk of drought – there is already some evidence of this happening in areas of rapid forest loss such as in Amazonia and Indonesia.

BIODIVERSITY, CONSERVATION AND NATURAL HABITATS

Conservation in the tropical forests is a complex management issue, and many LDC governments have been accused of using no substantial conservation policy. Broadly, there are two types of strategy which can be used, either separately or in combination – forest resource conservation and ecosystem conservation.

Forest resource conservation

The main aim of forest resource conservation is to manage the forests to ensure a sustainable supply of timber and other forest resources, including firewood. Of importance is the planning of a forest strategy to ensure that no more timber is removed from each area of forest each year than will be replaced by natural growth. A common problem is the effect of **clear felling** because, in most tropical forests, the number of useable trees is small – clear felling may be cheaper for logging companies, but destroys unnecessarily large amounts of other plants. 'Creaming', or selective felling, can help to overcome this problem.

Forest resource conservation can also be achieved by finding alternative sources of timber or alternative forms of income for governments. The planting of tree farms to provide local firewood, for example, can reduce tree loss from the forest, as can the development of alternative energy sources such as mini-hydroelectric power schemes or the use of biogas digesters using crop or animal waste. Alternative income might come from the development of wood-processing industries to produce veneer or plywood. These products generate much more income from exports than the sale of timber itself.

Even where strong conservation rules exist, however, a major problem is that of enforcement. Illegal logging, over-logging and logging of areas outside designated timber forests are problems in countries which are large and difficult to police. In some cases corruption involving logging companies and government officials has caused problems in managing the forest effectively.

Ecosystem conservation

This involves the protection of areas of the forest ecosystem and its species from human interference. By the late 1990s some 1200 protected areas had been established in tropical forests, varying in size from small reserves to large protected national parks. An example is the Korup National Park, which covers an area of 1250 square kilometres in Northern Cameroon, along the border with Nigeria. This area of forest has survived because its terrain was unsuitable for commercial agriculture and plantations, and its conservation is the result of funding by the Cameroon government, WWF, a range of international NGOs and aid from a number of overseas governments. In addition to preserving the forest and its species the area is being developed for limited tourism.

The conservation strategies described above have been developed in the forest countries by their own governments. A major challenge to the forests, though, is the fact that most of the forest products are destined for consumers in the MDCs. Changing policies and resource use in the consumer countries of the North, therefore, is at least as important for conservation of the tropical forests. Strategies that are being used to change consumption include:
- reducing consumption of tropical timber by using alternatives, often instigated by the publicity activities of environmental NGOs;
- changing domestic forest policy to enable more wood to be grown in the North; and
- promoting the use of timber products from the tropics rather than the purchase of raw timber.

Conservation in the world's wetlands

The word 'wetland' is used to describe any area where a key component of the ecosystem is the presence of water. It includes marshes, lakes, coastal mangrove swamps and river communities. There are many very large wetland ecosystems – for example, the Norfolk Broads and the Fenlands in the UK; the Florida Everglades and the Mississippi Delta in the USA; the Camargue area of southern France and the river valleys of northern Poland in mainland Europe; and the mangrove swamps of the Sundarban forests of the Ganges delta in Asia.

Wetlands are of importance for a number of reasons:
1. They are very rich as ecosystems, with diverse species of insects, fish and bird life, and high primary productivity because of the presence of substantial nutrients – they are therefore important for conservation because of their ecological value.
2. They are a source of natural resources such as peat.
3. Their location makes them especially vulnerable to human impact. Their sites are valuable for drainage and development, either for agricultural land or for urban development, and they are susceptible to the impact of water-borne pollution from nearby industrial and urban areas.
4. They are important as recreational resources, either for 'ecotourism' activities or for water-based recreation including sailing, fishing and other water sports. This makes them susceptible to the damaging impact of tourism and recreation.
5. They are often important in coastal protection against erosion.

The importance of conserving wetlands has been recognized by the Convention on Wetlands of International Importance, known as the **Ramsar Convention**, signed in 1971 by 64 countries. This contains a list of 542 sites of international importance, covering more than 32 million hectares, which are subject to national protection policies.

Of the 13 sites in the UK listed in the Ramsar Convention, two (Bure Marshes; Horsey, Hickling and Martham Broads) are part of the Norfolk Broads area of East Anglia. The Broads are waterways and lakes produced by peat cutting along the rivers Waveney, Yare and Bure during the Middle Ages, and the area includes extensive marsh areas and sedge and reed beds. The area is home to a number of rare species, including the swallowtail butterfly, the bittern, and the marsh harrier. The ecosystem is the product of human activity but has been maintained by animal grazing in the marshes, peat cutting and reed and sedge cutting over the centuries. During the twentieth century a number of important threats to the Norfolk Broads have arisen. These include:

- A decline in reed cutting as a result of the use of alternative materials for building and roofing. This has resulted in destruction of the reed beds by ecological succession to scrub vegetation.
- Pollution of the waterways. Some of this is from sewage pollution from local towns, but much is from nitrates and phosphates. These are the product of the use of inorganic fertilizers on local farmland carried as runoff into the Broads. The result initially is that the waterways become clogged as water plants such as algae grow rapidly in response to the fertilizers. Other plants and fish become crowded out. However, as the plants die, the decay process uses up the oxygen in the water, killing fish and other water creatures. This is the process of **eutrophication**.
- Bank erosion of the waterways because of the effect of the wash from visitor boats, for the Broads are an important recreation area, especially for boating. This bank erosion is made worse by the burrowing effect of coypu, a non-native species now endemic in the Broads after escaping from fur farms in the region.

The management of the Norfolk Broads falls to a large number of bodies, including local authorities, local naturalists' trusts and the Nature Conservancy Council. The region is now a National Park in all but name, and a range of management policies has been developed. These have included:

- dredging of phosphorus-rich mud from some of the Broads;
- removal of phosphates from sewage at local sewage plants;
- restrictions on speed limits for boats, to reduce the size of their wash; and
- bank restoration and protection using materials such as protective nylon matting.

A second example of wetland management is the Parc Naturel de s'Albufera in north-eastern Majorca, one of the Balearic Islands in the Mediterranean. This area of marshland is 177 hectares in size, and has historically been maintained by reed cutting, grazing and rice growing. When these industries ceased the marsh was still managed to retain a range of marshland plants and wildfowl throughout the twentieth century, but recent threats to its existence have arisen from pressure for development land in this tourist region of Spain. The government took the step of declaring the site a National Park in 1988, which has protected it from drainage and development.

Strategies for conserving natural habitats

Habitat conservation is an important part of the World Conservation Strategy, but many countries have a long history of attempting to protect natural areas from development or damage by human activity. Protected ecosystem are termed **biosphere reserves**, and include areas known as nature reserves, national parks, conservations zones, game reserves, nature parks and similar titles. Apart from a central focus on conservation such biosphere reserves are highly varied in terms of:

- *Size* – large national parks covering thousands of square kilometres (for example the Amacayacu National Park in Amazonia, which is 3000 square kilometres), and small patches of protected land, perhaps only a few square metres in area, can be biosphere reserves. The Wildlife Centre on Southampton Common in the UK is only a few hundred square metres in size.
- *Aims* – some biosphere reserves are intended to protect a single species in a unique habitat, such as many of the sites of special scientific interest (SSSIs) in the UK. Others may be representative areas of a large complex ecosystem, or a sample of one of the world's major biomes.
- *Management* – some biosphere reserves are operated by national governments or national bodies (as is the norm in the UK), others by local government (as in

Sweden), specially appointed bodies, NGOs, charities or even individual conservationists.
- ■ *Character* – some may be areas of wilderness which represent natural climax communities, as in most of the National Parks of the USA, while others may seek to preserve distinctive plagioclimax communities, as in the National Parks of England and Wales.
- ■ *Access and use* – some biosphere reserves are open to the public and encourage use of the reserve for recreation and tourism. Others seek to exclude most users, or confine them to specific parts of the reserve.

Biosphere reserves – case studies

To illustrate the contrasts in approach to conservation in biosphere reserves, a number of case studies are presented here. All have the common aim of conservation, but the methods and management they use are quite different.

National Parks in the UK

National Parks were first established in the UK in 1949. Few parts of the densely populated British Isles represent completely natural surroundings, and the landscape areas chosen for National Parks were (and are) characterized by distinctive human landscapes set in areas of great scenic beauty. The Lake District National Park, for example, includes the high fells and the lakes of Cumbria, but is a densely populated region dependent mainly on a rural economy of agriculture, forestry and tourism. Much of the land is privately owned, and at best the landscape represents a semi-natural ecosystem.

The aims of the National Parks are to preserve the character and way of life of the region and to protect it from inappropriate development or damage. This is undertaken through a joint planning board with representatives of the many local authorities, within whose area the Parks lie, and other conservation bodies

A major threat in National Parks in the UK is the impact of visitors, for most lie within access for a day visit by large numbers of people. The Peak District National Park, for example, has 17 million visitors each year. Much of the work of the National Park Authority, therefore, is traffic control, managing visitor movements and dealing with erosion problems resulting from visitor pressure in 'honeypot' sites.

National Parks in Botswana

Botswana is one of the world's poorest countries, situated in an area that includes savanna grasslands and parts of the Kalahari Desert of southern Africa. Since 1950 the government has established a series of Game Reserves and National Parks to protect areas of the major ecosystems within the country, and the distinctive suites of flora and fauna that they contain. In the north-east the Makaelelo Game Reserve protects herds of savanna grazers such as zebra and wildebeest, while in the north-west the Moremi Wildlife Reserve covers part of the marshlands of the Okavango Delta, a huge area of inland drainage. To the south the Central Kalahari Game Reserve has flora and fauna representative of a desert ecosystem.

All the reserves are intended to provide a focus for tourism, too, because the income generated from foreign visitors is important to the country's economy. Patterns and destinations of tourist visits are strictly controlled, however, to ensure that the aims of conservation and tourism do not come into conflict.

National Parks in the USA

National Parks in the USA comprise, principally, wilderness land, most of which is owned by the federal government. The first National Park was established in 1872 at Yellowstone, and there are now over 35. Most are preserved as examples of spectacular landscapes (such as the Rocky Mountains National Park), while others are preserved because of the distinctiveness of the environment and to enable preservation of rare species. The Everglades National Park in Florida conserves a region of swampland and coastal marshes with a distinctive flora and fauna, including alligators and the manatee.

While access is encouraged to some parts of National Parks in the USA, management by zoning is important: in this, natural, recreational and historic zones are identified and visitor access to each is managed in different ways. Figure 6.1 shows a model of zoning in a small biosphere reserve.

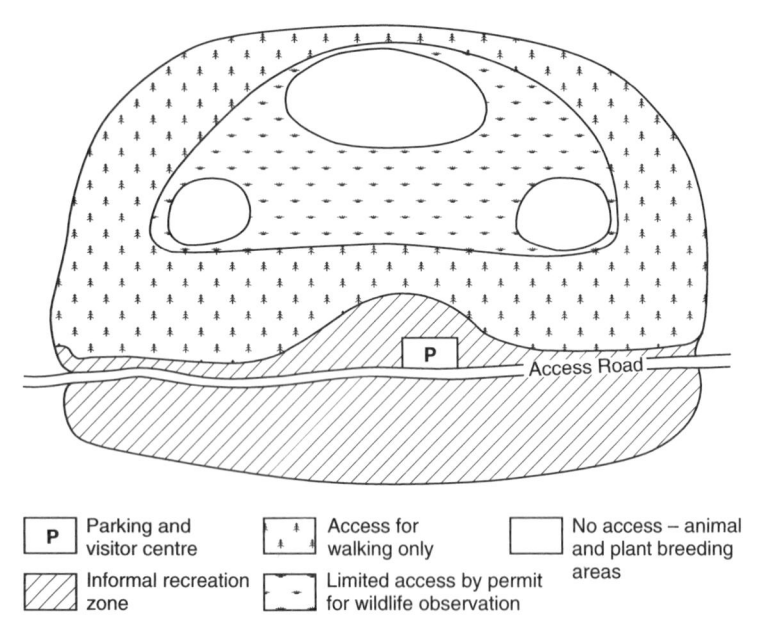

Figure 6.1 A model of zoning in a biosphere reserve

Les Mielles, Jersey

The final example is a biosphere reserve on a much smaller scale. The Les Mielles Area of Special Interest in Jersey was designated in 1978. If comprises, principally, an area of sand dunes with a rich and diverse wildlife in terms of the dune plants, the insects and the bird life which they support. Seventeen of the species found here are listed in the British Red Data Book (a register of rare and endangered species), and over 5000 species of insect are found in Les Mielles.

Les Mielles is under pressure from intense visitor activity, including walking, motor cycling and picnicking. Management strategies have therefore involved restricting the location of certain activities to defined areas in the locality (zoning), banning others, and steering visitors away from the most ecologically sensitive sites.

Soils, soil conservation and people

The conservation of natural habitats is an important aspect of conservation, which focuses on all the components of an ecosystem. Human impact is often responsible for producing a major change to a single component of an ecosystem, which in turn can threaten the whole community. Water pollution is one example of this, as is the issue of soil erosion. This section examines some of the global problems of soil erosion and some of the conservation strategies that can be used.

Soil erosion

Soil erosion occurs in most environments, and is part of the natural process by which the land's rock surface is broken down by weathering. Flowing water, wind and gravity carry (**transport**) grains of soil, often to streams or rivers, where it is carried away to be deposited elsewhere in lakes, or in the sea. In the UK average soil erosion removes between 5 and 25 tonnes of soil per hectare per year, which is the equivalent of the removal of a depth of soil of 0.2–1.0 mm per year. Since this does not exceed the rate at which new soil is formed, such erosion rates are not normally a problem: soil erosion becomes as issue for people only when increased rates of erosion interfere with human use of an environment. This usually occurs either as a result of extreme weather (for example, a severe rainstorm) or as the result of human 'mismanagement' of the soil. Such erosion issues may occur in a number of circumstances:

- ■ Where soil is washed or blown from farmland, reducing its potential use for agriculture.
- ■ Where large amounts of soil are carried into a stream or river, causing it to overflow its banks and flood. This

may occur at some distance from the site of erosion, and so may be a **downstream effect**.
- Where the eroded soil is deposited in a location which causes problems for people – for example, by accumulating behind a dam and reducing the volume of water that a reservoir can hold, or by being blown into urban areas or covering productive agricultural land.

The causes of soil erosion in any one place are often complex, but a key factor is changing use of the land – through changing agricultural practices, by removal of surface vegetation before building or farming, or by the impact of visitors using paths and tracks. Two examples illustrate these processes.

Wind erosion in the English Fens

The Fenland area of Eastern England is reclaimed peatland and is used for intensive and highly productive farming. In places wind erosion has removed up to 3 m of soil since 1750, with current losses of 10–18 mm per year. This is the result of a number of causes – the growing of spring-sown crops which leave the soil bare in winter (for example, spring wheat); the loss of soil quality as a result of not using a rotation system in which fields are left to grass periodically to retain fertility; the absence of hedgerows to act as windbreaks; the use of heavy farm machinery that compacts soil and allows it to be more easily eroded; the growing of crops that require a fine seed bed in the early stages of cultivation (for example, sugar beet).

Footpath erosion in the Cairngorm mountains

The impact of visitors in tourist 'honeypot' areas can lead to soil erosion through wear on footpaths and bridleways, through specialized recreational activities such as motor-cycle scrambling and pony trekking, and through vehicle access in official or unofficial car parks. On the Cairngorm–Ben Macdhui plateau in Scotland a 100-fold increase in visitors has been recorded since 1960, leading to substantial footpath erosion. Maps record no paths in the area between 1890 and 1940, and only 1.1 km of paths in 1960. Today over 20 km of path are in existence, and in places the paths have been eroded to a depth of 1 m.

Managing soil erosion

Most soil erosion results from inappropriate farming practices. In many locations the speed and impact of soil erosion can be reduced using fairly straightforward management approaches, such as:

- Preventing deep channels developing in the soil surface in a downslope direction by ploughing and planting across the slope of fields. The is a technique known as **contour ploughing/planting**, and avoids ploughing up and down slopes.
- Soils which become compacted do not allow water to soak in, causing it to run off across the surface and erode the soil. By deep ploughing, or by avoiding the use of heavy machinery, this can be prevented.
- Ensuring a good drainage system by digging ditches. This allows water to drain away, rather than running off across the surface.
- Keeping fields covered by planting crops or grass at all times, and avoiding periods where the earth is left bare. At the end of the growing season after harvesting, for example, straw and stubble can be left in the field to cover the soil through the autumn.
- Leaving hedgerows, or planting new ones, to act as wind breaks and to catch soil which may be picked up by the wind.
- Maintaining soil structure by the use of organic fertilizers or manures, and resting fields periodically. This prevents the soil breaking down into fine particles which are easily eroded by water, wind or gravity.

Using any of these approaches has economic consequences for farmers, however. Short-term pressures to use fields more intensively, without fallow (grass) periods, or to clear hedgerows to make larger fields where heavy machinery can be used, are intense. Only by recognizing the medium-term and long-term consequences of soil erosion, which reduces yields (and hence incomes) is the need for soil conservation acknowledged.

Managing soil erosion caused by visitor use requires management plans to control the movements and activities of visitors. These include restricting access to vehicles other than in designated car parks, re-routing footpaths regularly to ensure recovery of worn sections, or paving well used footpaths to prevent or slow down erosion.

Summary

The importance of preserving biodiversity has been recognized by a number of international agreements, including the World Conservation Strategy and the UN Framework Convention on Biodiversity. Preserving flora and fauna to preserve gene pools and to provide the possibility of future development of useful resources is important, but the moral imperative of conserving other species for their own sake is also a strong driving force. This chapter has examined, in particular, a range of approaches to protection of habitats and ecosystems through the use of biosphere reserves, and has also considered the management issues in relation to conservation in tropical forests and wetlands and in soil conservation. Chapter 7 considers the conservation of individual species in the context of biodiversity preservation.

Taking action

A number of actions by individuals can support conservation of natural habitats:

1 Contact a local naturalist society or conservation action group to undertake practical conservation work. In the UK groups such as the British Trust for Conservation Volunteers (BTCV) or the Groundwork Trust undertake conservation work in local environments. This work can include activities ranging from fund-raising to practical conservation – for example, clearing overgrown ponds and litter-strewn streams, or repairing eroded footpaths.

2 If you live in an urban environment, enhancing the range of wildlife in the local city ecosystem can be achieved by planting garden trees or flowers that attract insects or birds.

BIODIVERSITY, CONSERVATION AND NATURAL HABITATS

3 Support the work of NGOs in conservation work in environments overseas, either through offering volunteer help or through financial contribution.

4 Reduce or stop your own consumption of primary products from endangered environments. This might include hardwood timber products such as doors and window frames made from tropical timber.

ACTIVITIES

1 Choose one of the world's major biomes that interests you particularly – perhaps the tropical forests, or the ice-based environments of Antarctica. From the information provided by the major environmental organizations, identify the main conservation issues in that environment and the main conservation programmes being undertaken. Contact the embassy of one of the governments involved in this issue to discover its current policies.

2 Ask one of the major retail companies about its policy on conservation issues in relation to its purchase of goods. Does the company have a policy? If so, how does it ensure that its goods are as environmentally friendly as possible?

3 Try to undertake an outline **life cycle analysis** for a product that you use. This involves identifying the environmental issues in each stage of its production. For example, a life cycle analysis of newsprint paper would consider the environmental impact of coniferous forest plantations, forestry operations, the production of wood pulp, manufacture of the paper, the impact of the production of packaging and printing ink, and the environmental impact of its disposal (or recycling).

7 ANIMALS, PLANTS AND BIODIVERSITY

Introduction

The importance of retaining biodiversity is a key message that runs through most conservation policies. The ethical arguments of valuing diversity of living things is strongly underscored by the arguments for retaining as large a reserve of species for potential human use as possible and for retaining as wide a variety of strains of each species to maximize the **gene pool**. Biodiversity is both an ethical and a selfishly pragmatic approach. The previous chapter examined approaches to sustaining habitats, ecosystems and some of the non-living elements of ecosystems; here we shall consider issues of conservation of individual plant and animal species. These are not separate approaches, of course, for sustaining its habitat is essential to enabling a species to survive. We shall also examine the conservation implications of the growth of the animal rights movement.

Conserving endangered species

A number of approaches to preserving rare or endangered species have traditionally been adopted, ranging from game reserves to zoos and botanical gardens.

National parks and game reserves

This approach involves protecting the species **on-site**, and the habitat in which it lives – the game reserves of East Africa, for example, have as one of their aims the conservation of savanna animal species and the grasslands on which they survive. The advantages of this conservation approach is that the species are most likely to survive in their original habitat, but many management problems can arise:

1. In establishing such a reserve there is an inevitable conflict with the communities that live within the reserve, which must either be relocated or limited in their way of life so that they are not in conflict with the aims of the game reserve. Conflicts between elephants and the farmers whose crops they may graze or trample is a major problem in East African reserves, for example.
2. Protection can lead to overcrowding of species if they breed successfully. In the national parks of Zambia, for example, the success of elephant breeding has lead to overgrazing and disease, such that the numbers have to be reduced by culling to match the **carrying capacity** of the grassland.
3. Balancing the needs of conservation with the demands for tourism may lead to conflicts of interest and also to environmental damage in tourist 'honeypots'. **Ecotourism**, in which visitors are attracted by the wildlife or ecosystems, is an important growth area in the world tourist business, yet such visitors may damage the very environments they have come to see.
4. Policing such reserves to protect wildlife from poachers can be very difficult. The reserves can be very large, and the dangers to game wardens of dealing with armed poachers can be significant. Poaching of rhino and elephant, and game for food, are major issues in such reserves.

Single-species reserves are often the first sort of nature reserve to be established as a country begins to develop environmental concern and commitment to conservation, since they often occupy a fairly small area of land. In the UK, single-species reserves are often established for plants, and few (for example, the Farne Islands grey seal reserve) are focused on animals. Elsewhere, the reverse pattern is true and most reserves are animal based. Examples include the Wood Buffalo National Park in northern Canada, which preserves a large herd of North American bison, and the Kaziranga Sanctuary

Preserve in north-east India, which preserves the great Indian rhinoceros.

Zoos, aquaria and botanical gardens

These provide **off-site** protection, and provide a number of benefits. They protect species from disappearing, act as a location for conservation education in areas away from the species' own habitat, and provide opportunities for conservation research and for breeding programmes. In many MDCs, zoos and botanical gardens have a long history – Kew Gardens, in London, for example, was founded in 1761, and most of the major zoos (Washington Zoo, the Tiergarten (in Berlin) and London Zoo) date from the nineteenth century.

The major concerns about this approach to conservation relate to the scale of the operation that is possible and, for animals, the welfare issues of captivity outside their natural habitat. The limited size of such establishments means that only a small number of species can be the focus of preservation and breeding, and the need to combine conservation work with the preferences of visitors means that these are most likely to be the unusual, dramatic or most familiar species. For most species, zoos and botanical gardens will never be a part of their conservation.

The animal welfare issues are partly ethical and partly practical in nature. Recent publicity about zoos, especially in eastern Europe, keeping animals in overcrowded conditions or in inappropriate and barren environments, has raised great public outcry, and pressure is being placed on zoos to develop much more extensive and stimulating sites (as, for example, at Cabaraceno Zoo in northern Spain). Welfare issues may also link into the practical difficulties of getting animals to breed successfully in zoo environments. While there have been many failures, most notably in relation to giant pandas, there have also been many successes as, for example, with the breeding of Przewalski's horse for re-introduction to the wild. Failures are often attributed to the lack of a suitable habitat for the animals.

Rare breeds centres

One of the major concerns over biodiversity is that, of the many breeds of the most common plants and animals used in agriculture that have been produced over the centuries, very few provide the basis of modern farming. For example, in the UK almost all dairy farming involves only three breeds of cattle, and in the USA 75% of the potato crop is grown from only four varieties. While these breeds have been selected for their productivity, such a narrow base makes future production very vulnerable to disease. To sustain the existence of alternative breeds of farm animals, therefore, rare breeds centres have been established in many MDCs. These also serve as living museums.

Gene banks

Gene banks provide off-site storage for seeds, which are kept dormant at low temperatures. An international network of gene banks has been established by the UN Food and Agriculture Organization (FAO) to provide base collections of the world's major food and industrial crops. While gene banks are important, though, there are many species which cannot be preserved in this way, either because they do not reproduce from seed (for example, potatoes) or because they cannot be kept for long periods in storage under any conditions (for example, barley and maize).

On-site gene banks

The idea of on-site gene banks is that a diverse range of species and breeds is maintained as living samples in their original habitat, rather than off-site as seeds. Most farm crops can be traced to their original species in the wild in a number of key locations around the world – for example, many wheat species originate from the grasslands of tropical Africa. These areas of origin (known as **Vavilov centres**) are also the areas where there is the greatest diversity of genes in the original population, so on-site gene banks in these locations will prove to be particularly rich.

Species conservation – the international perspective

Concern for species conservation has lead to a number of international agreements on the protection of a wide range of species. The earliest of significance was the Convention on the

Preservation of Wild Animals, Birds and Fish in Africa, signed in 1900 to stop the activities of big-game trophy hunters. During the next 50 years a number of agreements relating to individual species were signed (for example, the International Convention for the Regulation of Whaling, 1946). More recently four major global agreements have been signed. These are:

The Ramsar Convention (1971)

This convention aims to protect wetland sites and species, and was described in Chapter 6.

CITES (1973)

CITES is the Convention on International Trade in Endangered Species, and has been signed by 110 countries. Its aim is to stop the trade in animals and animal products from species that are endangered by removing the market for such animals. Under CITES any trade in the 600 rarest species requires a licence, and these are rarely awarded. Illegal trade is then subject to substantial legal sanctions, including fines and imprisonment. CITES has certainly helped to reduce trade in endangered species overall, but has had the effect of driving such trade onto the black market. Rare species and their products can attract very high prices – the illegal killing of rhino in East African National Parks is driven by the high prices paid for rhino horn on the black market of eastern Asia, where it is sold as an aphrodisiac. Some governments are accused of 'turning a blind eye' to such illegal trade even though they are signatories to CITES.

The Bonn Convention (1979)

The Bonn Convention, more properly known as the Migratory Species Convention, was designed to protect migrating birds and animals which cross international boundaries in their travels. The Convention was handicapped by the small number of countries that signed it – by 1991 only 34 countries had signed, and this did not include the USA or Canada.

The Biodiversity Convention (1992)

This is the most significant of the four agreements, signed at Rio de

Janeiro in 1992 and covering a wide range of issues of species conservation (see Chapter 6).

As with all international agreements, there is much scope for individual countries to ignore their responsibilities even after becoming a signatory. Nevertheless, these conventions provide a broad framework for conservation at a global scale. In some cases this is added to by regional agreements, such as the Berne Convention on Conservation of European Wildlife and Natural Habitats (1979), and is reinforced by national legislation to protect species within individual countries.

Species conservation in action

The approaches to conservation considered above will be examined here by looking at a number of specific examples.

The case of primates

Primates are an order of mammals which includes some 220 known species, such as gibbons, chimpanzees, gorillas and baboons, together with *homo sapiens sapiens* – modern 'man'. Of these species approximately half are under threat in their natural habitat of tropical forest as a result of a number of human-induced pressures. Timber extraction, for example, removes their natural habitat, and some species are particularly under threat from this source, including orang-utan, gibbons and proboscis monkeys. The removal of forest to create farmland is also an important threat.

A third threat arises from hunting, which may result from conflict with farmers and competition for their food crops, but which is mostly either subsistence hunting or market hunting. Subsistence hunting involves the killing of primates for food, and is mainly confined to forest-living communities such as the Amerindians. Market or commercial hunting is a bigger threat, and in parts of West Africa (for example Sierra Leone and Liberia) large numbers of primates are being killed and sold to market as food. While this is mostly an illegal trade, it is still having a significant impact on primate numbers. A final threat from hunting is the live trade, in which young primates orphaned by the killing of their mothers for food are sold through the black market to collectors or as pets, mostly in MDCs. Chimpanzees and orang-utans are particular targets for this trade – it has been estimated, for example, that there are more orang-utans as pets in Taiwan than there are in the wild in Borneo!

Conservation work with primates is undertaken by a number of bodies. The IUCN coordinates much of the research and conservation planning work, but organizations such as the International Primate Society, the International Primate Protection League, the Primate Society of Great Britain and the Orang-utan Foundation undertake important work. All produce action plans for particular species or particular regions where primates are under threat, and support a range of conservation measures. These include:

Research

In order for plans for conserving endangered species to be developed it is important to know the present numbers of a species, its role within the ecosystems it inhabits and its own species dynamics – i.e. how, when and in what numbers it reproduces. This requires detailed research, often over long periods of time. An important idea in species conservation is that of **minimum viable population (MVP)**, which is an indication of how many individuals are needed to prevent the species declining and eventually becoming extinct. This is highly variable between species, depending on their ecology, but in the case of most primates is in the order of 10,000 individuals. Measuring this value for any species requires appropriate research programmes.

Reserves

Most nature reserves are designed for the preservation of a habitat or ecosystem, but there are a number where the primary focus is the preservation of primate populations. Examples include the Tiwai reserve in Sierra Leone, which has significant populations of diana monkeys and colobus monkeys.

Captive breeding

Captive breeding is undertaken either off-site in zoos or on-site in reserves in the primates' natural habitat. Establishing breeding programmes can be difficult because some animals find adapting to captivity very difficult, but some programmes have been more successful. Lion-tailed macaques and golden lion tamarinds have both bred successfully in zoos, and numbers in captivity exceed numbers in the wild. Some of the issues with captive breeding include the lack of environmental pressure to adapt to change, and the risks from breeding from a very small population. The co-ordination of breeding programmes between zoos to maximize the gene pool is thus very important. In practice, the number of species that can be supported in this way is not great, and most endangered species of primate are not involved in captive breeding programmes. Equally, many of the species of primate in zoos are not endangered species, so, while they contribute to the aesthetic aims of the zoos, they are not fulfilling any major conservation role.

One possible outcome of captive breeding programmes is reintroduction of the species and individuals into the wild. The IUCN coordinates programmes for reintroductions, but the costs and the risks involved have discouraged this sort of programme. For example, the release of chimpanzees into existing habitats can generate problems of the new arrivals being attacked and killed by established animals, and few reintroduction programmes have been successful. Overall, reintroduction is not seen as a major contribution to dealing with threatened extinction in the wild.

Education

Most NGOs and charities working with primates invest in public and school education programmes. This may be important in raising awareness of the issues, but there is little evidence that it has made much difference to the survival of individual threatened species.

The case of the Californian condor

The Californian condor's natural habitat is the mountains and coastal areas of the western seaboard of North America, and it was one of the main birds of prey in the region in the eighteenth and nineteenth centuries. Numbers declined because ranchers shot the birds, seeking to protect their animals, and by the middle of the twentieth century there were few breeding birds left. In the early

1980s, a series of bad winters reduced its numbers in the wild to three breeding pairs, then one. To save the condor from extinction, both of the remaining birds were captured and brought into captivity to support a breeding programme that also involved the 16 birds already in zoos in the USA.

The breeding programme has proved modestly successful, with the total population increasing from 27 birds to 52 birds by 1991 and to 90 birds in 1997. Attempts to release some of the birds to set up groups in the wild have been made, so far without success, but the ultimate aim of the programme is to establish two self-sustaining groups of 100 birds each in the wild.

The case of elephants

Of all the world's animals few evoke as much enthusiasm for conservation amongst people in the MDCs than the elephant. Elephants are an important component of the tropical savannas, but occupy a grazing niche, which means that their habitat is predominantly the wooded savanna and the tropical dry forest that merges with the grassland. Their principal food source is the leaves and shoots of the lower branches of trees.

In Zimbabwe, in southern Africa, rapid population growth and the expansion of agriculture has lead the government to create a number of nature reserves and national parks, which between them cover some 15% of the country. The aim of the parks is to preserve wildlife and habitats, to keep wildlife away from agriculture, and to provide a basis for environmental tourism. The Hwange National Park in the north-west of Zimbabwe lies close to the River Zambezi and the Victoria Falls, but is in an area of dry climate that merges to the west with the Kalahari Desert. Protected in the park, elephant numbers have grown from under 5000 in 1930 to almost 20,000 in 1980, and by the late 1980s the population was growing by 5% each year. The effect was that tree damage and trampling became major problems, leading to food shortage for the elephant and soil erosion around the water holes. The only realistic solution was to undertake emergency selective culling of the elephant to reduce the numbers to about 12,000. At this level of population the numbers could be sustained by the ecosystem in the park, and a net yield of 600 elephant per year can contribute to income for the local economy

ANIMALS, PLANTS AND BIODIVERSITY

from the sale of meat, skins and ivory. Figure 7.1 shows the impact of elephants in the Hwange National Park.

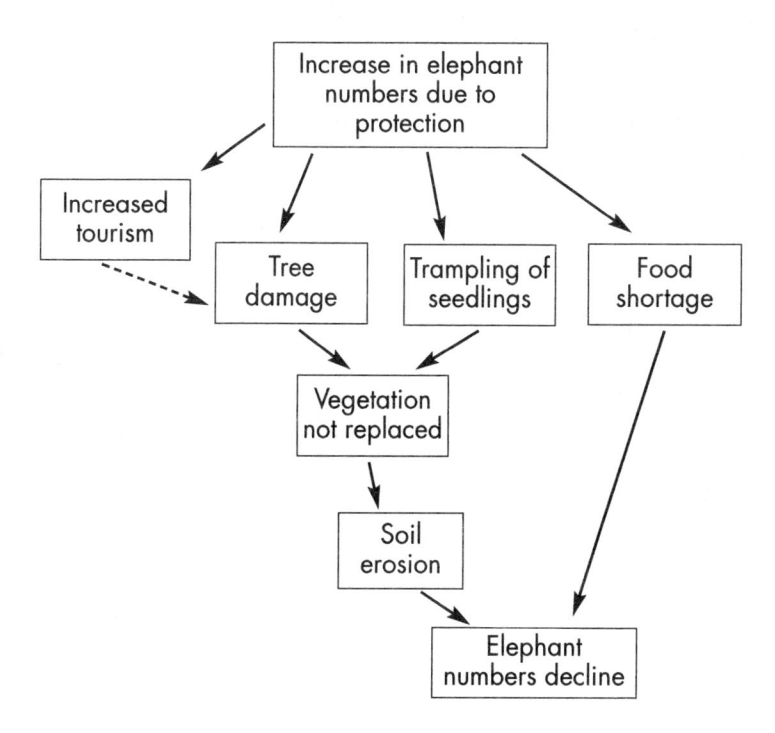

Figure 7.1 The impact of elephants in the Hwange National Park

The protection of the elephant provides an example of how the management of conservation is of critical importance. Simply protecting them in the National Park was not sufficient – although it allowed recovery of numbers unforeseen problems resulted. A more active policy of control by selective culling was essential to ensure that conservation of the elephant did not conflict with conservation of the habitat.

Conservation issues in farming

While the attention of much environmental concern is on conservation of species in the wild and their natural habitats, recognition that the artificial habitats created by people in their farming systems can create their own suite of environmental issues has begun to emerge. Three of these issues will be considered here – animal welfare issues relating to intensive farming methods; the development of health issues form manipulation of the food chain; and the question of the development of genetically modified organisms for farming.

Animal welfare issues and debates

Conservation of animals as a future resource and to preserve the gene pool raises important issues about the relationship between humans and animals. In particular, questioning the misuse of the environment has stimulated some groups to assert that environmental rights must be extended to all living organisms, and that the quality of life of animals within the human food chain needs addressing. Charity groups, such as Compassion in World Farming, have campaigned against intensive farming methods such as the raising of calves for veal in darkness to ensure that the meat is as white as possible, and the use of battery systems for poultry farming. Other groups have campaigned against the use of animals in scientific research. For the most part the arguments have been carried forward by protest, reasoned argument and debate. At its extreme a number of other animal protection groups have used direct action to free animals or to attempt to stop live animal transportation, especially the export of British calves to mainland Europe for veal production. The development of animal activism within the environmental movement is clear evidence of the diverse views of different groups.

An aspect of intensive farming which has been of particular concern in Europe in the 1990s has been the development of animal disease linked to some methods of intensive feeding. Two issues, in particular, have attracted media attention – Salmonella in poultry and eggs, and the development of BSE.

Salmonella is a bacterium responsible for food poisoning in humans. In the late 1980s concern was raised about the frequency of its occurrence in chicken meat and in eggs, and research demonstrated that as many as 75% of battery-produced hens carried the organism. This was attributed to the feeding of processed poultry back to the live poultry. As a result large numbers of birds were slaughtered and the market for poultry and eggs declined rapidly.

BSE (bovine spongiform encephalopathy) is a disease of cattle that leads to loss of control of the nervous system. Its occurrence in the UK in the early 1990s was linked to the feeding of cattle on commercial cattle feed made from processed cattle and sheep offal, including brains and spinal cords, through which the agent responsible was transferred. Of particular concern was the tentative link between BSE in cattle and a similar disease in humans called new-variant CJD (Creuzfeld-Jakob Disease). As a result sales of British beef to European markets were halted, and many cattle were slaughtered. Although BSE has now declined significantly in cattle as a result of the measures taken, there is concern that the number of cases of new-variant CJD will increase over the next two decades as the disease, which has a very long incubation period, emerges in people infected by beef during the early 1990s.

Genetic modification – the conservation issues

One of the major research areas in biology in the 1990s was in the field of genetics, and in particular in the identification of the genes linked to specific features in plants, animals and humans. This has lead to many important medical advances, and enabled the production of new varieties of species of plants for agriculture through genetic modification. Such species may have much faster growth rates or lead to larger crop yields. Two concerns have been raised about genetically modified (GM) crops:

1 As new species, their relationship with other species in ecosystems is unknown. Just as introductions of animals and plants into wild ecosystems can lead to extinctions or the domination of an ecosystem, so the effect that such crops may have is not clear.

2. The incorporation of GM crops into human food raises concerns about the interaction of such foods with human disease. Will they, for example, promote human genetic illness? Could they interact with disease bacteria and viruses in as yet unknown ways?

At present the arguments for and against GM crops are very strong. The pro-GM groups emphasize the careful testing of all new materials and foods before they are used, and stress the benefits of stronger, more productive crops. The anti-GM groups stress our current lack of understanding of the effects of GM foods and the potential health and environmental risks, citing the BSE issue as an example of the development of unpredictable consequences from using new foodstuffs.

The growth of GM foods has been strongest in the USA, where GM soya beans and GM maize are now important ingredients in animal feed, but some products have begun to appear in Europe. Most European governments are under pressure to halt the development of GM foods or to introduce strong labelling legislation to at least give consumers clear knowledge and allow purchasing choice.

Summary

The conservation of individual species is a central part of the arguments for maintaining biodiversity. Much media attention has focused on some of the most impressive animals under threat of extinction – such as tigers, giant pandas and rhinoceros – yet the issue of conservation stretches to all species, from bacteria to plants, insects and higher animals. The arguments for conservation of species are both pragmatic and ethical. The need to ensure a wide variety of species for future sources of food, drugs and raw materials is important, but the moral issue of sustaining all living creatures is of significance too. Linked to the moral issues is the question of animal rights and human manipulation of animals and plants or their genetics for human gain. Current important public debates concern this field in the arguments about BSE and about the development of GM species and the foodstuffs made from them.

Taking action

1 Most of the endangered species of mammals (tigers, rhinoceros, etc.) are the focus of specific conservation groups. Organizations such as Friends of the Earth and WWF can provide details of such groups for you to contact and support.

2 Support for research into conservation of less 'attractive' species, such as insects, is usually the focus of professional scientific research groups. Contact details for such groups can be found through the major web sites listed in Appendix 1.

3 Conservation of species depends on consumers' individual purchase decisions. It is important to avoid all products that might be linked to non-sustainable farming practice – for example, the purchase of timber from sustainable stocks prevents the loss of natural ecosystems and the animal species that occupy them.

4 Animal welfare issues can also be supported by consumer decisions. The purchase of organic, free-range or non-GM products emphasizes a concern for ethical practices in farming.

ACTIVITIES

1 For one animal or plant species that especially interests you (for example, chimpanzee or tiger) use libraries and conservation organizations to seek answers to the following questions:

  a How endangered is the species – what are its numbers and its distribution in the wild?

  b What are the major threats to its future survival?

  c What actions are being taken to sustain the species?

2 Contact a local conservation organization such as the local Naturalists' Trust. In your local region, what species are under threat of disappearing? What are the causes of this decline? What are local groups doing to deal with the issue?

8 THE WORLD'S SEAS AND OCEANS

Introduction

The Earth is sometimes described as the 'Blue Planet' because of its appearance in photographs taken from space, which show clearly that 70% of the Earth's surface is sea. Despite the extent of the seas, however, the **marine** world is still little known and understood in comparison with the land. The average depth of the ocean is 2500 m, and we are only just beginning to understand the variety of 'landscapes' beneath the sea and the complexity of the ecosystems that are found there. Most importantly, scientists are recognizing that the oceans are not just an unimportant wilderness offshore but are of critical importance in controlling the world's climate – and, therefore, all life and ecosystems on land. The science of the oceans (**oceanography**) is now an important branch of environmental science.

Marine ecosystems

Figure 8.1 is a simple cross-sectional diagram showing the main environments of the seas between the edge of a continent and the ocean depths.

- At the edge of the land are the **shallow seas** and **estuaries**. These are the areas of the sea most used by humans and, as a result, are the most threatened environments.
- Offshore from these shallow coastal area are the **continental shelves**, comparatively shallow seas which vary in area and width around the world, and which are important fishing areas.

■ Beyond the continental shelf lie the **ocean depths**, which make up the vast majority of the oceans. They are the least known parts of the sea, and include huge submarine mountain chains, extensive plains and deep trenches. Lines of mountains run down the centre of the major oceans. These **mid-ocean ridges** are volcanic in origin and contain mountains up to 10,000 m in height, but which break the surface only as relatively small peaks – as, for example, in Hawaii. The deepest ocean trench is the Marianas Trench, which reaches a depth of 11,000 m below sea level in the Pacific Ocean.

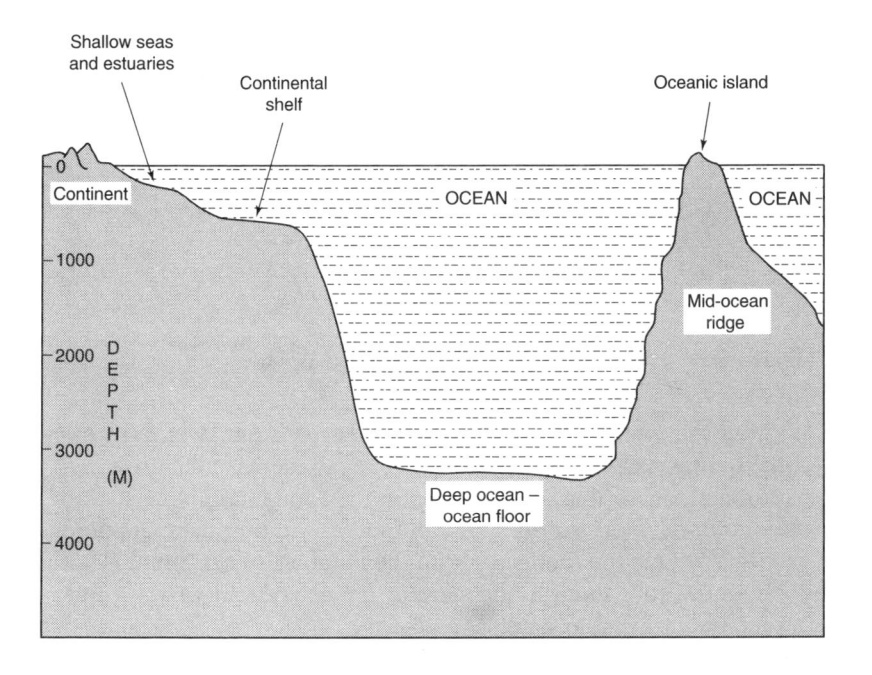

Figure 8.1　A diagrammatic cross-section of the oceans

Within these different environments many species of animals survive, and each location has its own characteristic ecosystem. Figure 8.2 shows a simple food web in a marine ecosystem in the oceans around Antarctica. Sunlight reaching the top layers of the ocean is absorbed by microscopic plants called **phytoplankton**, and is then converted into plant material. This is the food of microscopic animals, including **zooplankton** and **krill**. In turn, these make up the food supply for fish, shellfish, and some whales. Fish and shellfish are food for seabirds, seals and other whales, and at the top of the food chain are the carnivorous whales such as the killer whale.

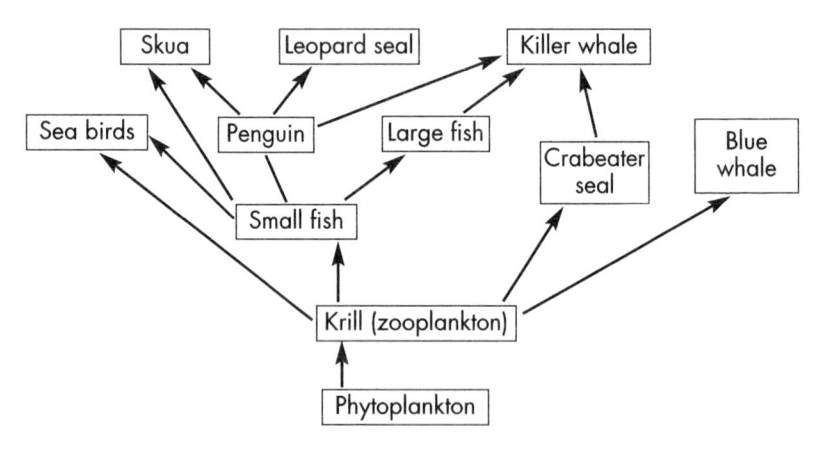

Figure 8.2 An Antarctic Ocean food web

Without the interference of humans the ecosystem is in **dynamic equilibrium**. For example, a warm year can increase the growth of phytoplankton so that all creatures in the food chain benefit from the increased food supply and can increase in numbers. A cooler year will reduce the food supply so the numbers of sea animals will decline. Overall, though, the state of the ecosystem varies a little but maintains a stable state.

The productivity of the seas varies between the main ocean areas. The deep oceans are the least productive, for the absence of sunlight in the depths limits the amount of life that can be sustained. However, where ocean currents come together, bringing plankton from a large gathering area, where rising currents (upwellings) bring large quantities of nutrients to the surface, or where surface temperatures are higher (as in the tropics), the ecosystems can produce more plankton and sustain greater numbers of sea animals. Between 50° and 60° south of the equator, for example, lies the Antarctic Convergence, where currents bring large quantities of nutrients and plankton and the environment is very productive. Nearer to the coasts the shallower seas and the flow of nutrients from the land to the sea in rivers mean that productivity is greater. The most productive areas are the river estuaries, including areas of mangroves, and areas of ocean convergence on continental shelves – for example, off the coast of Newfoundland and eastern Canada. Here, productivity can exceed 1500 $g/m^2/year$ in the deep oceans.

Marine resources

The world's seas are an important resource for humankind, and over the centuries have been used in many ways.

- Traditionally fishing in both coastal waters and the deep oceans for a range of species has provided a source of food. Although only a few species have been important as food sources and for other resources, the oceans are also important to us from the point of view of biodiversity and the range of living resources they may be able to offer in the future – if managed correctly.
- The oceans also provide a source of important minerals. This is a recent development as technology has enabled us to explore the ocean beds for minerals and to drill offshore oilwells.
- The oceans provide an important economic resource in terms of transport, which has also stimulated the use of coastal areas for large-scale industrial and urban development.
- The oceans provide an important potential source of sustainable energy (see Chapter 5), for the technology is now available for making use of the wind, waves, ocean currents, and thermal differences in the oceans to generate power.

- Finally, the sea is an important resource for recreation close to the coast, either through active recreation such as sailing and diving, or through environmentally-based activities in attractive and stimulating coastal environments.

We shall examine the issues of fish resources and mineral resources below.

Fishing and conservation

Fish have always been an important source of food, creating a livelihood for communities with access to the sea. In the twentieth century, the development of highly efficient fishing methods, fishing vessels that can fish anywhere across the oceans, and the increased demand from growing populations has stretched fish resources in some areas to their limit. In 1950 world fishing catches were 20 million tonnes per year. By the end of the century this increased to 95 million tonnes per year, close to the limit of 100 million tonnes per year which the FAO believes is the maximum yield that can be taken without causing permanent damage or loss of species. Although most coastal nations have fishing fleets, two-thirds of the world's catch is taken by just 11 countries. These countries have large fleets fishing around the globe serving large factory ships that follow the fleet. This use of factory-scale fishing is not the only technological advance, however, for most fishing by countries of the developed world uses advanced technology to track and catch fish.

Overfishing is caused by the increasing numbers of fishing vessels and their increased efficiency in catching fish, particularly the use of fine mesh nets which remove all fish, even the young and immature ones. The result is a decline in the numbers of many species. In European water, overfishing of haddock and plaice was first noticed as early as 1900, but catches of most popular fish have declined in the last 30 years. North Sea herring, for example, crashed in the 1970s, and haddock catches, having made a recovery through the 1960s, diminished rapidly through overfishing in the 1980s. Similar declines have occurred elsewhere in the world. In California, for example, the important sardine industry collapsed through overfishing in the 1930s and did not recover until the

1980s. Off the coast of southern Africa the rich pilchard stocks were overfished by a combination of local fishing fleets and international fleets during the 1960s and 1970s and were substantially lost by 1980.

Overfishing isn't the only reason for the drop in fish stocks. Other human activities also have an effect. For example, the building of the new High Dam at Aswan in Egypt reduced the flow of nutrients from the Nile into the Mediterranean Sea. This led to the collapse of the sardine fishing industry in the Nile delta region within one year.

Management of fish stocks for future use has not yet proved very successful, despite the large number of international fishery bodies. Agreement on maximum fish catches and on minimum net mesh sizes have been difficult to introduce because of disagreements about the scientific evidence of the impact of fishing on fish stocks – and also because some countries wish to protect their national fishing industry. The 'cod wars' between the UK and Iceland in the 1970s, for example, resulted from Iceland's extension of its territorial waters to protect its fish stocks and the determination of the British fishing fleets to retain access to traditional fishing grounds.

Amongst the countries of the European Union, fishing is controlled by the **Common Fisheries Policy (CFP)**, first established in 1983. Fishing employs 300,000 people in the EU, and the CFP tries to conserve fish stocks and the fishing industry by a number of measures:

- technical measures – limiting the types of fishing gear that can be used, fixing the minimum size of fish in each species that can be landed, and periodically closing some areas for fishing;
- reducing the overall fishing capacity by imposing quotas on the number of vessels that can be licenced;
- limiting the total allowable catches (TACs) for each species in each fishing area;
- negotiating agreements with other fishing nations (for example, Norway, Iceland, Canada) to limit their access to European fisheries; and
- providing money for restructuring, in which people in the fishing industry are encouraged to move into other employment.

During the 1980s and 1990s the CFP was partially successful, but by the mid-1990s scientific evidence showed that catches of some species, especially plaice, whiting and mackerel, were continuing to fall and that some spawning stocks were falling rapidly. While pollution may be a partial cause, the CFP has been accused of failing by not allowing strong enough action against overfishing and quota breaches, by not identifying fraud in the recording of quotas, and by not preventing fleets from other countries fishing in European waters. The introduction of more sophisticated monitoring of quotas using satellite tracking of fishing vessels and computer logging of catches may help to police the fishing industry more carefully, but there is a genuine fear in many coastal areas of Europe, for example northern Spain and south-west England, that the traditional fishing industry on which whole communities depend may diminish permanently.

Whaling

Whaling has been an important issue to conservationists in recent years. Every part of a whale is useable in some way, but its main value lies in its meat for food, its skin and, traditionally, its fat (blubber) as a source of oil. As result, in the twentieth century, whaling has pushed many species to the edge of extinction As large whales (blue whales and humpbacks) declined in numbers the large whaling fleets moved on to smaller species such as fin whales and minke whales. In the 1940s, 25,000 fin whales were caught per year – today almost none are caught. The **International Whaling Commission (IWC)** was established in 1946, and has 37 member states. As a result of international pressure it introduced a worldwide ban on commercial whaling in 1983, but in 1993 three nations (Iceland, Norway and Japan) tried to overturn the ban. This was resisted because there was no scientific evidence that whale stocks had recovered. This is an example of the **precautionary principle** in conservation. Whaling does continue for scientific research, and there is some illegal whaling, but increasingly it is recognized that there is more money to be made from whale watching by tourists than by whaling.

Oil and minerals from the oceans

In the second half of the twentieth century developments in technology allowed exploitation of minerals from the seabed or beneath the ocean floor. Oil is the main resource that has been exploited in this way, and the growth of the oil industry in, for example, the Gulf of Mexico and the North Sea has been important for the world's economy. The continental shelves contain half of all known reserves of oil and natural gas. The main environmental issues that arise from this are the risks of pollution from accidents in extracting or transporting the oil.

Most of the other minerals currently taken from the sea come from gravel dredging in shallow coastal waters. These are important to local communities but their environmental effects are small in scale. However, the oceans are now being recognized as holding great potential for other minerals – precious metals may be obtained from muds and sediments on continental shelves, and uranium, magnesium and bromine can be obtained from seawater itself. The deep ocean floors have areas covered by manganese nodules, small pebbles rich in metals such as copper and molybdenum. At present, although the technology exists to extract these resources, the costs are too great, although proposals for dredging manganese nodules in seas off Papua New Guinea have been put forward.

Obtaining resources from the sea raises important issues about ownership of the oceans. While countries have rights to the minerals close to their coastline, many resources lie beneath open sea and international waters. The UN has tried to regulate the use of the oceans through three United Nations Conferences on the Laws of the Sea (UNCLOS). The latest of these (UNCLOS III) reached agreement on controls for 40% of the oceans, by defining four 'zones':

- ■ *Territorial Sea* (0–12 miles from the coast), where countries have complete authority over all uses and environmental issues.
- ■ *Contiguous Zones* (12–24 miles from the coast), where countries have limited controls.

- *Extended Economic Zones* (normally up to 200 miles from the coast), in which countries have controls over resources and environmental issues.
- *Continental Shelves*, on which countries can exploit the sea bed resources up to the edge of their shelf.

While these 'rules' have been accepted by most countries, the setting up of an International Seabed Authority (ISA) to control resources in the deep oceans ('the common heritage of mankind'; Ambassador Pardo of Malta, 1967) has been resisted – mainly by developed countries who do not wish to share their technology and seabed resources with less developed countries. So far, therefore, UNCLOS III has not come into force because insufficient states have signed the agreement.

Marine pollution

A major concern about the world's seas is the effect of pollution on the marine ecosystems. Traces of pollutants have been found in Antarctic penguins, many thousands of miles from any source of pollution, but most of the areas of concern are in coastal waters, estuaries and in the seas of the continental shelf, particularly in the developed world. Particular areas of severe pollution in Europe are the Mediterranean Sea, the North Sea and the Baltic Sea, where pollutants become trapped and are not flushed into the large oceans. In North America the estuaries of New York and Chesapeake Bay, and the Caribbean Sea have particularly high levels of pollution. Pollution reaches the seas from four sources:

- direct discharge of waste products into the sea from coastal towns or industrial plants;
- waste carried into the sea by rivers that have flowed through industrial or urban areas;
- dumping of wastes at sea deliberately; and
- airborne pollution that settles into the sea.

Some examples of important marine pollutants are described below:

PCBs – polychlorinated biphenyls

These organic substances are by-products of the plastics industry, and are also used in paper products, inks, paints and electrical equipment. PCBs are easily absorbed by animals, but remain in fatty tissue – they are extremely toxic and carcinogenic. In the North Sea PCBs have been linked with increased death rates in seabirds and the deaths of seal pups – the decline in the population of seals in the Waddensee in The Netherlands between 1950 and 1975 has been strongly linked to the build up of PCBs in the population.

Tributyl tin oxide (TBT)

TBT was developed to prevent the build up of creatures and weed on the hulls of boats (an anti-fouling agent) and replaced highly poisonous arsenic and copper paints. Evidence in the 1970s, however, suggested that TBT was responsible for female dogwhelks developing male features and becoming sterile. A ban on its use on small vessels was introduced in the UK in 1987, and there is now evidence that dogwhelk populations are recovering.

Phosphates and nitrates

These chemicals are washed into the sea by rivers draining farming areas where artificial chemical fertilizers have been used. The load of phosphates and nitrates of the River Rhine, for example, increased five-fold between 1950 and 1990. These chemicals stimulate the growth of marine plants such as phytoplankton in coastal waters, producing what is know as an **algal bloom**. This in itself is unsightly or unpleasant, but two further effects can result.

1. It can produce changes in the ecosystem which encourage the growth of minute creatures called dinoflagellates, whose red colour produces so-called **red tides**. The dinoflagellates also produce poisonous compounds (toxins) which can kill shellfish or cause severe illness in humans who eat them. Such red tides are most common in tropical waters, but have been recorded in the North Sea and the estuaries of north-eastern USA.

2 When the algae die, their decay on the seabed can remove all the oxygen from the water (**eutrophication**), leading to the death of many larger sea creatures.

Sewage

In many coastal areas the discharge of raw sewage into the sea has had important effects on marine plants and animals – as well as on the use of beaches and inland waters for recreation. Treatment of sewage before discharge, and the use of long outfalls so that the sewage is released in areas where wave action will break it down, are important, and water authorities in the UK have undertaken large capital schemes to deal with such sewage problems. The EU has strong regulations on sewage discharge which it requires the governments of member states to meet. The award of EU 'Blue Flags' to beaches that meet minimum standards for cleanliness for bathing has become important for tourist resorts. Sewage in bathing waters has also become an important focus of activity by environmentalists, with groups such as 'Surfers against Sewage' campaigning strongly for action to clean up coastal waters.

Managing marine environments

The management and conservation of marine environments is not an easy task. Within the waters that belong to single countries, policing and enforcing conservation regulations is very difficult. In the waters beyond exclusive economic zones it is almost impossible, for no single country has legal authority. In sea areas close to continents, where several countries are competing for marine resources or wish to ensure that their own national interests are not affected by restrictions, agreement on conservation is very difficult indeed. The issues of managing the oceans through initiatives from UNCLOS have been described above. Two examples of managing coastal waters are presented here.

Coastal waters of the USA

Most of the coastal waters of the USA do not border those of another nation, but even so management is difficult. The management problems are large, too, for one-third of the US population lives in coastal counties, and its 189 ports move over 1.3 billion tonnes of cargo each year. The task of protecting living marine resources, reefs, wetlands and estuaries falls to the Federal Office of Coastal Zone Management (OCZM), which provides services and funds to individual states. These coastal management programmes have included reductions in pollution into coastal waters, cleaning of beaches, and protection of inshore fisheries – as, for example, in Chesapeake Bay, Maryland. By enabling planning to consider all aspects of the management of coastal waters, the work of the OCZM, despite funding limits, has been quite successful.

The European Union

In the EU managing the seas is more complex because of the large number of nations with coasts on the two main sea areas – the Mediterranean Sea and the North Sea. The North Sea, in particular, has many conservation issues, ranging from overfishing to pollution. The major rivers draining into the North Sea include the Rhine and the Thames – the Rhine carries large quantities of heavy metals and the Thames very high concentrations of nitrates from fertilizers. During the 1990s three North Sea Conferences set targets to reduce chemicals reaching the North Sea by 50% by the year 2000, but by the time of the review conference in Esbjerg in 1995 few of the goals had been reached. A large number of EU directives (such as Directive 76/160 on the quality of bathing water) require national governments to introduce controls on such environmental issues, and all are based on the precautionary principle.

The main threats to the Mediterranean are from sewage, industrial pollution and growth of the tourist industry. Only 20% of coastal towns have plants to treat sewage, and over 650,000 tonnes of crude oil is discharged into the sea each year. Attempts to control pollution have been hindered by countries wishing not to do anything to slow down their economic growth – for example, a proposal by Spain to halt all dumping of toxic waste in the Mediterranean by the year 2005 was rejected by most countries. Management of the Mediterranean was established by the 1976 Barcelona Convention, updated at Genoa in 1985. This established measures to:

- build sewage treatment plants for all the area's major cities;
- establish 80 laboratories to research and monitor important environmental issues;
- protect endangered species, such as the Mediterranean sea turtle; and
- reduce the discharge of chemicals into the sea.

An important approach to dealing with marine problems has been the idea of **coastal zone management (CZM)**, in which all of the environmental issues – both on the land and the sea – in the coastal areas are managed together. Although France, The Netherlands and Denmark have passed legislation making CZM a requirement, most countries still leave such planning to different groups, making overall management of conservation issues very difficult.

Summary

The oceans and seas cover over two-thirds of the earth's surface, and most people live within 200 km of the sea. Environmental pressures on the oceans include not only their use for resources such as fish and minerals, but also the damaging effects of pollution on marine plants and animals and on their recreational and landscape value close to coastlines. Managing the seas is difficult because so much of their area is outside the legislation of a single country. Action by the UN has made some progress in providing controls up to 200 miles offshore, but managing the open oceans is an important issue for the future. Steps have been taken by international bodies to deal with issues of overfishing and pollution of coastal waters but there is much progress to be made. Integrated plans for coastal zone management may help, but most countries have not yet developed such planning schemes.

Taking action

How can individual people take action to help in conservation of the seas and oceans? A number of practical steps can help:

1 Take care in buying fish products so that, where possible, they have been produced as farmed fish or have been caught using environmentally friendly methods – tuna fish caught using a rod and line, for example, avoids dolphins and other fish being caught in the large tuna nets.

2 Support government and NGO action in reducing pollution into rivers, which will eventually find its way into the sea.

3 Reduce energy and resource consumption by, for example, recycling or using fuel-efficient vehicles, so that the demand for oil and oil transport is reduced.

4 Support local action, and place pressure on water authorities to improve sewage disposal systems.

ACTIVITIES

1 Contact your local water authority to obtain information on:
   a sewage disposal
   b river pollution in your region.
   Have these improved in recent year?

2 Contact one of the major environmental and conservation NGO groups to find out what current issues they are trying to lobby government about in relation to the seas.

3 Scan the national media for reports of pollution incidents at sea. For one incident try to identify its cause. Also identify the main groups of people who are involved in the issue – for example, coastal holiday resorts, oil companies, marine pollution cleaning companies.

9 ATMOSPHERE, WEATHER AND CLIMATE

Weather, climate and conservation issues

The Earth's atmosphere is a key part of our environment. It provides the basic necessities of life through air and water, and its movements and processes produce the world's patterns of weather and climate that have a large effect on how people live. In recent years media attention has focused on extreme events (severe storms such as Hurricane Andrew, floods such as those in Bangladesh or the River Mississippi, droughts such as those in Britain and the Sahel), and on the evidence that pollution is causing changes to the atmosphere. Talk – of the ozone 'hole' over Antarctica, with its potential for causing increases in human disease, especially skin cancer, and of the 'greenhouse effect', with its potential for increasing global temperatures – has raised the possibility of long-term harm to people as a result of our pollution of the atmosphere.

The atmosphere pays no attention to national boundaries and is part of the world's 'common inheritance'. Dealing with the damaging effects of human activity on the atmosphere, and managing the Earth's envelope of air to conserve it for the future, require international co-operation as well as action in each country. The atmosphere is the one component of the whole world ecosystem that links all places together. Long-term changes to the atmosphere in any part of the world may, therefore, change the patterns of weather and climate, the patterns of animal and plant life and the economies, ways of life and standards of living that depend on them.

Understanding how the atmosphere works, how human activities may affect it, and how those actions can be reduced or modified is a major conservation challenge. In this and the next chapter, we shall examine each of these questions.

The energy of the atmosphere

The atmosphere provides a thin layer around the Earth, less than 100 km deep, and most of the processes that affect people and produce the weather we experience occur in the lowest part of the atmosphere, known as the **troposphere** (8–15 km deep). The atmosphere is a mixture of gasses, mostly nitrogen (78%) and oxygen (21%), the rest being a number of gases which are of great importance to the climate, including water vapour, carbon dioxide and ozone.

We think of the atmosphere as something constantly in motion, for our weather is made of wind, moving clouds, storms and rain. The energy to keep it in motion almost all comes from the sun. Of the energy reaching the top of the atmosphere from the sun most is reflected back into space as light from clouds, dust or the ground surface. Less than half (47%) is converted into heat by striking water vapour, dust or, mostly the Earth's surface. The atmosphere is heated from below, therefore, and its temperature declines the higher in the troposphere you go. Most of this heat energy powers the cycling of water in the atmosphere, with only some 1% driving the winds. Less than 0.1% is absorbed by plants to provide the energy for life itself.

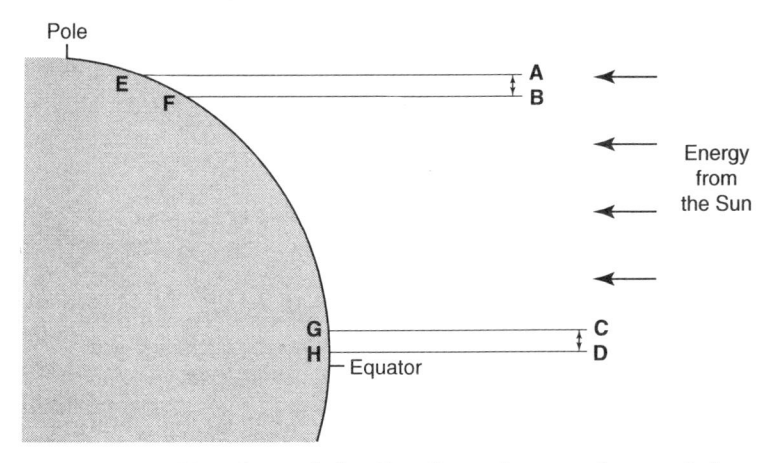

Figure 9.1 Heating of the Earth at the tropics and the poles

The tropics are warmer than the areas near to the poles. Figure 9.1 shows how sunlight reaching the Earth's surface near the poles is 'spread' across a larger area of the Earth's surface than that near the tropics. The amount of energy reaching A–B is the same as that reaching C–D. However, the area of the Earth's surface near the pole (at E–F) is much greater than that at the equator (G–H) because of the curvature of the Earth. As a result each square metre of the Earth near the poles receives less energy than a similar area near the equator, and is therefore colder. The difference in temperature between the poles and the equator is what drives the motion of the atmosphere, because the winds and the storms in the atmosphere are the way in which energy is transferred from the tropics to the poles.

Modelling the global climatic system

Although the world's atmosphere changes constantly (it is **dynamic**), it is possible to identify particular features of the atmosphere which are more or less permanent, so that a **model** of the global climate system can be constructed. Figure 9.2 shows a generalized picture of the wind zones and pressure patterns on the Earth's surface, with major belts of winds blowing from high-pressure areas to low-pressure areas. Major pressure features are the low-pressure zone near the equator, the high-pressure zone near the tropics of Cancer and Capricorn, the low-pressure zone in the mid-latitudes (45–60°) and the high-pressure zones at the poles. The wind belts have familiar names:

- the *Trade Winds*, blowing from the sub-tropical high to the equatorial low;
- the *Mid-latitude Westerlies*, blowing polewards from the sub-tropical highs;
- the *Polar Easterlies*, blowing from the high pressure at the poles.

These winds do not blow north–south, since their movement is deflected by the spin of the Earth (this is known as the **Coriolis effect**).

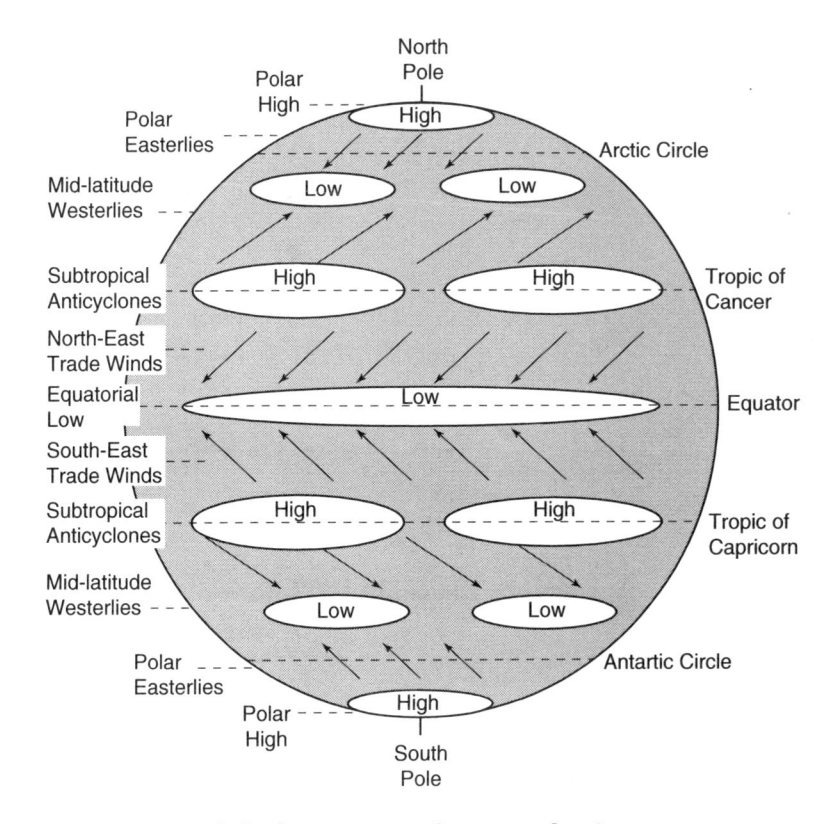

Figure 9.2 Global patterns of atmospheric pressure and wind

These features of the atmosphere do not stay in precisely the same position throughout the year; they move a little north and south with the seasons. The British Isles, for example, lies in the belt of south-westerly winds for much of the year, bringing winds (and rain) to much of the country. In summer, though, the sub-tropical high-pressure area may drift over the country, bringing periods of warm settled weather.

Understanding the working of the weather involves a knowledge of the atmosphere in three dimensions. Figure 9.3 shows how air doesn't move straight from the equator to the pole but gets involved in upward and downward movements in a number of **circulation cells**. Three main cells can be seen on the model:

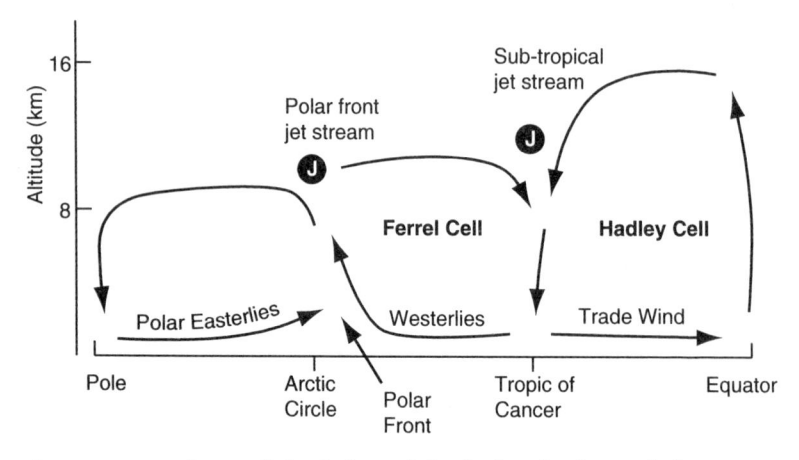

Figure 9.3 A model of the global circulation of the atmosphere

1 The **Hadley cell**. Hot air at the equator rises (as hot air always does), then travels at high altitude to the tropics, where it sinks, forming high-pressure areas. Air from the high-pressure areas travels at the surface back towards the low pressure at the equator as the Trade Winds.
2 The **Ferrell cell**. Air from the sub-tropical high-pressure areas travels at the surface towards the poles as the Mid-latitude Westerlies. Where it meets the cold air from the poles it is forced to rise, and returns to the tropics at high level.
3 The **Polar cell**. Air from the polar high-pressure areas travels towards the equator at low level as the Polar Easterlies, until it meets the Mid-latitude Westerlies at the **polar front**, where it is forced to rise. This air returns to the poles at high level.

Figure 9.3 also shows the position of two other important features of the atmosphere – the **jet streams**. These are narrow bands of fast-moving winds, with wind speeds at their core of 200–400 kph, which lie near the top of the troposphere at a height of between 3 and 15 km. The **polar front jet stream** blows from west to east above the boundary of the Mid-latitude Westerlies and the Polar Easterlies at the Earth's surface. The **sub-tropical jet stream** blows east to west above the sub-tropical high-pressure areas. Both jet streams play a vital role in transferring energy from the equator to the poles, and are very important in influencing the nature and position of weather patterns at the surface. The exact course of the polar front jet stream, for example, varies throughout the year, but it always forms a pattern of waves, known as the Rossby Waves. The position and intensity of the Rossby Waves controls the formation and movement of mid-latitude depressions, and is therefore of great importance in directing the weather of much of Western Europe, North America and the southern half of Australia.

The role of the oceans

Although the atmosphere is important in this transfer of energy from tropics to pole, it does not do it alone. The oceans, although they move more slowly than the air, also provide energy transfer, with ocean currents moving energy towards the poles. Recent scientific research has demonstrated that the atmosphere and the oceans are not separate systems but are intimately linked. Understanding the atmosphere–ocean system has become an important priority in research, both in oceanography and in meteorology and climatology. Meteorologists regard the oceans as the 'flywheels of climate', for 80% of the energy received at the Earth's surface is absorbed by the oceans. This heats the top 100 m of the sea, and is then released back into the atmosphere as heat. Sea surface temperatures (SSTs) appear to be linked very strongly to weather and climate patterns, and variations in SSTs (sea surface temperature anomalies, or SSTAs) can produce effects both locally and across the globe. The SSTs in the central Pacific Ocean appear to be particularly important.

Storms and storm tracks

An important feature of the atmosphere are the storms of various sizes and intensities that occur around the world. They bring much of the weather that is hazardous to human beings, and there is concern that their intensity or location may change as a result of global warming. The general position of these storms can be explained by the main features of the model of the atmosphere, but their precise location, track and intensity depends on the exact conditions of the atmosphere at any one time – the position of the Rossby waves, or SSTAs, or the season will all have an important effect on storm characteristics. Four main types or groups of storms will be described here:

Mid-latitude depressions

These storms bring the pattern of wind and rainfall to mid-latitude regions such as Western Europe, most of North America and Australasia. They form at the polar front where cold polar air meets warm air carried by the Mid-latitude Westerlies, and are characterized by a low-pressure area around which air circulates in an anticlockwise direction, with associated fronts (Figure 9.4). The fronts occur where air of different temperatures comes into contact but cannot mix because of their different densities – a warm front occurs where warm air lies to the rear of cold air, and a cold front occurs where cold air lies to the rear of warm air. In each case the less dense warm air is forced to rise over the cold air, and as it rises it produces cloud and rain. Travelling west to east, these depressions develop, mature and decline over a period of 3–8 days. While most simply bring cloud, rain and wind, intense depressions can form. In these there are strong differences in temperature between the tropical air and the cold air within them, or the jet stream is very strong, and they can cause severe damage. In the UK, for example, the severe storms of 15 October 1987 and 25 January 1990, with wind speeds of 100–120 kph, caused great damage. An important concern in the debate over the effects of global warming from the greenhouse effect is whether it will result in more frequent very severe depressions in the mid-latitudes.

ATMOSPHERE, WEATHER AND CLIMATE

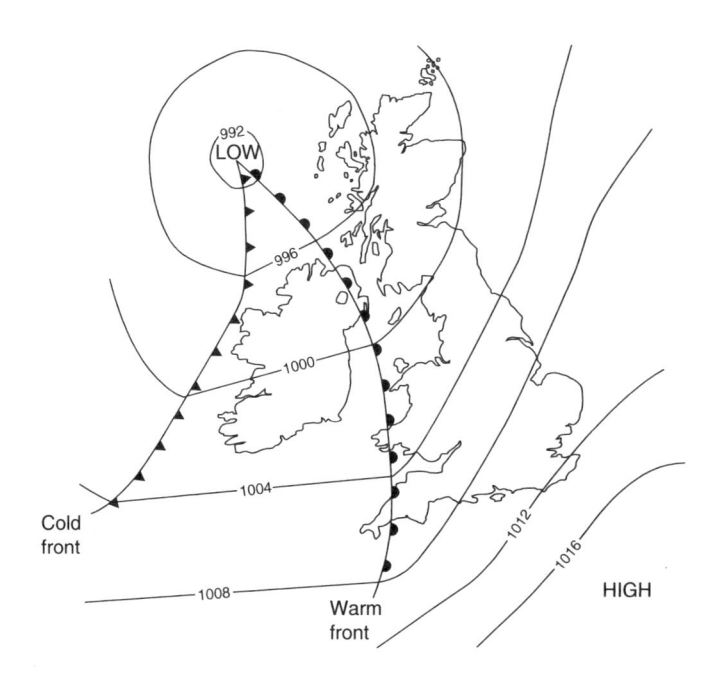

Figure 9.4 A typical mid-latitude depression

Hurricanes

Hurricanes (known as cyclones or typhoons in the Pacific Ocean) are depressions (low-pressure areas) that occur in sub-tropical areas, travelling westwards and curving away from the equator in their track. They occur in the summer months, with an average of 79 hurricanes each year in the northern hemisphere and 24 in the southern hemisphere. Their strength, intensity of rain and great wind speeds are well known, with wind speeds of up to 150–175 kph and rainfall of up to 400–500 mm per day. They form under specific conditions:

- over the oceans, where there is a supply of warm moisture to 'fuel' the hurricane;
- where there is a large area of sea with SSTs more than 27°C;

- at least 5° north or south of the equator; and
- on the western side of oceans.

Hurricanes are responsible for severe damage and loss of life – from the storm winds, from flooding and from landslides when they strike land. In an average year hurricanes cause some 20,000 deaths worldwide – 96% of these in Asia, with most occurring in Bangladesh. In the Caribbean, recent very severe hurricanes have included:

- *Hurricane Gilbert* in 1988. This was a Category 5 hurricane on the five-point Saffir/Simpson Damage Potential Scale, with wind gusts up to 320 kph. Its track caused severe damage in the central Caribbean, especially Jamaica and Mexico.
- *Hurricane Mitch* in 1998. This was a category 4 hurricane, which caused severe damage and loss of life in Central America.

Those concerned about global warming (see Chapter 9) have suggested that one effect will be an increase in the frequency of very severe hurricanes and cyclones.

Tornadoes

Tornadoes are small-scale local storms with an intense swirl of wind only a few tens of metres in diameter, with a distinctive 'funnel' appearance. They form in mid-latitudes where there are very strong temperature differences between tropical warm air and polar cold air. The most favoured location is the central states of the USA, where many dozens occur each year, each one carving a swathe of severe damage over a distance of a few miles.

Other tropical storms

Although the processes of storms in the mid-latitudes are better understood than those in the tropics, there are several distinctive types of storm which occur in the tropical and sub-tropical regions.

- **Wave disturbances** (also known as Easterly Waves) are linear features up to 3000 km in length, bringing rain and cloud, common in the Pacific and in the Caribbean.

- **Monsoon depressions** are large (1000–1250 km in diameter), slow moving areas of low pressure that form during the south-west Monsoon over India and Bangladesh, producing long periods of rainfall.
- **Squall lines** (known in West Africa as disturbance lines) are smaller features, lines of cloud and rain a few hundred kilometres in length, travelling westward at 50–60 kph.

El Niño and the Southern Oscillation

Research into the operation of the ocean–atmosphere system has been very extensive in the last two decades. Large-scale international projects have been funded by the UN through the World Meteorological Organization (WMO), including the World Climate Research Programme (WCRP). Research within this programme has included the TOGA Project (Tropical Ocean/Global Atmosphere) and the WOCE Project (World Ocean Circulation Experiment). Such research has provided a much more detailed understanding of El Niño and the Southern Oscillation (ENSO), which appears to be a major driving force in the world's climate despite being a feature of the atmosphere–ocean circulation in the Pacific Ocean.

El Niño is an event which occurs every 3–4 years and in which large areas of the upper parts of the ocean in the tropical eastern Pacific Ocean have much higher temperatures than average (+1–4°C). This event is called El Niño because it brings warm water to the coasts of Ecuador and Peru around Christmas time, the celebration of the young Christ child (El Niño). The Southern Oscillation is a pattern of changing atmospheric pressure across the Pacific. When the differences between atmospheric pressure between the eastern Pacific and Indonesia are smaller than usual, the effect is to draw warm water into the eastern Pacific – El Niño. The El Niño of 1997–8 was amongst the most intense ever recorded, with SSTAs over the eastern Pacific of up to +5°C over an area 1.5 times the size of the USA. The energy transferred from this water to the atmosphere may have been a major influence on producing the world's warmest year in 1997.

El Niño has been linked to other patterns of severe weather elsewhere in the world, including:

- dry conditions over northern Australia, Indonesia and The Philippines;
- dry conditions over south-east Africa and northern Brazil;
- lower rainfall than usual during the Indian monsoon;
- wetter weather along the west coast of tropical South America, the Gulf Coast of the USA, southern Brazil and Argentina; and
- reduced numbers and intensities of hurricanes in the Caribbean, but increased numbers of cyclones and typhoons in Asia.

Although the ways in which these events are linked has not yet been established, it seems clear that an understanding of ENSO is important, and much research needs to be done. In particular, the links between global warming and the frequency and intensity of El Niño need to be established, for there may be a direct link between human impact on the environment and severe climatic and weather consequences.

Major climatic zones

The workings of the atmosphere mean any particular place on the Earth's surface has a general pattern of weather that it experiences from year to year. This is the **climate** of a place, and is usually described by showing the changing patterns of temperature and precipitation (rain, snow, hail, etc.) in a typical year. It is possible over a period of time (normally 30 years) to measure the average (mean) temperature of each month of the year, the average precipitation in each month, and the average annual temperature and total precipitation. Other aspects of climate might include the mean number of days of sunshine or the average cloud cover, average atmospheric pressure, and patterns of humidity or frost.

Over the globe it is possible to identify many regions with similar climates. Understanding these climates is important, because they distinguish the types of natural vegetation and animal life which

ATMOSPHERE, WEATHER AND CLIMATE

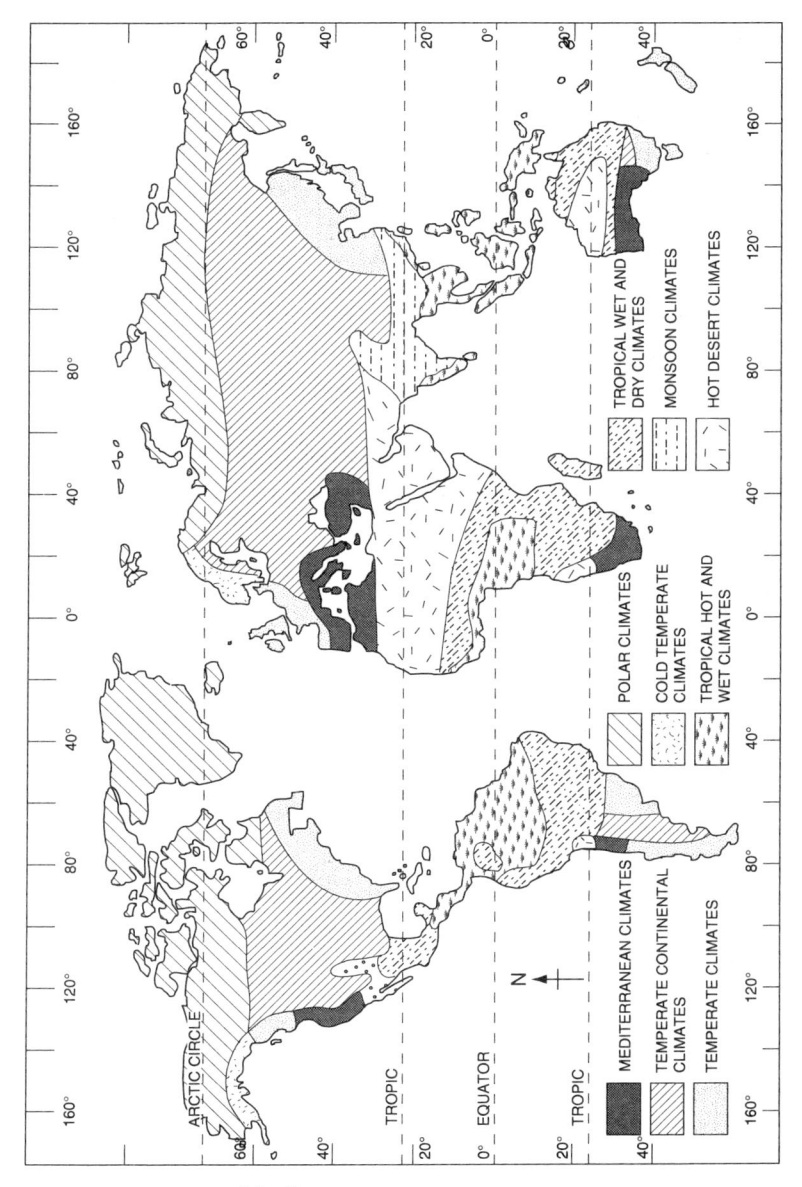

Figure 9.5   World climate zones

may live in that region, and they have an impact on how people might use their environment. For example, the crops that can be grown or the amount of energy needed for heating will depend on temperature patterns, and the supply of water resources for industry or people will be strongly affected by the amount of rainfall. Figure 9.5 shows the distribution of the main climate zones of the Earth, the main characteristics of which are described below.

Tropical hot and wet climate

These are the areas close to the equator which are hot and wet throughout the year. Temperatures typically average about 25–28°C, and annual rainfall is 2000–4000 mm. The dominant natural vegetation is tropical rainforest.

Tropical wet and dry climate

This climate, sometimes called a savanna climate, is hot throughout the year, but has one or two distinctive wet seasons. The major natural vegetation is open woodland or tropical grassland.

Monsoon climates

The Monsoon climates are best known in southern and eastern Asia (India, Pakistan and China). They are characterized by a marked change in dominant wind direction throughout the year. In India, for example, the months of June to September are characterized by south-westerly winds bringing heavy rainfall to the region (the south-west Monsoon). In winter, however, the winds blow towards the equator from northern India, bringing high temperatures and almost no rain (the north-east Monsoon).

Hot deserts

The world's hot deserts occur beneath the sub-tropical high-pressure areas, where sinking air produces clear skies, high temperatures and almost no rainfall. The great deserts of the Sahara, the Kalahari, and south-west USA are typical of such regions.

Mediterranean climates

On the poleward side of the deserts are regions which are dominated in summer by the sub-tropical highs, but which in winter experience the passage of mid-latitude depressions in the belt of south-westerly winds. Summers are hot and dry, therefore, but winters are mild and wet. This climate is typified by the Mediterranean climate of Italy, Spain and Greece, but is also found in California, South Africa and Western Australia.

Temperate climates

These regions lie for the whole year in the band of the Mid-latitude Westerly winds, but in summer may periodically have fine weather if the sub-tropical highs reach the regions. In winter mid-latitude depressions regularly pass through the area. Rainfall can occur at any time of year. The typical range of temperature is 0–25°C. Regions a long way from the sea (central Asia, central Russia, and the mid-west states of USA) do not gain benefit from the way in which the sea moderates extremes of temperature on adjacent land areas. As a result, winters in these regions may be very cold, but summers may be very hot. The climate in such regions is often known as a **temperate continental climate**. The typical vegetation in temperate climates is deciduous woodland or grassland.

Cold temperate climates

Between the temperate areas and the poles are zones which are colder because of their latitude and which are throughout the year in the paths of mid-latitude depressions. These areas, such as northern Canada and Scandinavia, have much colder winters even near the coast, and the main vegetation found is coniferous trees.

Polar climates

Close to the poles the climate is cold throughout the year, and vegetation is limited by the shortness of the growing season. In favoured areas scrubby tundra vegetation may grow, but in many areas there is little or no ground cover except ice.

Climate change

The pattern described here provides a broad picture of weather and climate around the globe. Climate, however, is not constant, for even without the interference of human beings the climate can (and does) change. There is a great deal of evidence for changes in climate within human history, and geologists can show evidence from the rocks of periods when the climate may have been very different from that experienced today. In Western Europe, the sixteenth and seventeenth centuries have been described as the 'Little Ice Age', for wetter and cooler summers and much colder and snowier winters were more common. Glaciers reached much further down Alpine valleys than they do today. Failed harvests in France in the 1780s may have been an important cause of the French Revolution, while the snow scenes common on Christmas cards date back to the period of the Little Ice Age. In contrast, the eighth to tenth centuries were rather warmer and wetter than today – and the retreat of ice from the North Atlantic enabled the Vikings to 'discover' Greenland, Iceland and North America.

On a longer time scale, there is much information about the last Ice Age (the Pleistocene period of geological time), when ice sheets expanded several times during the period from 2 million years ago to 10,000 years ago to cover large areas that now have temperate climates. Evidence from the analysis of oxygen isotopes in ice cores drilled in Greenland also shows how the climate has fluctuated – between times when the world was 4–6°C warmer on average than today and times when it was 4–6°C cooler.

The causes of these changes are complex and not really fully understood. Some of the small changes are simply the result of the dynamic nature of the atmosphere. Climate figures and data are averages, and in any year different temperatures or amounts of rainfall may occur. On a longer scale the effect of changes in the Sun's output of energy, or natural cycles in the amount of energy the Earth receives because of its precise position in the solar system relative to the sun (**Milankovitch cycles**) may be important. Similarly, periods of intense volcanic activity can reduce temperatures by blocking out sunlight. What is clear, though, is that no *single* explanation is enough to account for the known patterns of climate change.

The issue of climate change is particularly important for those interested in conservation. A concern linked to the impact of pollution and other human activity on the atmosphere is that it may change patterns of weather and climate. However, if climate varies and fluctuates naturally it is hard to know how much any change is due to human activity. Furthermore, understanding climate change may help us know how our impact on the environment may change climate, and what evidence we should be looking for. These are all issues which are considered in the next chapter.

Summary

This chapter has examined how the atmosphere works as a system and how it produces the patterns of weather and climate that we experience. Since many aspects of the natural environment are strongly influenced by weather and climate, it is important for conservation to understand how atmospheric processes work. The role of people in altering those processes will be examined in Chapter 10.

Taking action

This chapter has mainly identified the natural processes that drive weather and climate. There is little that an individual can do to affect this. However, the next chapter examines the impact of humans on climate, where a whole range of individual actions can contribute to conservation. The major action that can be taken is to support research into meteorology and oceanography, and to urge both national governments and international bodies to support research in these areas. Lobbying local and national representatives to promote policies and funding to support this research can be important in emphasizing your concerns.

ACTIVITIES

1 Obtain from your local library or local newspaper data for the climate of your own region.

2 Look at the literature in your local library for historical evidence of extreme weather events in your region, or evidence of climate change.

3 Keep a diary of significant weather events (e.g. floods, droughts, storms) from around the globe that have been reported in the national media. Identify which of the aspects of weather and climate covered in this chapter may be the major cause of a particular event (for example, a hurricane).

4 For the events you have identified above, look at how far the media try to link them to evidence of natural climate change or climate change produced by human activity.

10 CLIMATE CHANGE AND HUMAN IMPACT

Introduction

Wherever people live they pollute the air by their activities. Even in the earliest societies of prehistory smoke from the burning of wood for heat and light and soil blown off the land from farming added pollutants to the atmosphere. Air pollution is recorded as long ago as Roman times – Nero's tutor, Seneca, wrote of how smoke affected his health, and the courts dealt with cases of smoke pollution and its effects on those living close to forges and workshops. As industrialization has grown in the last two centuries, the effects of burning fuels such as coal, oil and natural gas, and the release of waste gases from industrial production, have rapidly increased atmospheric pollution. With this increase have come major air pollution disasters, such as Seveso (1976), Bhopal (1984) and Chernobyl (1986), and the damaging smogs of London in the first half of the twentieth century and Los Angeles today. More worrying, though are the long-term effects of air pollution on human health (links are established between increases in car exhaust pollution and asthma) and on climate, as a result of the ozone hole and the greenhouse effect. Such long-term effects are less visible day to day but may in the end be very serious. The impact of pollution on the atmosphere from the burning of fossil fuels was considered in part in Chapter 5, where the issue of acid rain was discussed. Here we shall look at two specific issues in more depth – the destruction of ozone in the upper atmosphere, and the concern about the greenhouse effect – both of which raise questions of long-term climate change as a result of human activity.

Ozone depletion

Ozone in the stratosphere

Ozone is a form of oxygen in which three oxygen atoms are joined together (O_3) rather than the more usual two (O_2). Within the layer of the atmosphere known as the **stratosphere**, at a height of 50 km above the Earth's surface, ozone is formed by the effect of sunlight on oxygen, then slowly destroyed by chemical reactions with certain naturally occurring gases such as nitric oxide. As a result of mixing and movement in the stratosphere this produces a maximum concentration of ozone at a height of about 20–25 km. Despite the popular use of the phrase 'ozone layer', the ozone is simply one component of the atmosphere even at 25 km, where it is only 0.0001% of the volume of the air. In a completely 'natural' state, the overall rate of formation and destruction of ozone in the stratosphere is balanced, although the amount of ozone varies throughout the year according to changes in the amount of sunlight being received.

The importance of ozone lies in the way it absorbs some of the ultraviolet radiation that comes into the atmosphere in sunlight, and particularly ultraviolet-B (UVB). If it reaches the Earth's surface UVB is potentially harmful to both human and plant health, and is strongly linked to the development of skin cancer and eye cataracts.

The ozone hole

The first evidence of a fall in the amount of ozone in the stratosphere came in 1977, when the British Antarctic Survey, as part of their regular atmospheric monitoring, recorded a reduced concentration of ozone over Antarctica at heights of about 20 km. This raised many concerns amongst scientists and environmental groups. With development in satellite technology during the 1980s a more detailed picture began to emerge, and detailed mapping of the amount of ozone depletion was possible. In the winter and spring of 1987 (July to November in Antarctica!) satellite readings showed that over a very large area the amount of ozone in the stratosphere had fallen by over 97% between August and October. This reduction in ozone concentration is typically described as the 'ozone hole' because it is an area that allows more UVB through the atmosphere – in a strict sense, though, despite the popular image, it is not a hole at all.

Observations over subsequent years confirmed the appearance of this ozone hole over Antarctica every year. Its development is encouraged by the long Antarctic winters, which produce very low temperatures in the stratosphere – which, in turn, reduces the formation of new ozone to replace ozone that is lost. Observations have also taken place in the Arctic, where conditions in winter may be very similar, and an ozone hole of similar size but showing less depletion of ozone has been found each winter. Of concern is the observation that this hole can extend over parts of Western Europe, particularly the British Isles, and North America, and as far south as 30° north (the latitude of north Africa and Florida).

A review of the state of the ozone layer was undertaken in 1998 by the WMO. They concluded that:

- during the 1990s total ozone levels in northern polar latitudes declined in the winter and spring to 25–30% below the averages for the period before 1975;
- in the Antarctic, the ozone loss in the winter and spring (peaking in September and October) usually exceeds 50%. However, in the winter of 1998, the area of the ozone 'hole' was the largest ever recorded, and in some locations ozone had almost completely disappeared in the layer 14–22 km above the Earth's surface;
- only over the mid-latitudes has the decline in ozone become less during the 1990s, possibly as a result of international action to reduce the pollutants that cause ozone loss (see below);
- overall, the decline in stratospheric ozone is approximately 1–2% per year across the globe.

The depletion of the ozone layer has raised serious concerns about human health. UVB reaching the surface can cause skin cancer and eye cataracts, and the United Nations Environment Programme (UNEP) has estimated that the damaging doses of UVB have increased by 5% near to the tropics, by 10% at the North Pole and by 40% over Antarctica Their estimate is that a 10% reduction in stratospheric ozone around the globe will result in an extra 300,000 cases of skin cancer and 1.6 million cases of cataracts each year.

The destruction of the ozone in the stratosphere is largely the result of the presence of compounds called **chlorofluorocarbons (CFCs)**. These contain chlorine, which speeds up the breakdown of ozone. The main sources of CFCs are propellants in aerosol sprays, some components used in the electronics industry and coolants in refrigerators. From these sources over 1 million tonnes per year of CFCs are released into the atmosphere. Other chemical compounds that cause ozone destruction are oxides of bromine.

The Montreal Protocol and beyond

Concern about the possible impact of ozone depletion grew rapidly during the 1980s, even though the evidence of ozone loss was not easy to obtain and there had been no measurements of increases in UVB. In 1987, the Montreal Protocol on Substances that Deplete the Ozone Layer was signed by 75 nations, committing every signatory to cut its use of the most damaging CFCs to half of the 1986 level of output by 1999.

This agreement is regarded by many conservationists as an example of speedy action amongst countries to respond to an environmental crisis. The lead-up to the signature of the Montreal Protocol, and the years that followed, are a good example of the complex way in which international environmental and conservation politics operate – O'Riordan (1995) suggests that 'environmental diplomacy is a cat and mouse game operating at many levels.' Some parts of this 'cat and mouse' game were:

- disagreements between scientists about the atmospheric processes at work;
- disagreements between scientists about whether the limited amount of data was enough to show ozone depletion or increases in UVB conclusively;
- disagreements about whether it was even possible to measure changes unless measurements were taken over decades rather than just a few years;
- the use of this scientific uncertainty by companies to argue for no change in CFC production;

- employment by the chemical companies manufacturing CFCs of scientists sceptical about the reality of destruction of ozone;
- promotion of CFC reduction measures by companies manufacturing alternatives to CFCs;
- political arguments from less developed countries that halting CFC production, especially for refrigeration, was a ploy by the developed countries to slow down their economic growth;
- arguments that the production of CFCs was mainly a developed world business, so the developed countries should pay for the solutions by giving aid to the less developed countries to develop and use alternatives to CFCs. An important factor in persuading many less developed countries to sign the Montreal Protocol was the setting up of an international fund to support them in actions taken to reduce CFCs; and
- concerted action by NGOs such as Greenpeace and Friends of the Earth to raise public awareness of the issue and to persuade governments to take action.

The fourth meeting of the countries who had signed the Montreal Protocol, held in Copenhagen in 1992, agreed a new set of measures to speed up the phasing out of ozone-destroying chemicals. In particular, this brought the date for reaching the 50% of 1986 output levels forward, from 1999 to January 1996.

By 1996, most countries had made some progress in reducing CFC production, but had not met the targets set. However, by 1998 the WMO showed that the combined total of ozone-depleting substances in the troposphere had peaked in 1994 and had started to decline slowly, with the exception of bromine which was continuing to increase. In the stratosphere it was expected the peak would be reached in 2000, but the evidence to confirm this may not be available for many years. The WMO, however, also noted that the decline in ozone may be helping to counteract global warming (see below), and may be reducing the warming at the surface by up to 30% – this simply illustrates how complex many environmental and conservation issues are.

Carbon dioxide and the greenhouse effect

The greenhouse effect

A second concern about human impact on the atmosphere and on climate has been the issue of global warming resulting from the so-called 'greenhouse effect'. The greenhouse effect is a natural atmospheric process. The atmosphere is heated mainly by sunlight striking the Earth's surface and being converted into heat (infrared energy) – and is therefore, in effect, heated from below. This heat would normally be gradually lost out into space, but some is absorbed by gases in the atmosphere (mostly water vapour and carbon dioxide, but also methane (CH_4), nitrous oxides (NOx) and ozone) and is trapped there – just as heat is trapped in a greenhouse since little of it can return through the glass the light came in through. Without the intervention of humans the processes in the atmosphere keep the temperature within a narrow range. Indeed, it is this process which keeps the temperatures high enough for human life to survive on Earth – without it the average temperature of the surface would be $-18°C$ (compared with the present average of $+15°C$). However, pollution has increased the amount of some of the main gases trapping heat in the atmosphere, and the result is a concern that the atmosphere is getting steadily warmer – what is properly called the 'enhanced greenhouse effect'.

The increase in greenhouse gases is the result of the burning of fossil fuels (coal, oil and natural gas) for energy, and industrial pollution. In 1992, it was estimated that key gases were increasing at the following rates each year:

CO_2 0.5%;
CH_4 0.5%;
NOx 0.25%.

These gases do not contribute equally to potential global warming, however, and it is estimated that 72% of any global warming will be due to CO_2, and 18% due to CH_4. It is for this reason that conservationists have most concern about carbon dioxide emissions.

Figure 10.1 shows the increase in atmospheric CO_2 over the last 40 years. Before the industrial revolution natural levels of CO_2 in the atmosphere were about 280 parts per million (ppm – i.e. in every million 'units' of air, 228 would be CO_2). By the late twentieth century this increased to over 350 ppm, mainly from the burning of fossil fuels. Most CO_2 emissions are produced by the countries of the developed world, with the USA accounting for 24% of the total and the EU producing 13%. Current rates of increase of CO_2 output suggest that its concentration in the atmosphere may double within 50 years.

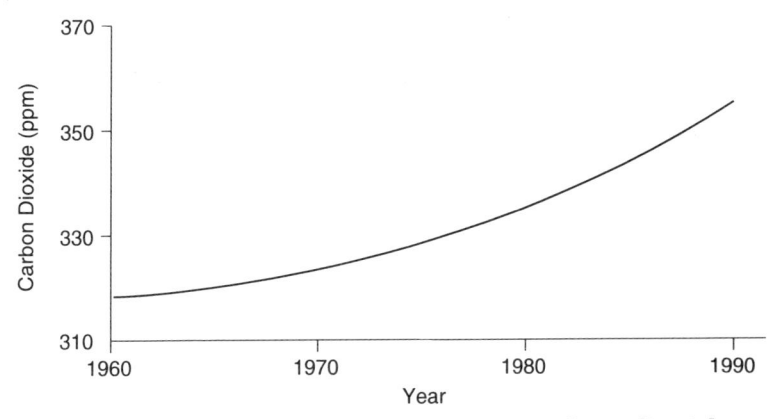

Figure 10.1 Increases in atmospheric carbon dioxide since 1960

The impact of global warming

Growing concern about the possible impact on climate of the growth in CO_2 concentrations lead to the establishment of an **Intergovernmental Panel on Climate Change (IPCC)** in 1990. Its role was to collect all the scientific evidence about the effects of an increase in greenhouse gases and to predict their likely impact on climate. The initial report predicted that in a 'business as usual' situation (i.e. with outputs continuing to increase as at present with no attempt to reduce CO_2 output):

- global temperatures will increase by 0.2–0.5°C by 2050;
- CO_2 concentrations will double by the year 2025; and

- sea level will rise by 10–30cm by the year 2030 and 33–75cm by the year 2070, as a result of the seas becoming warmer and expanding in volume.

By 1992 new research evidence was available, however, which suggested that the oceans absorbed more of the extra CO_2 than had previously been estimated, so that the impact on the atmosphere would be less than originally predicted. As a result, in the IPCC's second report in 1992 predictions were reduced to:

- a doubling of CO_2 concentrations by 2050; and
- a rise in sea level of 8–15 cm by the year 2030 and 16–30 cm by the year 2070.

During the 1990s scientists and governments tried to identify evidence of climate change as a result of global warming. Figure 10.2 shows the pattern of global temperatures over the twentieth century and suggests a steady increase in temperatures, with most of the warmest years on record occurring in the 1990s. The occurrence of severe Caribbean hurricanes in the 1990s, and widespread reporting of weather extremes are also often portrayed as evidence of climate change.

However, a number of issues arise with this evidence.

1 Climate changes naturally over time without human interference. Evidence from carbon dating of tree rings and from the measurement of oxygen isotopes in ice cores in the Arctic confirms these changes. Figure 10.3 shows the pattern of climate change in recent Earth history. From this, it is not possible to be sure that recent changes are any more than part of a natural fluctuation in climate.

2 Globalization of news and media means that we are made aware of weather events around the world that would not have reached our attention in the past. It may be that such events are not becoming more frequent but are simply being reported more widely.

3 Our weather records are very short, stretching back only two centuries at most, and much less in the developing world. We have only recent data to

compare today's events with, therefore, so we are not able to tell whether events are extreme in the long term.

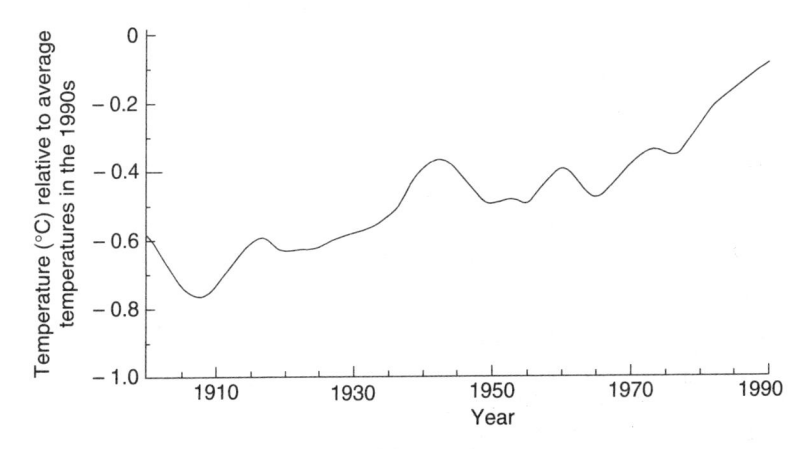

Figure 10.2 Average world temperature during the twentieth century

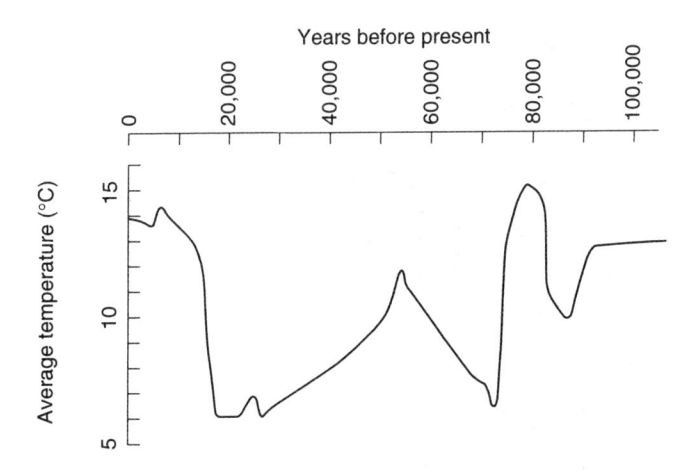

Figure 10.3 Global temperature over the last 100,000 years

If climate *is* changing as a result of global warming then predicting the likely pattern of change is difficult. The IPCC has run computer models to make predictions of the patterns resulting from different temperature increases. Under any change some predictions are possible:

Climatic zones

The location of climatic zones will shift. The British Isles, for example, may develop a climate more like that of the Mediterranean, and people will be able to grow olives and grapes. Some areas will become drier than at present (for example, much of China), while other areas will become wetter (for example, northern Australia). As a result areas which are currently important grain areas (for example eastern China or the Great Plains of the USA) may be less able to produce the volume of crops they do at present. There are clearly great implications of such changes for world patterns of food production, hunger and trade, and many geopolitical issues may arise.

Sea level changes

The ice sheets of Antarctica and the Arctic will melt and reduce in size, leading to sea level increases. This change has been predicted to be between 10 cm and 1.5 m over the next century, and it is possible that low-lying countries such as Bangladesh and some islands in the Pacific Ocean could be flooded. The IPCC predicts that by the year 2100 much of the Nile Delta, and 80% of the land of the Marshall Islands in the Pacific Ocean, will be lost. In addition, most of the world's major cities stand on coastal sites, and the cost of flood protection may be very high. A 1.5 m sea level rise would destroy 80% of Japan's sandy beaches, with a large impact on both its coastal ecosystems and its tourist industry.

Weather extremes

Extremes of weather may become more frequent because the temperature differences between the tropics and the poles will be greater. More severe hurricanes, and more intense mid-latitude depressions may result from global warming, with a potentially large impact on regions in the tracks of such storms. Areas such as

Bangladesh, where most of the world's deaths from hurricanes occur, will be particularly badly affected because of concurrent rises in sea level, as will the countries of the Caribbean and Central America. Intense mid-latitude depressions may have a significant effect on coastal areas of north-west Europe and Iceland.

Biodiversity

Biodiversity will be affected, for as climate zones shift, so animal and plant species are affected. While plants and animals can move with the climate zones where change is slow, the changes in climate may be too fast for some species to adapt. As a result some species may become extinct.

Action on global warming

The reports of the IPCC were produced to inform the 1992 UN Framework Convention on Climate Change, part of the Rio Summit. This convention agreed to reduce emissions of CO_2, CH_4 and NOx to 1990 levels by the year 2000. Some 160 countries signed the Convention, but most have not ratified it because of concern over measuring pollution outputs and the economic impact of trying to slow down the use of fossil fuels. Some countries prefer to take radical action now, believing that the **'no regrets'** policy of taking early action is better than a **'wait and see'** approach, where more evidence is thought necessary before action should be taken. The Canadian government, for example, has a target of reducing CO_2 emissions to 20% below its 1990 levels by the year 2000. International meetings to review progress on reducing greenhouse gases have taken place in Kyoto, Japan in 1997 and in Buenos Aires, Argentina in 1998. Despite the arguments about the lack of reliable data about global warming and CO_2 emissions from individual countries, and about the particular problems developing countries face in cutting back on energy use, both meetings produced agreements on future monitoring of CO_2 emissions, and set up programmes to monitor emissions around the globe. This will also help to identify the regional patterns of climate change that may occur from global warming, and so help individual countries to plan for their new environments.

Summary

Concern about changes in climate is perhaps the greatest conservation and environmental issue as we enter the twenty-first century. The causes of climate change are rooted in issues of pollution and the use of fossil fuels. Its consequences are potentially global in effect, affecting the developed and the less developed world, and every part of the human environment may be changed as a result. Its consequences are also unpredictable, as scientists try to unravel the processes at work and predict the likely environmental effects. Climate change is also a major political issue, for it brings the world's nations into discussions about what should be done, who is responsible for the causes and solutions, and who should pay. It has potential for conflict between peoples and states.

While most scientists are agreed that changes are taking place in the atmosphere (increasing CO_2 and destruction of stratospheric ozone), little has been agreed beyond that. Because evidence of change will only truly emerge over decades, and changes over a few years cannot be distinguished from natural climatic change, there is scope for many disagreements between scientists and between politicians. Those in the debate all have their own veiwpoint and are seeking particular answers and outcomes – they have vested interests. Industry and business, and most politicians, do not wish to take actions that slow down economic growth. Companies that manufacture CFCs wish to continue in business, as do companies making alternatives to CFCs. Even environmental and conservation groups have vested interests in pursuing the greening of society.

The choice is between adopting the precautionary principle of taking early action, and taking a 'wait and see' approach to see what further evidence emerges. The political scene has caused the precautionary principle to be applied to the ozone issue, yet has allowed many countries to adopt a 'wait and see' attitude to carbon dioxide emissions. By the twenty-second century we shall be able to judge their decisions with hindsight!

Taking action

Individual action to support conservation in relation to climate change can involve a number of approaches:

1 Reducing household and personal energy use to assist in the reduction of CO_2 production from the burning of fossil fuels.
2 Reducing the use of aerosol sprays, or using only those labelled as ozone friendly, which do not contain harmful CFCs.
3 Disposing of old refrigerators through local authorities or private companies which undertake to dispose of the coolants without releasing CFCs to the atmosphere – and replacing the refrigerator with one with ozone-friendly coolants.
4 Supporting pressure groups and political groups promoting reductions in CO_2 emissions through international political action and agreement.

ACTIVITIES

1 Use the Internet to identify the most recent developments in international policy on reducing CO_2 emissions. Possible websites and addresses are included in Appendix 1.
2 Contact your local Agenda 21 group and identify what activities it is undertaking to promote awareness of global warming.
3 Contact the public relations department of a local or national company and obtain a copy of their environmental policy. What does it say about reducing emissions to the atmosphere?
4 Use the Internet or your local phone book to contact one of the main environmental NGOs. Find out what current campaigns they have in relation to global warming issues.

11 MANAGING ENVIRONMENT AND RESOURCES

Introduction

The interaction of people with their environment has generated many conservation issues for the future. In the chapters in Part 2 of this book we have looked in detail at the causes of these issues and have identified many of the approaches being used to tackle the problems that arise. If we are to move towards a more sustainable society, then it is essential that we develop management approaches and strategies that promote sustainability and support conservation work. This chapter describes some of these strategies and looks at some of the strategies in action.

Uncertainty and the precautionary principle

A key component of conservation is to minimize the levels of pollution that are emitted from the activities of society – from its industries, its farming and its social environment. A major challenge is to balance the risks from pollution against the costs and benefits to society of the activities generating that pollution. However, in many cases the science is not sufficiently well developed to provide exact predictions. In some cases this is because we simply do not have enough data to fully understand the situation – for example, we do not know the possible impact of GM crops on local and regional ecosystems. In other cases it may be that, although we understand the broad principles of the science, the models that have been produced are not able to predict with enough accuracy what will happen – our models of climate change, for example, although rapidly improving, are still not able to make predictions in enough detail, or with enough confidence, for us to rely on them. In addition, there may be aspects of the science which, as O'Riordan (1995) suggests are 'beyond the knowable'. In other words, we may not yet know enough of the overall principles of science to know what will happen in radically different circumstances – do some environmental changes, for example, happen suddenly and catastrophically to fundamentally change the whole set of principles on which our current scientific knowledge is based?

Because of this problem of uncertainty an essential part of environmental management, the **precautionary principle**, needs to be applied, and has become part of the environmental policy of many nations and organizations. O'Riordan (1995) suggests that this involves four components:

1. In the absence of scientific proof, always erring on the side of caution in decisions that are taken.
2. 'Leaving ecological space as room for ignorance.' This suggests that no resource should be extracted to the limits, even where current science suggest this is possible – we may simply not yet know the effect of such extraction or use.
3. Involving the whole of society in discussing and being aware of environmental decision-making, to emphasize the lack of certainty and to clarify that lack of certainty in people's minds.
4. Putting the onus on developers to prove that their developments and plans do not cause environmental harm, rather than letting the burden of proof fall on society as a whole to show that they do. In essence, developments should be assumed guilty of environmental damage until proved innocent, rather than the other way around.

Risk assessment and environmental management

The precautionary principle requires that any development that will impact on the environment should be examined in terms of its likely effects. We need to know, for example, what the possible effects of particular actions or decisions might be, and what the likelihood is of environmental damage occurring. If damage may occur we need to know what levels of damage could occur with different levels of activity. Trying to estimate or calculate this is the process of **risk assessment**.

Risk assessment is a highly complex and technical field, for there are many difficult questions that must be asked about risks and potential hazards – for example:

- *When does a 'risk' become a 'hazard'?* Risk is a measure of the chances of a particular event occurring, such as a devastating hurricane resulting from global warming. A hazard is when an event becomes sufficiently likely to require action to reduce its possible effects. How often does a devastating hurricane have to occur for it to become a hazard rather than a risk – once a decade, once a century, or once a millennium? This then raises questions about whether there is sufficient data available to scientists to measure risk, and whether the variability of the natural environment means that even measures of probability are not especially helpful for planning purposes.

- *How safe is 'safe enough'?* If we measure risk we have to make judgements about the limits of safety. However, safety is a matter of personal judgement, and will vary from society to society and individual to individual. What is safe for a government in terms of reducing the costs of protection to society overall may leave some individuals or groups at very high risk. For example, allowing a nuclear waste dump in one location may be best for society as a whole, but will not be best for those who live in the locality. Risk is very much dependent, therefore, on precise circumstances.

- *How do people perceive risk?* Much research is being done into the psychology of risk, for it is important to understand how people form their ideas of risk. The role of the media may be important here because their portrayal of risk, perhaps through the sensationalization of headlines, can form and shape people's views. Research in the USA suggests that people's reactions to plans to create nuclear fuel dumps are influenced most by their images of nuclear warfare and the dropping of the first atomic bomb on Hiroshima, rather than on objective knowledge of the process of dumping nuclear waste.

A number of management approaches have been developed which build in the idea of risk assessment, and which are used in making decisions about environment activities. These are mostly known by their acronyms – ALARP, BATNEEC, and BPEO.

The ALARP principle

ALARP means **as low as reasonably possible**, and is the principle that any development will be tolerated only where risks have been minimized as part of the planning and design process, or where the cost of reducing the risks further would be disproportionate to the benefits gained from the project. In all cases there will be a point at which the risks, even with ALARP, make a project unacceptable.

The BPEO principle

BPEO stands for the **best practicable environmental option**. The main idea behind BPEO is that any development must take account of the full range of scientific evidence and the attitudes and views of different social groups to identify which option goes furthest to meeting all environmental requirements. The word *practicable* is important, for it recognizes that there may be technical and financial limits to achieving the very best or optimum solution.

The BATNEEC principle

BATNEEC is the **best available technique not entailing excessive costs**. This requires developers to try to identify the best means for reducing pollution or environmental impact as they plan their project, but it also recognizes that the *ideal* solution may be so expensive that it would make any development impossible. As with ALARP and BPEO, simply choosing BATNEEC does not guarantee that a project will be approved by the authorities, who might believe that even with the best available technique the environmental impact will be too great to permit development.

Quality standards and environmental management

A common approach to managing environmental impact and pollution is the idea of **quality standards**. This recognizes that cutting out all pollution or having zero environmental impact is almost impossible with any development. The quality standards approach involves setting standards, or levels of pollution or environmental damage, which must not be exceeded.

The traditional approach to pollution control has been the **uniform emission standards approach**. This sets standards for the highest levels of pollution output from an activity, and these standards are applied to all such activities wherever they occur. An example of a uniform emission standard is the limits on the pollution allowed from city waste incinerators, imposed by an EU Directive in 1989.

An alternative approach is the **quality standards approach**, which is based on the idea that pollution is a problem because of the impact it has on various elements of the environment, not because of where it comes from. What is important, therefore, is not how much pollution has been produced, but that this should be kept to a level where the impact on the environment, plants and animals does not exceed certain maximum levels. In different places, therefore, different levels of pollution output might be allowed. For example, a city disposing of its treated sewage into seas with stormy weather and strong tides to dilute the effluent might be allowed to have higher pollution output than a city discharging into a calm lagoon. What is important is to keep the measurement of impact on beach pollution or marine animals to within specified limits.

While this seems a sound approach, it does raise the questions of how easy it is to predict the impacts of pollution, how easy it is to measure pollution and, in the long term, how we can know what quality standards are appropriate for a sustainable environment. Despite these concerns, the quality standards approach is now the usual way of setting pollution standards in Europe, while in other parts of the world a mix of the two approaches is used.

Environmental planning techniques

In most countries of the world today there is a requirement that no development will occur without some form of assessment of its environmental impact. Environmental scientists, therefore, have developed a number of techniques that can be used in making such assessments, and which can be used by business, by developers or by government in preparing their proposals. Three of these techniques will be considered here – life cycle analysis, environmental auditing, and environmental impact assessment.

Life cycle analysis

Life cycle analysis (LCA) involves the examination of a new product at every stage of its manufacture, marketing, consumption and disposal to try to measure the impact on the environment of each part of that process. By doing this it is possible to measure the overall impact of a product on the environment, and the analysis helps businesses to identify the areas where taking action to improve the product's **environmental performance** is particularly necessary or may be especially helpful. To promote this approach the EU, for example, developed an ecolabelling scheme in 1992, through which products which have good environmental performance throughout their cradle-to-grave life cycle can be labelled as such. In this way business is encouraged to promote environmentally friendly production, and consumers are helped to make environmental purchasing decisions – for example, is a wooden window frame more environmentally friendly than an aluminium window frame?

LCA involves three stages:

Inventory

This involves identifying all the ways in which the product affects the environment from extracting its raw materials to disposing of its waste products and packaging. Five stages in the life cycle are identified: pre-production (e.g. extracting raw materials); production; distribution (which includes packaging); utilization; and disposal.

Evaluation

This involves measuring environmental impact at each stage of the life cycle. The EU requires each stage to be assessed in terms of its impact on waste production, soil pollution, water contamination, air contamination, noise, energy consumption, natural resource consumption, and effects on ecosystems. Through this stage the major problems in the process can be identified.

Response

This is the stage in which the manufacturer identifies what it will do to address the issues identified by the evaluation.

LCA has not yet been adopted very widely, but it is growing in use and is promoted by amongst others, the International Chamber of Commerce. Only if it becomes a statutory requirement, however, is it likely to become an important tool for business to use.

Environmental auditing

Environmental auditing is a process in which an organization or business reviews its environmental performance in each part of its activities. There are many types of audit, varying from a **comprehensive business audit**, where every aspect of the business is reviewed, to a **compliance audit**, which simply checks whether legal environmental requirements are being met, to an **occupational health audit** in which the health and safety of the workforce is reviewed. Many companies have undertaken partial environmental audits as part of the greening of their business, but as yet there is no legal obligation on them to do so. Although the process itself may be expensive, most businesses report that there are economic gains in the long term from improvements to environmental performance that such an audit can recommend. In Norway and Sweden all businesses are required to undertake such an audit, but there is no system as yet for verification of the process.

Environmental impact assessment

Environmental Impact Assessment (EIA) is the process in which any proposed development is examined to consider the impact it may have on every aspect of the environment. EIAs were first developed in the USA where the National Environment Policy Act (1969) requires all national (Federal) agencies to prepare an EIA for any proposed developments. Its use spread in many MDCs, and in 1985 EIA (or Environmental Assessment (EA) as the EU calls it) was made obligatory in the EU. This directive was implemented in the UK through the Town and Country Planning (Assessment of Environmental Effects) Regulations of 1988.

EIA is not a single technique, but rather a broad approach to analysing environmental impact, and many different methods have been devised. These include, for example, comparing projects with a long checklist of environmental factors or using mapping overlays to show the areas in a proposed project where environmental effects might occur. All EIAs, though, comprise a number of stages:

1 *Preparing an environment statement.* This is the identification and measurement of the likely environmental impacts of a project. Identifying the impacts is usually termed **scoping**, and the impacts themselves are measured in terms of their **magnitude** (i.e. the size of the impact) and their **significance** (i.e. how important this impact may be in informing a final decision about the project).

2 *Consultation.* This involves discussing the environment statement with other organizations and the public, so that a full range of views on the proposal has been identified and additional aspects of the scope of the EIA can be raised by other bodies.

3 *Incorporation* of the EIA into the decision-making process, to help decide for or against a particular proposed development. This is the final and critical stage of the process, for it is here that the project is accepted, modified or rejected by official planning bodies.

EIAs are now an important part of planning and conservation, especially in MDCs. They enable a more objective view of a development, and this can help to inform decisions. Despite this positive view of EIA, though, it is important to remember that such an assessment is only as good as the data that goes into it and the knowledge of environmental science that we currently have. In addition, producing an EIA doesn't mean that when a final decision is made it will only be the environmental factors which are taken into account. Some people believe that EIAs only improve the amount and quality of information available to decision-makers – bad decisions can still result! Political or economic pressures may lead to an EIA being largely ignored or the importance of some of the factors in the EIA being changed. Finally, there is concern that because EIAs are applied to individual projects they may overlook wider environmental issues. An EIA on a road proposal will look at local impacts, but will not examine the global climate implications of increasing car numbers, for example. It has been suggested, therefore, that national and regional governments need to develop **strategic environmental assessments** (**SEAs**), which can take such broader issues into account. SEAs are now required as part of planning in The Netherlands, and some local authorities in the UK (for example, Kent County Council) have developed SEAs within their structure plans. This can provide a more strategic, long-term view of environmental priorities against which any individual proposal can be compared.

Managing environmental developments – a case study

The management processes described above can be seen in operation in most planning developments in the MDCs. As an example, we shall consider the planning of a new local sewage disposal scheme in Cornwall, in south-west England. Figure 11.1 shows the region concerned and the organization of the scheme.

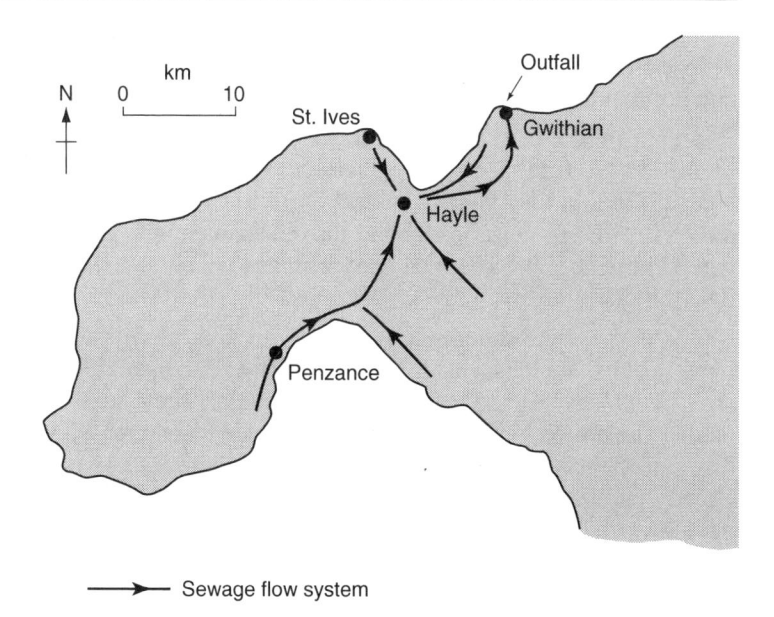

Figure 11.1 West Cornwall's new sewage disposal system

West Cornwall's economy is very dependent on tourism, both on the south coast around Penzance and Marazion and on the north coast around Hayle and St. Ives. An important part of the tourist industry is the region's bathing beaches. Two water-quality directives from the EU set standards that most of the region's beaches and waste water could not meet, which posed a major threat to tourism in the region. The Bathing Water Directive of 1975 set minimum quality standards for any beach where bathing could be allowed, which had to be met by 1995, while the Urban Waste Water Treatment Directive of 1991 set a uniform emission standard for waste water following sewage treatment.

To meet these standards the regional water company, South West Water, planned a scheme to redirect all sewage via a new sewerage system to a treatment works at Hayle on the north coast, with waste water then discharged via a 3 km pipeline into the sea near Gwithian. As a result no sewage would be discharged from the south coast, all sewage would be subject to treatment at a new sewage processing works, and the effluent would be discharged into deep water where the prevailing currents would carry it out to sea and break it down still further.

In preparing the plan South West Water undertook an EIA, which identified the final proposed scheme as the BPEO. In addition to meeting the quality standards and emission standards of the EU directives, the proposal exceeded the emission standards for waste water imposed by the UK government's Department of the Environment.

Concern about the scheme, however, centred around issues which local groups, such as Surfers Against Sewage, considered created significant environmental risks. In particular, they believed that inadequate protection had been taken to prevent the increased sewage disposal on the north coast from increasing pollution at St Ives, which already had bathing beaches meeting EU standards, and which had been awarded EU 'Blue Flag' status. The difficulty of measuring precisely the flow of the treated water after discharge into the sea was emphasized, and independent consultant engineers indicated that South West Water's predictions of impact might be incorrect.

After extensive discussion and a number of rejections of the proposals by Cornwall County Council, the scheme was finally approved, and completed by 1996. South West Water and relevant regional and national government agencies now monitor the levels of output from the scheme and the occurrence of pollutants on the beaches of north Cornwall.

Summary

Planning for conservation requires the use of a range of management approaches and techniques. These have to deal with a number of uncertainties about environmental impact and at the same time seek to make estimates of risk and potential impact from developments. Despite these uncertainties, EIA is now widely used in both MDCs and LDCs and makes a useful contribution to the planning of projects. Other techniques, such as LCA and environmental auditing, are available to organizations, and are becoming more important in their use.

Taking action

1 All organizations and businesses can undertake an environmental audit. Whether you are self-employed, work for a small business or a large multinational company, in the public sector or are a student, you can undertake such an audit for at least part of your organization.

2 For a local development project where you live (such as proposals for a new supermarket, new road or a new industrial estate) identify from the developers and from the planning authority what environmental management approaches have been used in planning the project. If possible, contribute to the process by writing to the planning authority with your views, or attend any public meetings where the project is being discussed.

ACTIVITIES

1 Undertake an environmental audit for your own home. Try to identify all the ways in which your lifestyle might impact on the environment, and identify any ways you can reduce that impact.

2 Choose a development project which has attracted national media attention, such as the construction of the Millennium Dome in London, or the building of new stadium facilities for the next Olympic Games. Use the Internet or direct contact with the developers to identify what environmental management processes were used as part of the development.

3 Undertake a brief survey of about ten local businesses and find out how many have undertaken any form of environmental audit.

Part Three
POLITICS, CONSERVATION AND THE LAW

12 ENVIRONMENTAL ISSUES AND CONSERVATION – INTERNATIONAL PERSPECTIVES

Introduction

The first chapter in this book examined some of the key environmental and conservation events which have raised the awareness of individuals and governments. This third section looks at approaches to tackling the major environmental and conservation issues through international dialogue, agreement and legislation. Action for conservation has taken place around the world at four different levels:

1. At the *global* scale, where the United Nations and its agencies such as UNEP have organized conferences and international agreements.
2. At the *continental* scale, where organizations such as the EU have developed agreements amongst the countries of a continent.
3. At the *national* scale where individual countries have taken action, including passing laws to protect the environment.
4. At the *local* scale, where organizations, individuals or local/regional government has taken action for conservation in the local area.

These actions are often linked, and many environmental issues are being approached with action at each level. In this way the slogan 'Think Global, Act Local' is more than just a reflection of the need for each individual to take responsibility for conservation – it is confirmation that actions are being taken at every scale. This chapter looks at some of the developments at the global and continental level; Chapter 13 looks at national and local developments.

Global action for conservation

Action to protect the environment at local and national levels can be traced back, to some extent, over the last two centuries, for organizations such as the Audubon Society in the USA, and the forerunner of the Royal Society for the Protection of Birds (RSPB) in the UK (founded in 1889) have long histories. International agreement and action is much more recent, however, and has largely been driven by the UN and its various agencies. We shall examine here some of the major events in such international activities.

Conservation – the origins of international action

International concern about conservation and environmental issues is not a new phenomenon, and the past two centuries have seen a number of initiatives to push countries to co-operate in this field. Much of the early work was undertaken by national societies for preserving flora and fauna, and one of the earliest international groupings was the International Committee for Bird Protection, formed in 1922.

However, it was not until after the Second World War, with the rise of a new culture of international co-operation, that developments began to grow substantially, mainly through the work of the UN. The FAO, for example, was formed in 1945 with a clear mandate to tackle food supply and malnutrition issues, with a focus on the environmental management necessary to achieve this. Resource conservation was at the heart of the FAO's work.

UNESCO (the United Nations Educational, Scientific and Cultural Organization) was founded in 1946 to promote co-operation in the fields listed in its title, and some 12% of its initial budget was for conservation and science. With a small budget and limited expertise UNESCO recognized the limitations to its work, but it was instrumental in supporting the development of the International Union for the Preservation of Nature (IUPN) to take forward work in the conservation field. The IUPN, later the IUCN – the word 'preservation' was replaced with the word 'conservation' – was a strong catalyst to conservation work over the next two decades, despite financial constraints. Successes included the establishment, in conjunction with other bodies, of the International Biological Programme in 1964 to promote research on the use of natural resources and how humans could respond to changing environmental conditions.

The growth of 'doom'

The 1960s were a period in the developed world of rapidly changing social conditions, of economic growth and of concern for large-scale issues such as nuclear proliferation/disarmament and civil rights. Towards the end of the decade a number of eminent scientists and social scientists raised concerns about the environment and its ability to sustain humanity into the future as a result of population growth and pollution. Many of the ideas linked strongly to the views of Thomas Malthus (see Chapter 4), whose predictions of doom have never materialized. The 'Prophets of Doom' (McCormick, 1995) of the 1960s raised the spectre of 'neo-malthusian' ideas. The writings of these people were highly influential in both the scientific and political arenas, and stimulated much debate between those who saw them as accurate predictions and those who saw them as highly pessimistic doomsday publications. They stimulated great public interest in the environment, too, and provided an important background to the Stockholm Conference in 1972.

Paul Ehrlich

Ehrlich's book *The Population Bomb* (1968) predicted that disaster would befall humanity unless control of population growth could be achieved, and he predicted that during the 1970s and 1980s hundreds of millions of people would face starvation.

Barry Commoner

Commoner's paper *The Closing Circle* (1971) predicted major pollution problems as a result of the increasing effect of waste disposal and the dumping of the by-products of modern society.

Garrett Hardin

Hardin presented a paper to the American Association for the Advancement of Science in 1967 on the **tragedy of the commons**, in which he predicted that misuse and exploitation of the Earth's common resources, such as pastureland or the oceans, would lead to major environmental problems. The major problem, he believed, was the lack of international agreement on the use of such resources.

The Club of Rome

This grouping of 75 scientists and politicians from 25 countries met in Rome in 1968 and produced for publication in 1972 their book *The Limits to Growth* (Meadows et al, 1972). This book predicted environmental catastrophe by the end of the century because of the rapid increase in population and pollution and the limited nature of resources available.

Barbara Ward and Rene Dubois

Ward and Dubois were commissioned to produce a report in preparation for the Stockholm Conference in 1972, which was published as *Only One Earth* in 1971. This emphasized the gloomy predictions of earlier writers, and used the concept of 'spaceship Earth' to show the limits of resources. However, it suggested that if governments could adopt collective international responsibility and 'loyalty to the Earth' then actions could help delay or prevent some of the worst predictions.

Stockholm, 1972

The first international meeting on the environment was the UN Conference on the Human Environment, held in Stockholm in June 1972. Although a benchmark as the first such event, its achievements were limited. This was mainly because the LDCs were suspicious of the motives of the MDCs, and saw limiting resource useage as a way of constraining their economic growth. After all, they argued, most environmental problems were caused by excessive resource use by the countries of the North. The MDCs, in turn, were resistant to providing ways of supporting the LDCs economically and financially in dealing with environmental concerns. The success of the Stockholm Conference lay in the creation of UNEP, which was charged with monitoring environmental change, taking action to reduce environmental damage, and supporting controls in resource exploitation. Some follow-up conferences during the 1970s and 1980s focused on issues such as desertification and womens rights, but were seen by many simply as events to exchange views, with little resulting action on the environment.

The United Nations Environment Programme (UNEP)

UNEP's work in the 1970s and 1980s was important to the advancement of conservation work. Despite being handicapped by political in-fighting, the differing objectives of the MDCs and LDCs and limited funding, it still managed to promote a number of international research programmes. Its Regional Seas Programme, launched in 1974, sought to undertake research and promote co-operation between neighbouring countries to resolve pollution and resource problems in seas around the world. Its programme to tackle desertification, however, which grew out of the International Conference on Desertification in Nairobi in 1977, was less successful because of its failure to fully understand the social and political causes of the problem, and because of lack of money. More recently, though, UNEP has been instrumental in the Montreal Protocol, and the Framework Convention on Climate Change, which have moved forward a range of climate issues.

The World Conservation Strategy, 1980

During the 1970s UNEP worked with the IUCN and WWF to develop The World Conservation Strategy (WCS), which was published in 1980. The strategy aimed to enable society to meet genuine human needs, while at the same time assuring the healthy survival of the biosphere. The WCS had three main objectives:

- to maintain basic life support systems such as the climate, water and soils;
- to maintain all plant and animal species to preserve genetic diversity for the future;

- to support all species and populations to become sustainable for the future.

Sustainable development (see Chapter 2) was an important idea embodied in the WCS, and now forms the lynchpin of many national and international conservation agreements and policies. More than 60 nations now have national conservation strategies that are based on the WCS, and many others use its principles in conservation planning. Its success and worldwide appeal lead to the development of a second World Conservation Strategy, entitled *Caring for the Earth* and published in 1991 by the same organizations.

The Brundtland Report, 1987

In 1983 the UN established the World Commission on Environment and Development, chaired by Gro Harlem Brundtland, the Norwegian Prime Minister, to promote the cause of sustainable development (see Chapter 2). It believed that environmental policy was given lower status than other social and economic policies, and criticized governments for being too concerned with dealing with the *effects* of environmental damage rather than trying to identify and deal with the *causes*. The Brundtland Report made a number of important recommendations:

- that national environmental protection agencies should be strengthened;
- that UNEP and its work should be strengthened;
- that closer links should be formed between governments and NGOs; and
- that a Universal Declaration should be developed by the UN on environmental protection and sustainable development.

The Brundtland Report was an important benchmark in the history of conservation because it had greater international support than the Stockholm conference and pushed nations to underpin their economies with the concept of sustainable development. This pressure was important in shaping the aims of the Earth Summit in Rio de Janeiro, Brazil, in 1992.

The Rio Earth Summit, 1992

The United Nations Conference on Environment and Development (UNCED, also known as the Earth Summit) was held in Rio de Janeiro in June 1992, and brought together 30,000 delegates from 178 countries, including the leaders of over 100 countries and the heads of state of most of the major world economic powers. In a parallel conference, 1500 NGOs from 163 countries attended the Global Forum. UNCED's aims were to produce agreements on responding to environmental and development problems, and it lead to five main outcomes:

- *The Rio Declaration on Environment and Development.* This built on the Stockholm Declaration from two decades earlier, and comprised 27 principles for action to support environmental and development issues. The Rio Declaration was signed by all participating countries.
- *Agenda 21.* Agenda 21 is an agenda for action for the twenty-first century to promote sustainable development. This huge document (40 chapters!) provides guidance and principles on promoting sustainable development in almost all aspects of society and the economy (industry, education, etc.) and is intended to lead to action in every nation. Each country was encouraged to set up national and local Agenda 21 schemes. To support this, the UN established the UN Commission on Sustainable Development later in 1992, with representatives from 53 countries, to oversee Agenda 21 and to meet each year to review progress.
- *The Framework Convention on Climate Change.* This agreement provided the principles for action and discussion about climate issues (see Chapter 10).
- *The Convention on Biological Diversity.* This convention was aimed at preserving biodiversity, and contained principles for action, signed by 155 nations. The USA, however, refused to sign because they believed that it would be a threat to their biotechnology industry.

- *The Forest Principles.* This set of principles provided each country with the rights to exploit its forest resources, but established some general principles of forest management.

The Rio Earth Summit was a major landmark in the history of environmental issues and produced many important documents and sets of principles to guide future action. However, it has been criticized by many observers for a number of reasons:

- Most of the agreements were strong on principles but weak on tying countries to specific actions. Many of the outcomes were seen as simply rhetoric, and many of the phrases in the agreements were seen as controversial, difficult to interpret and easy for countries to avoid or wilfully misinterpret. Many contained 'opt-out' clauses that would be easy for countries to use.
- It was clear that the LDCs emphasized the development principles, while the MDCs emphasized the environmental principles. This raised concerns that any later moves towards implementation would bring the countries of the North and South into disagreement about real action.
- The cost of implementations of the agreements was seen as too large. The UN estimated that implementing Agenda 21 in full would cost the world's nations US $125 billion per year, making it an unrealistic hope.
- Many of the agreements, and especially the Convention on Biological Diversity, were seen as minimalist – they made very little demand on countries, and did not go far enough in seeking to protect the environment.

Global co-operation beyond Rio

Each of the agreements and conventions signed at Rio de Janeiro included systems to review achievements and actions and to monitor progress. Reviews of the Framework Convention on

Climate Change culminated in a major international meeting in Kyoto, Japan, in 1997, and a follow-up meeting in Buenos Aires, Argentina, in 1998. Both meetings made progress in bringing together the evidence of climate change, and made some movements in agreeing action to deal with the causes of climate problems. However, both were still criticized for failing to make critical agreements. In particular, the unwillingness of some of the MDCs, most notably the USA, to speed up the reduction in carbon dioxide emissions from burning fossil fuels, and the concern of many LDCs to be able to develop their industrial base, including the expansion of energy use, made agreement very difficult.

The five-year review of Agenda 21 was organized by the UN Commission on Sustainable Development in Washington, USA, in 1997. This demonstrated that, while progress had been made in many areas, many of the concerns raised after the Rio Summit had become real problems. UNEP had encouraged progress on many issues and believed there had been many achievements – in particular a new emphasis on preventative rather than 'curative' actions by governments. However, it has recorded a number of concerns about global co-operation on environmental and development at the end of the twentieth century. In particular it is concerned about:

- the gap between growing public and media interest in the environment and the limited actions by government;
- the faltering of the political drive captured by the Rio Summit; and
- the large gap between political commitment and real action.

The development of principles and practice for environmental protection clearly varies across the globe. While much of the action is dependent on the activities of individual countries, developments in Europe provide a good example of conservation policy at a continental scale. The role of the EU in this field will be examined in the next section.

The EU and the environment

The EU came into existence in 1993 as a result of the Treaty of Maastricht (1992) and is the successor to the European Economic Community, which had been established under the Treaty of Rome (1957), later known as the European Community (EC). It now comprises fifteen states (Austria, Belgium, Denmark, Finland, France, Germany, Greece, Ireland, Italy, Luxembourg, The Netherlands, Portugal, Spain, Sweden and the UK), with a population of 325 million.

As one of the world's most developed economic areas, the EU is also a key source of pollution. The scale of the problem can be seen through the figures below, which show that the countries of the EU, which have 7% of the world's population and 2% of its land area, produce:

- 2 billion tonnes of waste and chemical substances per year – 5 tonnes per person;
- 33% of the world's sulphur and nitrogen gas emissions;
- 35% of the world's CFCs; and
- 25% of the world's carbon dioxide.

The EC first adopted a formal environmental policy at its Paris Summit in 1972, in which it set in train the processes leading to its First Environmental Action Programme covering the period 1973–7. This set the framework within which EC policies in all economic and social spheres should take account of environmental issues, and also provided the background to a series of EU directives. Directives are legal requirements from the EU which member states are required to implement by legislation in their own country – for example, a directive of 1988 requires an Environmental Impact Assessment (EIA) to be undertaken in the planning of a number of specified projects (for example, the construction of a power station or a motorway). Every country now has its own national laws or rules which require this to happen.

The First Action Programme laid down eleven principles on which EC environmental policy should be based, and these have remained as guiding principles in the EU.

1 The principle that **prevention is better than cure** shall apply.
2 Environmental effects should be taken into account as early as possible in planning and decision-making.
3 Exploitation of nature or natural resources which causes significant damage to the ecological balance must be avoided. The natural environment can only absorb pollution to a limited extent, and is an asset which may be used but not abused.
4 Scientific knowledge should be improved to enable action to be taken.
5 The principle of **the polluter pays** must apply.
6 Activities carried out in one member state should not cause deterioration of the environment in another.
7 The effects of environmental policy in member states must take account of the interests of developing countries.
8 The EU community must act together in international organizations to promote international and worldwide environmental policy.
9 The protection of the environment is a matter for everyone. Education is therefore necessary.
10 The principle of **the appropriate level** shall be applied. In each category of pollution it is necessary to establish whether action is most appropriate at local, regional, national, community or international level.
11 National environmental policies must be co-ordinated within the EU, without hampering progress at national level.

Since 1972, five Action Programmes on the Environment have been established. The Fifth Action Programme, entitled Towards Sustainability, and covering the period 1993–2000, marked a significant change in emphasis, in enshrining the principles of sustainable development, and placing less importance on legislation and more on political and social change to alter attitudes to the environment as a way to ensure environmental protection. This supports two key constitutional developments that resulted from the reorganization and restructuring of the EC during the 1980s and 1990s. Firstly, the Single European Act of 1987 introduced a specified area of EC practice and policy entitled Environment and in Article 130R(2) requires that 'environmental protection requirements must be integrated into the definition and implementation of other Community policies'. Secondly, the Treaty of European Union (the Maastricht Treaty) of 1992, which established the enlarged EU restates Article 130R(2), and in Article 2 makes a clear requirement that 'economic development within the EU must be sustainable with respect to the environment'.

Environmental protection and conservation, set in a context of sustainable development, are key concerns of the EU, therefore. This is supported in a number of ways. Firstly, EU directives on the environment are important in establishing the laws of the EU. Water quality, for example, is governed by a large number of directives on standards for bathing water, the suitability of fresh water for fish life and the quality of water that can be used for drinking, and since 1976 a list of over 125 substances that must be removed from water has been produced (including, for example, mercury and PCBs). The 1991 Nitrates Directive requires all states to draw up codes of agricultural practice for their countries to reduce nitrate pollution of water, and to establish legal limits on levels of nitrate pollution. While the **principle of subsidiarity** means that each country must produce its own systems for reaching the standards required, such directives do provide minimum standards.

Secondly, the EU provides funding to assist environmental improvements. Between 1994 and 1999 it spent ECU7000 million on constructing water cleaning and sewage schemes in the EUs poorest regions. In Ireland, for example, the proportion of urban waste water that met EU standards rose from 20% in 1993 to 80% in 1999.

Thirdly, the EU has established a European Environment Agency, based in Copenhagen, Denmark. Its purpose is to support research on environmental issues in the EU, to provide environmental information to EU countries and institutions, to promote the development of EU environmental policy, and to raise public awareness about the environment.

ENVIRONMENTAL ISSUES AND CONSERVATION – INTERNATIONAL

Finally, the EU is involved in environmental protection elsewhere in Europe and at a global scale. It provides funding for environmental protection programmes in eastern Europe and Russia, and has strongly supported two agreements on environmental protection across the whole of Europe:

- **The Dobris Agreement (1991)**, which is an agreement on co-operation between 36 European nations;
- **The Environmental Action Programme (EAP)** for eastern and central Europe (1995), which funds and supports environmental protection and conservation actions.

At a global scale the EU is a signatory of most of the global conventions on the environment, such as the Montreal Protocol.

Despite the high profile of environmental matters within the policies of the EU, however, the Union faces a number of difficulties in dealing with environmental issues:

- The policing of environmental directives is very difficult. The principal of subsidiarity leaves most of this to individual countries, and standards therefore vary.
- Some desirable environmental changes are not politically acceptable in some or all of the EU countries, for example the promotion of smaller fuel efficient cars.
- Some desirable changes would have adverse consequences for another sector of the EU. Organic farming makes up about 2% of all farms in the EU. Promoting organic farming, however, would reduce the use of chemical fertilizers, with a negative effect on the fertilizer industry, and would also reduce yields such that the EU as a whole would need to import more food from abroad.
- The EU's neighbours in eastern Europe (Hungary, Poland, the Czech Republic, etc.) have major environmental problems caused by air pollution from industry, producing acid rain and low air quality

standards. Air movements take these pollutants into the EU. Supporting environmental protection in eastern Europe is a major priority for the EU.

- Some of the major environmental issues in the EU are international ones. Pollution of the River Rhine, for example, which flows through three EU nations, and pollution of the North Sea, the Baltic Sea and the Mediterranean Sea, must be controlled by co-operation between countries. Managing such co-operation is very difficult.

Conservation, the environment and education

The sections above have looked at global environmental developments and at those in the EU. From the beginning of such developments, the importance of environmental education has been strongly emphasized, not just through schools and colleges but also through training in business and industry, through community activities and through raising public awareness of the environment. Principle 19 of the Stockholm Declaration says:

> Education in environmental matters for the younger generation as well as adults, giving due consideration to the underprivileged, is essential.

This idea was developed further in the Rio Declaration, which promoted public knowledge and understanding of environmental matters (Principle 10), and agreed that:

> the creativity, ideals and courage of the youth of the world should be mobilized to forge a global partnership in order to achieve sustainable development and ensure a better future for all (Principle 21).

Following the Stockholm Conference in 1972, UNESCO organized the International Workshop on Environmental Education in Belgrade in 1975. They key outcome of that conference was the **Belgrade Charter**, which set a number of objectives for an international environmental education programme. These objectives were:

- to foster clear awareness of, and concern about, economic, social, political and ecological interdependence in urban and rural areas;
- to provide every person with opportunities to acquire the knowledge, values, attitudes, commitment and skills needed to protect and improve the environment;
- to create new patterns of behaviour of individuals, groups and society as a whole towards the environment.

The principles in the Belgrade Charter were extended to cover education beyond school following a conference in Tbilisi in 1977, attended by representatives of 66 countries, and the Belgrade Charter and the Tbilisi Agreement still underpin environmental education and training around the world. Both encourage:

- education *about* the environment, to develop knowledge of environmental matters;
- education *in and through* the environment, to develop active experience of the environment; and
- education *for* the environment, to develop a sense of responsibility and a wish to take action for conservation.

The development of environmental education and training since the Belgrade Charter has been very varied around the world. Its importance has varied as environmental issues have become high-profile public issues or waned in significance. Even in the EU, where environmental education has been promoted since an agreement of education ministers in 1988, its role is still not significant in most schools. In the UK for example, environmental education was included in the National Curriculum in 1990 but effectively excluded in the 1995 curriculum revision. Many large companies have a strong environmental training programme, but this is frequently limited to those needing technical environmental knowledge, for example to limit pollution from a company's plants, or those involved in marketing.

Public interest in the environment remained high throughout the 1980s and 1990s, yet the development of public understanding programmes through the media or through community education has not been extensive. Much has been targeted on those already possessing good environmental knowledge. In the LDCs, some community development programmes have included a strong environmental education element (for example in community programmes in Imizamo Yethu, a township in Cape Town, South Africa), but environmental education reaches few people in most countries.

Summary

The high profile of conservation and environmental issues in the last quarter of the twentieth century has stimulated a number of responses at an international level to seek solutions to global environmental problems. The initiatives of the 1972 Stockholm Conference and the 1987 Brundtland Commission Report underpinned the Earth Summit at Rio de Janeiro in 1992, and provided the framework of many international agreements. While these agreements are a tribute to success in bringing countries around a discussion table, they are frequently criticized for their strong rhetoric but limited powers to enforce countries to comply with decisions. The EU is one international group which has sought to incorporate environmental action into the heart of its social and economic policies, but it still faces many political challenges if it is to make better environmental improvements. The next chapter will examine conservation at a national level by examining particular countries and their environmental practices, and will also look at the role of local initiatives and NGOs in the politics of conservation.

ACTIVITIES

1 Obtain a copy of the EU Fifth Environmental Action Programme. What initiatives does it seem to be proposing?

2 Read a copy of *The European Union and the Environment*, obtainable from your nearest EU Commission Office:

England: Jean Monnet House, 8, Storey's Gate, London SW1P 3AT

Ireland: 18 Dawson St., Dublin 2

USA: 2300 M Street, NW, Suite 707, Washington DC 20037.

3 Obtain a copy of the Rio Declaration through your local library. What do you believe are its strengths and weaknesses?

4 Contact your local Chamber of Commerce to find out what training businesses in your local area provide to develop environmental knowledge for their staff.

5 Contact your local college, local education authority or school district to find out what environmental education programmes are available in the local area.

6 Contact local environmental groups to see what conservation courses or activities they run.

13 ENVIRONMENTAL ISSUES AND CONSERVATION – NATIONAL AND LOCAL PERSPECTIVES

Introduction

One of the traditional catchphrases of the conservation movement has been 'Think Global, Act Local'. This phrase recognizes that it is the actions of individuals and groups in their own local areas and day-to-day lives that, together, impact on the whole world's environment. The meetings and agreements of nations, prime ministers and presidents only have meaning when they are turned into action in each country, each region and each town or village. Key players, therefore, in conservation are governments, NGOs, community groups and enthusiastic individuals, for together they translate global ideas into local actions (**top-down model**), or put pressure on government and politicians to take action or contribute to global decisions (**bottom-up model**). This chapter looks at how conservation and environmental protection have been undertaken in a number of contrasting countries, and looks, too, at the central role of NGOs and community groups in shaping conservation in practice. It seeks to place the global and continental developments looked at in the previous chapter in a national and local context.

Conservation and environmental protection in the UK

Key developments

The UK is often thought of as the cradle of the industrial revolution, where industry and urban growth first emerged in the eighteenth and nineteenth centuries. It was first, too, at creating major environmental problems, therefore, and also first at taking steps to deal with some of the pollution created. The world's first pollution control agency was **The Alkali Inspectorate**, created in 1863, and the post Second World War period saw three important Acts of Parliament that were models for similar legislation in other parts of the world:

- The **1947 Town and Country Planning Act** gave strong controls on building and industrial development to local authorities;
- The **National Parks and Access to the Countryside Act, 1949** created the ten National Parks in England and Wales and opened many areas of upland Britain to public access.
- The **1956 Clean Air Act**, passed in the wake of the great London smog of 1952, created smokeless zones in cities and towns and gave local authorities control over smoke pollution.

Despite these landmarks in conservation, however, there was no strong central government drive on conservation. Much of the enforcement was undertaken by local authorities, where local political factors often influenced how much or how little control was exercised. There was also little co-ordination and co-operation between the various bodies involved, and many areas of pollution were dealt with by a wide range of agencies. Air pollution control, for example, was dealt with at a national level in part by The Alkali Inspectorate (a central government body), in part by the Ministry of Housing, and in part by the ministries of Transport and Agriculture.

In 1970, partly in response to the growing interest in the environment, the government established the Department of the Environment, the first in the world, by bringing together a number of existing ministries (e.g. Housing, Local Government and Transport). Despite its name, very little of its activity was about environmental policy, for it dealt mainly with managing local government. However, in the following few years it passed important controls on water pollution by setting up regional water authorities to manage water supply and quality through the 1973 Water Act, and by imposing a wide range of pollution controls through the 1974 Control of Pollution Act. The work of the Department of the Environment has been important in the development of conservation activities, in the protection of the rural environment, in pollution control and, more recently, in the integration of ideas of sustainable development into government policy and planning. Each of these will be examined here.

Protecting rural Britain

Protecting the landscapes and wildlife, and the associated rural ways of life, has always been an important conservation aim in Britain. SOme of the earliest public bodies and conservation societies were formed for this purpose – the National Trust, founded in 1895, had as one of its aims the protection of Britain's natural heritage, and the Council for the Protection of Rural England (CPRE) was founded in 1926 to promote countryside preservation, give advice to landowners, and press for new laws to protect rural life and landscape. Pressure from these bodies was important in the setting up of the Addison Committee, which in 1931 proposed the idea of National Parks, although this idea didn't come into reality until after the Second World War.

Following the 1949 Act, responsibility for managing the protection of natural environments was given to two bodies:

1 **The Nature Conservancy**, later the Nature Conservancy Council (NCC), and reconstituted as English Nature in 1991, with responsibility for:
- national nature reserves (NNRs), sites protected by the NCC because of their specific wildlife characteristics. Over 200 such reserves were designated by the early 1990s;
- sites of special scientific interest (SSSIs); individual sites, often very small, but with some distinctive environmental characteristic. Nearly 6000 such sites exist.

2 **The National Parks Commission (NPC)**, later the Countryside Commission, with responsibilities for:
- national parks – classical areas of distinctive natural beauty. Ten such areas have been designated, including Snowdonia and Dartmoor;

- areas of outstanding natural beauty (AONBs); smaller areas of distinctive landscape beauty – for example the North Downs of Surrey and Sussex;
- heritage coasts.

A major development in conservation was the passage of the 1981 Wildlife and Countryside Act to provide protection for a range of rare species and habitats. This was the result of widespread concern expressed by a number of conservation organizations, including the CPRE, that many SSSIs were being damaged and lost, highlighting the need to protect biodiversity. However, despite its importance the Act was criticized for not providing strong enough powers of enforcement on landowners who might choose to destroy important sites, particularly those designated as SSSIs. A three-month consultation period between identification of an SSSI and its formal designation gave landowners time to destroy them, and the cost to the NCC of managing the sites or supporting landowners to manage them proved very high.

In 1986 a further form of landscape conservation was created with the designation of ESAs – environmentally sensitive areas. These areas (for example, the Somerset Levels) are areas in which agricultural development in keeping with the traditional landscape is funded by government agricultural agencies to prevent major environmental change. While providing a lesser form of protection than SSSIs or AONBs, ESAs are an important aspect of landscape conservation.

The conservation of the natural environment and landscape in the UK has thus a long and chequered history. Conflict between conservation groups and landowners has been frequent, and there are still concerns that individual landowners can make or break prospects of conservation.

Pollution control and monitoring

Although the UK has a long history of action on pollution control, most of the developments since joining the EC have been in response to pressure from EC Directives – some 80% of British pollution control legislation now in effect originated in Brussels.

The principle of subsidiarity means that legislation or regulation is enacted in the UK by appropriate means, and the UK has now implemented some 90% of EU environmental directives (in comparison with 95% in France and 80% in Italy), through, for example, the 1990 Environment Protection Act.

Pollution control in the UK is still disjointed, lacking the co-ordination that the European Environment Agency believes is essential for effective monitoring and control. Pollution and environmental damage is still monitored by many different agencies and by local authorities. This has changed a little since the establishment of the Environment Agency following the 1995 Environment Act. This agency is charged with monitoring and assessing the state of the environment, and regulating, through its new Pollution Inspectorate, a large number of particular processes, including:

- 2000 industrial processes;
- disposal of radioactive waste from 8000 sites;
- 8000 waste management sites;
- 100,000 water discharge agreements;
- 50,000 water abstraction licenses; and
- 43,000 km of flood defence works.

Promoting sustainable development

The UK has been a signatory to most of the global environmental agreements of the last two decades, and has also absorbed the principles of EU environmental policy into its own regulations and practice. In both these spheres, the concept of sustainable development is central. The first appearance of the idea in UK government policy was in the publication of a White Paper, entitled *This Common Inheritance*, in 1990, which outlined broad environmental policies in relation to water, air, land use, and recycling. This reflected the main ideals established by the Brundtland Commission in 1987. In response to the Rio Declaration and Agenda 21, the government was able to respond quite quickly, therefore, and in 1994 published the *UK Strategy for Sustainable Development*. This was built around a number of general principles drawn from both Rio and from the EU's 5th

Action Programme on the Environment:
- the use of the precautionary principle;
- the emphasis on scientific evidence as a requirement for decision making;
- the sharing of responsibility for the environment between government, business, local authorities, NGOs and other organizations;
- the integration of environmental policy into all aspects of government;
- a preference for the use of market mechanisms rather than government regulation; and
- environmental policy should not inhibit wealth creation or national economic competitiveness.

These principles have been criticized for emphasizing economic growth and erring on the side of caution, and for offering no additional resources to partners to develop environmental policy and practice. In particular, local authorities were charged with developing local Agenda 21 programmes, but these were not resourced to any substantial degree by central government.

Further development of strategies for sustainable development were built around a number of cabinet level committees and also around the establishment by the Environment Act, 1995, of a new Environment Agency whose principal aim is:

> to protect or enhance the environment, taken as a whole, ... to make (a) contribution towards attaining the objective of achieving sustainable development.

Despite these developments, by the time the UK government had to submit evidence to the Washington Earth Summit +5 meeting in 1997 it could report that its actions were still mainly to do with policy preparation rather than real environmental improvement. With a new government in office from May 1997 the pace of change has altered very little, and although the Deputy Prime Minister has a brief that includes overall responsibility for environmental matters, environmental issues have not had a high profile in recent policy developments.

Environmental protection in the UK, therefore, is characterized by slow progress towards incorporating sustainable development ideals into policy and practice, and by the continuing use of a wide range of pollution control regulations. Legislation still dominates the scene even though the pursuit of consensus and agreement is promoted by most environmental groups and declarations. The UK is sometimes described as 'the dirty man of Europe', and many environmental and conservation groups suggest that much of the apparent environmental protection activity is only rhetoric. Nevertheless, many environmental improvements can be recorded, including reductions in carbon dioxide emissions, and improvements in coastal bathing waters and in drinking water standards.

Environment and conservation in the USA

The context of conservation in the USA is rather different from that in the UK. First, the relative autonomy of the individual US states in the federal system means that the response to national government pressure may be highly variable across the nation, and the ability of national government to be prescriptive in its legislation is less than in the UK. Second, the complex relationship between states, federal government, the White House, Congress and the legal system while providing important checks and balances often limits the ability of single groupings to assume strong national co-ordinating roles. Third, the principles of open government and active participation by those affected by public policies in the USA means that environmental pressure groups (the environmental lobby) have been much more influential than in the UK. Finally, in the UK the role of the EU in shaping and driving policy is of great importance, but the USA, while having agreements with other American nations, does not have legal obligations as part of a larger scale political and economic group.

A result of these differences is that environmental responsibility lies with a large number of bodies and organizations – at a federal level almost 30 different organizations have responsibility for implementing environmental legislation, ranging from the Department of the

Interior to the Army Corps of Engineers to the Food and Drug Administration (FDA).

In 1970 the National Environment Policy Act was passed which attempted to restructure the way in which environmental issues were managed in the USA. This Act established a number of key components of future policy:

- It required all government departments and agencies to identify the environmental impact of activities in their field of operation.
- It required all major federal programmes to produce an Environmental Impact Statement (EIS) for any major development activities.
- It established a Council on Environmental Quality (CEQ) based in the White House to advise the President.
- It led to the establishment of the Environmental Protection Agency (EPA), reporting directly to the President. By the 1990s the EPA had become the largest federal regulatory agency, and the largest such body in the world with a staff of 20,000 and a budget of nearly $8 billion per year.

Since 1970 the effectiveness of the EPA has varied according to the political leadership in The White House. During the 1970s, despite anti-environmental pressure from the business community, the EPA pushed through a wide range of environmental legislation, including important acts in the areas of toxic waste disposal, water pollution and pesticide controls. An example of its work was the so-called 'Superfund' legislation, the 1980 Comprehensive Environmental Response, Compensation and Liability Act. This takes a levy or tax on all organizations disposing of toxic waste that could result in long-term water pollution. The Superfund is then used to assist in dealing with pollution incidents where no individual organization can be identified as the pollution cause. By the mid-1990s the Superfund had assets of $15 billion, but environmental groups were still concerned that this would not be enough to deal with the pollution problems that were being generated by toxic waste.

Action on the environment has not had as a high a political profile since the end of the 1970s. The Republican administrations of Presidents Reagan and Bush in the 1980s reflected the same view of environmental issues as that of the UK Conservative government under Margaret Thatcher, in that they believed strongly in deregulation and the power of the market to develop appropriate controls. As a result the activities of the EPA were more constrained, as it was reduced in staff numbers and budget, and the CEQ was of little influence on policy. While this has been addressed to some degree during subsequent Democratic administrations, economic and business lobbies have constrained environmental legislation.

At the global level, the USA has been a signatory of most of the major agreements, and was highly influential in promoting the debate leading to the Montreal Protocol on ozone emissions. However, as the world's most developed economy, it produces a high proportion of the world's carbon dioxide emissions, and its role in implementing many of the global agreements is central to achieving political success and real progress on environmental improvement and conservation. Following the Earth Summit at Rio, concern was expressed at the USA's unwillingness to sign the Convention on Biological Diversity, and at the review meetings on Rio in Washington in 1997 and at the Kyoto and Buenos Aires reviews of the Framework Convention on Climate Change, concern was expressed at the relative lack of progress on reducing carbon dioxide emissions by the USA. As with the UK, some progress is being achieved, but the political limitation of the need for government to deal with highly varied interest groups makes progress slow.

Environment and conservation in the South – the case of India

Environmental protection and conservation is often quite incorrectly thought to be something that the developed countries have taken forward, while the countries of the South have been too busy tackling poverty and basic economic issues to be very concerned. The explosion in environmental interest took off in the 1970s in the LDCs just as it did in the MDCs. By 1980 over 100 LDCs had established national environmental protection agencies, and by the mid-1990s the vast majority of countries had such an organization in place. However, the view of the causes and possible solutions to environmental problems and the ways of achieving environmental protection is often quite different in the LDCs. India provides an interesting example of such differences.

India's first notable environmental protection dates back to 1853 with an act of parliament (in London!) to protect the use of the shore in Bombay. More recently, though, through the direct interest of Prime Minister Indira Ghandhi in environmental matters, the key benchmark was the creation of a National Committee on Environmental Planning in 1972 to advise the government. This was a predecessor of the national Department of the Environment set up in 1980, reporting directly to the Prime Minister, and with responsibility for:

- monitoring pollution;
- establishing biosphere reserves;
- protecting marine ecosystems; and
- reviewing large development projects.

This central government initiative encouraged similar actions in each of India's states; by the mid-1990s all states had an environment department and more than 450 state laws on environmental regulation had been passed. However, success in setting up the systems was not matched by achievement, and a number of problems persisted through the 1980s:

- Environmental issues were still largely ignored by most policy makers at national and state level.
- The lack of a requirement for environmental impact assessment meant that many large developments were approved without proper consideration being given to their effects.
- Enforcement of laws was very difficult.

These limitations were highlighted by the Bhopal accident in December 1984 when the Union Carbide pesticide plant accidentally released methyl-isocyanate, causing the deaths of 2500 people living close to the plant, and damaging the health of up to 200,000 in total.

India's commitment to environmental matters at a political level is demonstrated by their actions in signing most of the international agreements during the 1980s and 1990s. At grassroots level it is demonstrated by the many thousands of community groups committed to direct action in protection of the environment, such as the famous Chipko Andalan (mainly village women committed to tree protection) and the People's Science Movement, dedicated to bringing appropriate technology to rural India. In addition the NGO Centre for Science and Environment has been amongst the most active NGOs in global politics from the South.

India's poverty and social economic problems give it a different perspective on many world issues. In the negotiations before the signing of the Montreal Protocol on controlling ozone depletion, Indian representatives coined the phrase 'rich-man's problem – rich man's solution'. They believed it unfair that India should have to give up basic necessities such as the use of CFC-based food preservatives and refrigeration, then be expected to buy Western-manufactured CFC substitutes – particularly when most of the ozone problem had been caused by the countries of the North. They demanded, and eventually obtained, agreements from Western nations to provide both financial aid and technology transfer to assist India in helping with the solutions to the ozone problem. It was not that India did not recognize that ozone depletion was occurring – they simply insisted that the solutions had to recognize who had caused the problem and who could most easily afford to support the solutions. This view is widely held in the LDCs, but India's relative power in world politics because of its population and economic size means that its voice is especially important – and, along with China, these views have been expressed at Rio, Washington and Kyoto.

NGOs, environmental protection and politics

NGOs are an important part of the political scene in conservation and environmental issues. Oxfam has calculated that there are over 12,000 *international* NGOs worldwide, and there are tens of thousands of others which operate within single countries. NGOs are non-profit-making bodies, supported by the work and financial support of members. They may be single-issue groups (for example the Japan Tropical Forest Action Group, JATAN) campaigning and working on only one single environmental issue, or they may operate across a wide range of environmental matters (for example, Greenpeace). Some, for example Oxfam, may have interests that go beyond the environment. NGOs vary hugely in size, too, from a few members and no paid employees to having a large paid staff. For example, the Bangladesh Rural Advancement Committee (BRAC) has a full-time staff of over 2000, and is one of the largest NGOs in the world; Greenpeace has full-time offices in 30 countries, 4.5 million supporters in 143 countries and an annual turnover of over US $100 million.

The growth of NGOs in terms of both their numbers and their membership has been very rapid over the last two decades and their influence on the shape and direction of environmental politics has been very important. This reflects:

- the focus they have – in contrast to most political parties, which are trying to balance environmental issues against other social and economic pressures;
- the power of popular support, because of their membership numbers;
- their expertise both in the science and technology of the environment and in campaigning and lobbying methods; and
- their ability both to act quickly on issues and to sustain campaigns over long periods.

The impact of NGOs in galvanizing world opinion to promote the global-scale meetings at Stockholm (1972) and Rio (1992) is widely acknowledged. Their influence on specific issues has also been great. A good example of such an impact has been on the policies of the World Bank, an international body whose role is to provide development funding to the countries of the South. Concern over the lack of environmental requirements it imposed on countries receiving loans and grants lead to it being pressured over many years by NGOs to change its policy. By 1993, the World Bank had changed its position to include environmental aspects in most funding and was directly funding over 100 environmental projects.

NGOs operate in a number of ways, and many are involved in several strategies at the same time.

Direct conservation and protection work

Groups work on conservation projects and manage nature reserves or protected sites. In the UK, for example, the RSPB has over 100 nature reserves, and the Groundwork Trust supports active conservation projects in urban areas.

Education

Most NGOs have a substantial education dimension to their work, producing information materials for teachers, young people and the public.

Campaigning

This occurs at all levels of politics and through all types of action. The lobbying of local and national politicians in support of particular actions is important, and the large NGOs have developed sophisticated campaigning departments employing the techniques of professional advertising, promotion and lobbying. This campaigning is directed not only at government but also at individual companies. In North America, for example, the campaigning of a number of environmental NGOs has been important in influencing policies on maintaining the water quality of the Great Lakes. Major pollution problems have affected the Great Lakes because of the industrial and urban development along their shores. The USA and Canada have responded at government level through the Great Lakes Water Quality Agreement (GLWQA), signed in 1972. However, concern in the 1970s and 1980s about increasing pollution led to campaigns by three major NGOs (the

Sierra Club, Great Lakes United and the National Wildlife Federation), and their work persuaded the governments to impose much tighter restrictions on pollutants, the use of the shoreline and the preservation of wetlands.

Direct action

Although not especially common, NGOs may take direct action against organizations they believe to be undertaking environmentally-damaging activities. On 30 April, 1995, for example, Greenpeace protesters boarded and took over the disused Brent Spar oil platform to protest at the environmental risks of disposing of the platform by sinking it. Their action eventually persuaded the oil companies to seek alternative disposal methods.

NGOs, of course, are not without their critics. Governments criticize them for oversimplifying complex political problems and ignoring economic realities. The media may present some of their actions as destructive in a way that may be counter-productive in swaying public opinion. The groups themselves are not without management problems, and internal politics about the nature and focus of activities can be very important. The range of environmental philosophies (see Chapter 1) which exist also means that different NGOs working in the same field may have quite different, even contradictory, aims.

Grassroots movements and conservation

An important element of conservation politics in the last two decades has been the development and influence of grassroots movements. These movements involve the spontaneous emergence of a common focus for action amongst local people, usually in response to a pressing environmental need. Many have developed from community groups in the LDCs – the Naam movement in Burkina Faso, West Africa, for example, grew from frustration with government failures to deal with environmental issues, and mobilized villagers to build their own water conservation systems (small dams) and grain warehouses, and to provide their own local system of loans and financial support. Other groups have grown in the MDCs, for example the women's movement to prevent the establishment of nuclear weapons at the Greenham Common airbase in England during the 1980s.

The growth of the Chipko Andalan movement in northern Uttar Pradesh in India illustrates well the work of grassroots movements. The roots of the movement lie in the formation of the Dasohli Gram Swarajya Mandal (DGSM) in the mid-1960s to promote cottage-based industry for local villagers to use forest products. Frustration at the way in which local landowners by-passed DGSM and local people to sell forest products and timbers to outside contractors lead to the growth of a local resistance movement in 1974, originating in the village of Reni in Chamoli District. Chipko Andalan means 'movement to hug trees' and involved mainly local women in forming protective cordons around trees to prevent them being felled. Its actions, based on Gandhian principles of non-violence, attracted world-wide attention through the media. Its impact on forest policies and community groups elsewhere in the world was substantial. The movement succeeded in protecting 12,000 square kilometres of forest from clearance in the River Alakananda basin, but, ironically, it failed to achieve any real changes in local state policies and practice in Uttar Pradesh in the long term. The movement still exists to provide advice and support and the management of reafforestation programmes elsewhere in India.

A second example is that of the rubber tappers of western Brazil. Mobilized by their leader Chico Mendes, they campaigned against the spread of cattle ranching and rainforest clearance in the Amazon region. The high profile of the campaign resulted in Mendes being murdered in December 1988, but the effect on world environmental policies on forest protection was substantial.

Local conservation in action

Much of the contribution to conservation comes through the work of local groups and the actions of individuals, either through political involvement or through active conservation work. Local projects organized through NGOs and charities are an important component of the local scene. Co-ordination between groups has often been a problem, but the development of Local Agenda 21 programmes has assisted this co-ordination. In the UK, implementation of Agenda 21 at a local level was delegated to local authorities (councils), most of whom set up steering and co-ordinating groups. The guidance given to authorities suggested six possible actions:

1 Improving the local authority's own environmental performance.
2 Integrating sustainable development into local policies.
3 Awareness raising and education.
4 Consulting and involving the general public.
5 Forming partnerships for environmental action.
6 Measuring and monitoring progress towards sustainability.

Durham County Council in north-east England launched its local Agenda 21 in November 1994, and now involves over 250 local organizations in its programmes. Projects include, for example, developing cycle routes for children travelling to school, and funding research into developing 'biodiesel' by using waste vegetable oil from local food-processing industries. It has also identified a set of 25 sustainability indicators against which to measure its progress – including, for example, local river water quality, the percentage of businesses with waste-reduction programmes and the prevalence of asthma in the local community. Local Agenda 21 has made good progress in this example, but the picture is not necessarily as positive elsewhere. However, the principle of co-operative working between groups to deal with local environmental and conservation issues is important, and is one that is accepted by most political groups.

The green parties

The growth of official green parties in politics was a strong feature of the 1980s in Europe. Official green parties are often seen as originating in West Germany where *Die Grunen* grew from a combination of strong anti-nuclear campaigning groups and the grassroots support of the peace movement in the late 1970s. However, other groups, including the People Party (later the Ecology Party) in the UK and the Values Party in New Zealand, can trace their origins back to the early 1970s. Other European green parties grew from pre-existing 'socialist' groups which took on the environmental focus, and new parties formed specifically with an environmental brief.

The success of green parties in the 1980s has been attributed by Inglehart to the growth in Europe of an affluent middle class with liberal values developing a concern for 'quality of life', and hence the environment. This perspective was not supported by traditional political parties, and the 'niche' for environmental parties was created. In 1979 the Greens had their first successes in election to the European Parliament, and by 1994 they achieved as much as 10% of the votes in European elections in Germany and Belgium, ending up with 22 seats in the European Parliament. At national elections, though, their success has been rather less, as voters appear less willing to focus their national political decision-making through green parties. Even in Germany, where the green vote has traditionally been strong, national and regional elections in the late 1990s have seen a relative decline of the greens. This has been explained by the traditional parties taking environmental issues into their policies.

In the USA formal green politics has never had a success in the way that it has in Europe, despite the relatively high profile of the environment movement. This may be explained by the political system, in which strong lobby groups are important in the formation of policy in government. As a result the influence of the NGOs may have acted as a substitute for the growth of formal green parties.

Summary

This chapter has looked at the politics of conservation at national level and has considered the experiences in a number of different countries. The roles of NGOs and grassroots movements and the official parties have also been considered. What has emerged is a picture of varying experiences in different national situations, and evidence of a wide range of responses from governments and other groups. This emphasizes the complexity of the politics of environment and conservation, and the need to look at every situation individually to identify the various political forces, organizations and interest groups involved. The next chapter will look at some of the issues this raises for the future of conservation and environmentalism in the political arena.

ACTIVITIES

1 Use one of the Internet addresses in Appendix 1 to contact one of the major NGOs. What are its current major campaigns about? From the information they provide, what are the main strategies they are using to get their message across (lobbying parliament, poster campaigns, news coverage, direct action)? Compare the activities of two different groups in relation to one of the major issues.

2 Obtain the manifestos of each of the candidates in your next local, regional or national election. How far do environmental issues feature in their campaigns? How knowledgeable do they seem on environmental issues?

14 CONSERVATION, ENVIRONMENT AND THE FUTURE

Introduction

This book has examined a wide range of conservation issues. It has looked both at the science of conservation and at the politics and economics of environmental issues. Conservation is a combination of science, economics and politics in practice, underpinned by a concern for moral and ethical issues about people and their relationship with their human and physical environment. Furthermore, environmental issues and development issues cannot be separated.

There are many important and pressing environmental issues that we must face as we enter the third millennium. Simply talking of doomsday scenarios, though, while having some initial effect in attracting attention, runs the risk of frightening individuals and governments into inaction. The gloomy predictions of Malthus and of the neo-malthusians of the 1970s, have not been realized, and 'crying wolf' is a certain way of creating greater long-term problems.

What is needed is concerted, planned and integrated actions by individuals and governments to address conservation issues at local, national and global levels. In particular, changing the way people think about the environment and about quality of life will be important tasks, and real challenges to political will. This final chapter makes some suggestions for the way forward.

Priorities for action

The conservation of the environment to provide for a sustainable future raises many challenges for individuals, for business and for governments. Each locality, region, country and continent will have

CONSERVATION, ENVIRONMENT AND THE FUTURE

its own particular priorities which arise from the combination of issues that are most pressing for its own communities. In a country like Indonesia, for example, key pressures will be coping with a rapidly growing population and balancing the need to make best use of the country's natural resources while still preserving ecosystems and the country's biodiversity. In the USA the priorities will be rather different, and will focus on dealing with issues such as atmospheric pollution in the cities, reducing the nation's contribution to greenhouse gases and, because of its political and economic power, seeking to play a central role in moving the world economy towards sustainability. In the UK important national issues will be reducing greenhouse gases, managing the resources of the regional seas such as the North Sea, and dealing with the environmental challenges of pressure for living space in a small country and the threats that brings of urban development in rural environments.

Globally, we can identify a number of key priorities for action, which will be essential areas for improved performance if we are to approach sustainability through the twenty-first century.

Action on global population growth

Population growth is largely occurring in the LDCs. While it is argued that people in the LDCs consume far fewer resources than those in the MDCs, sheer numbers of people pursuing improvements in quality of life and standard of living will pose a major resource pressure in the future. The world can do nothing about past issues of population growth, but it can take action to minimize future growth. This must be the contribution of the LDCs to a sustainable world.

Action on sustainable growth

Reducing the demand for resources per capita must be the major contribution of the MDCs to promoting sustainable development. The incorporation of the principles of environmental economics into resource planning by governments and business is essential if this is to be achieved – for it will, ultimately, only be the operation of economic systems that drives sustainability. Those economic systems must, therefore, fully enshrine environmental principles.

Action on emission reduction

Pollution of the land, air and waters is a major threat to the future. The use of emission controls, quality standards and EIA as part of future planning will be essential if this problem, at its most severe in the MDCs, is to be tackled.

Action on global warming

Global warming, as a result of the emission of greenhouse gases, is a key threat to sustainable development. As evidence accumulates of its reality, the need to recognize its social, economic and political implications becomes greater. It is in the unstable human systems that the biggest threat from global warming comes, as issues of food and water supply in changing climatic conditions become potential sources of conflict.

Action on biodiversity

The survival of humanity so far has been built on creativity and technological skill, making use of the wide range of natural resources available. Central to this is the gene pool of potential future resources which, if lost, deprives people of important future developments. This issue has been likened to the dangers of throwing away a library before reading many of the books, and in this way not knowing what important information they may hold.

Action on global poverty

Amongst the major conservation threats, global inequalities in quality of life and the threat of global poverty are both pressing environmental issues and crucial humanitarian and moral issues. The poverty in the poorest thirty countries of the world is an environmental issue in itself, and risks people in these countries misusing the natural environment in trying to cope with the challenges of poverty.

Action on education for sustainability

The role of education in economic and social development has long been recognized. Along with health care, education is seen as the key to individual achievement, which in turn supports the well-being of the community and society. Education for sustainability is prioritized in Agenda 21 and in most of the other international environment and development agreements. Education *about* and *for* the environment are key components of this, through formal education (schools and universities, and training for business and industry) and through informal education (developing public understanding, and community education).

Political will

The last quarter of the twentieth century has seen the growth of international engagement with conservation issues. The growth of international NGOs and the meeting of governments around the globe to consider ways of tackling environmental issues and signing protocols and agreements is a first step, for it is in the actions of governments that real change occurs.

Two important concerns have been identified by environmental and conservation groups, though. Firstly, the actions taken so far are but a first step, perhaps little more than a gesture of goodwill towards conservation issues. As Jeremy Leggett of Greenpeace wrote after the 1992 Earth Summit:

> We have to climb a mountain, and all governments have succeeded in doing here is meander in the foothills having barely established a base camp.

Secondly, it is political decisions at national and international level that will make the biggest change towards global sustainability, yet politics must be seen as 'the art of the possible'. All governments seek to balance their ideologies and beliefs, the pressures from within their own countries to address a full range of social and economic issues, and the need to take actions that will ensure they can retain political power. These provide constraints on action which almost inevitably mean that the hardest decisions are rarely taken quickly, if at all. As Andrew Lees of Friends of the Earth said following the Earth Summit:

> The Earth Summit has exposed the enormous gulf that lies between what the public want and what their leaders are willing to do.

In the late 1990s the reviews of progress five years after Rio demonstrated clearly many of these difficulties. Some governments had made progress in some areas, mainly by setting up working groups, seeking to identify current performance against sustainability indicators, and supporting scientific research in the field of conservation. Others had done little, however, and the commitment to supporting conservation and sustainable development remained as rhetoric and signatures. The Earth Summit +5 meetings also demonstrated that fundamental issues of the relative responsibilities of the countries of the North and South had not really been resolved at all.

In 1992 the team that had produced *Limits to Growth* in 1972 identified a number of conditions that were necessary to underpin future government action towards sustainability. These were:

- developing a vision of the future which involves what they *really* want in terms of sustainability
- developing networks for communication, discussion and action, at every level from local to global;
- committing to telling the truth, using honest and open language, about environmental realities, and neither deceiving themselves or their peoples nor overplaying those realities;
- committing to learning as much as possible, as quickly as possible, about the environment, and sharing that knowledge with all; and
- learning to love the environment and to celebrate both the diversity of humanity and the common ground that joins peoples together around the world.

While these are emotive and emotional aims, which may not sit easily with the traditional views of politics, they may provide a basis for future action.

Think global, act local

The role of the individual is important in conservation and the establishment of sustainability. Global economic activity is simply the sum total of the actions and decisions of individual people. In their roles as consumers, and as members of communities, they contribute to national and world patterns of behaviours and action. A key priority, therefore, is the support of action at grassroots level, whether in village communities in rural China and India or in the most affluent parts of London, Sydney and Washington. Of most importance, is the individual's role in politics – as activist, as lobbyist and as elector. Changing the views of politicians about what the priorities are or should be is probably the key to creating a sustainable society.

Sustainability and the city

Much of the action on sustainability will be carried through in a small part of the Earth's surface – in its cities. The world's people are increasingly living in cities. In 1900 only 15% of the world's people lived in cities. By the beginning of the twenty-first century the figure is 50%, and this will continue to grow to 60% by 2020. Many of these people live in 'mega-cities' with more than 5 million people, of which most are in the LDCs. The world's largest city, Mexico City, has a population in 2000 of almost 26 million. Growth rates of cities in many of the LDCs are over 3% per year as people migrate in from the countryside. Establishing sustainable development depends, therefore, on creating sustainable cities, and much of the effort and resource input towards sustainability will need to be directed at cities. The sustainable city will have a number of characteristics:

- sustainable systems for the provision of food and water and for the disposal of waste;
- transport systems that minimize private car use, and therefore reduce both local air pollution and contributions to greenhouse gases;
- good quality and accessible services such as health care and education;
- a strong commitment from local authorities and business to minimizing waste and pollution and promoting green practices;
- provision of adequate open space and wild areas within the city;

- a commitment to raising the quality of life for citizens, both economically and socially; and
- redevelopment within the city to ensure that both housing and commercial activities are present, thereby reducing commuting.

These issues are becoming political priorities in a number of Western cities, but there is, as yet, little vision in many LDCs of what a sustainable city may be. Achieving the sustainable city in the LDCs is, of course, related to the resolution of many of the environmental and development issues highlighted elsewhere in this book. While the problems sit in the countries of the South, the solutions lie in the hands of the consumers and governments of the North. Creating sustainable cities in the LDCs, therefore, needs to be a political priority in the MDCs, too.

In conclusion

Development, environment, conservation and sustainability are interconnected ideas. Progress in science will help understanding, but progress in politics and economics and in the attitudes of individual people will be what produces lasting change. Our final view is a quote from Chief Seattle of the Susquamish Indians, addressing a meeting of United States congressmen over issues of land rights in the mid-nineteenth century. His view is as true today and will be so in the future.

> There is no quiet place in the white man's cities. No place to hear the unfurling of leaves in the spring or the rustle of insects' wings. And what is there to life if a man cannot hear the lonely cry of the whippoorwills or the argument of the frogs around the pool at night? Whatever befalls the earth befalls the sons of the earth. If men spit on the ground they spit on themselves. This we know – the earth does not belong to man, man belongs to the earth. All things are connected like the blood which connects one family. Man did not weave the web of life; he is merely a strand in it. Whatever he does to the web he does to himself.

APPENDIX 1
CONTACTING
CONSERVATION GROUPS

Addresses

United Kingdom

**British Trust for
Conservation Volunteers
(BTCV)**
36 St Mary's Road
Wallingford
Oxfordshire
OX10 0EU

**Centre for Alternative
Technology**
Llwyngern Quarry
Machynlleth
Powys
SY20 9AZ

Council for National Parks
246 Lavender Hill
London
SW11 1LN

**Council for the Protection of
Rural England**
Warwick House
25 Buckingham Palace Road
London
SW1W 0PP

Countryside Commission
John Dower House
Crescent Place
Cheltenham
GL50 3RA

**Countryside Commission for
Scotland**
Battleby
Redgorton
Perth
PH1 3EW

Earthwatch
57 Woodstock Road
Oxford
OX2 6HJ

English Nature
Northminster House
Peterborough
PE1 1UA

Forestry Commission
231 Corstophine Road
Edinburgh
EH12 7AT

Friends of the Earth
26–28 Underwood Street
London
N1 7JQ

Greenpeace
Canonbury Villas
London
N1 2PN

London Wildlife Trust
80 York Way
London
N1 9AG

Population Concern
231 Tottenham Court Road
London
W1P 9AE

Royal Botanic Gardens
Kew
Richmond
Surrey
TW9 3AB

Royal Society for Nature Conservation
The Green
Witham Park
Waterside South
Lincoln
LN5 2JR

Scottish Wildlife Trust
25 Johnstone Terrace
Edinburgh
EH1 2NH

Transport 2000
3rd Floor
Walkden House
10 Melton Street
London
NW1 2EJ

Ulster Wildlife Trust
Barnett's Cottage
Barnett Demesne
Malone Road
Belfast
BT19 5PB

United Nations Information Centre
20 Buckingham Gate
London
SW1E 6LB

Urban Wildlife Trust
Unit 213, Jubilee Trades Centre
130 Pershore Street
Birmingham
B5 6ND

The Wildfowl and Wetlands Trust
Slimbridge
Gloucestershire
GL2 7BT

Worldwide Fund for Nature (UK)
Panda House
Weyside Park
Godalming
Surrey
GU7 1XR

Australia

Australian Trust for Conservation Volunteers
13 Duke Street
South Caulfield 3162

Department of Conservation and Environment
Information Centre
240 Victoria Parade
East Melbourne 3002

Environment Protection Agency
6th Floor, 477 Collins Street
Melbourne 3000

Friends of the Earth
222 Brunswick Street
Fitzroy 3065

Greenpeace Australia
389 Lonsdale Street
Melbourne 3000

Worldwide Fund for Nature
1st Floor, Ross House
247 Flinders Lane
Melbourne 3000

Canada

Environment Canada
Information Directorate
Ottawa
Ontario
K1A 0H3

New Zealand

New Zealand Natural Heritage Foundation
Massey University
Palmerston North

United States

Earthwatch
PO Box 403
680 Mt Auburn Street
Watertown
MA 02172

Friends of the Earth
218 D Street SE
Washington DC 20003

Greenpeace USA
1436 U Street NW
Washington DC 20009

National Audubon Society
950 Third Avenue
New York
NY 10022

National Wildlife Federation
1400 16th Street NW
Washington DC 20036

Sierra Club
730 Polk Street
San Francisco
CA 94109

United Nations Environment Programme
2 United Nations Plaza
Room DC2–303
New York
NY10017

World Resources Institute
1709 New York Avenue NW
Suite 700, Seventh Floor
Washington DC 20006

Worldwide Fund for Nature
1250 24th Street NW
Suite 400
Washington DC 20037

Internet addresses/websites

African Water Page	http://www.sn.apc.org/afwater/index
Agenda 21 (Global/National)	http://www.nies.go.jp/english/lib-e/agenda-e/agend36.html
Agenda 21 (Local, UK)	http://www.hants.rov.uk/environment/
Amazing Environmental Organisation	http://www.webdirectory.com/
Earthwatch	http://www.uk.earthwatch.org
EcoSchools Manual	http://www.act.gov.au/environ/esml
EcoWeb	http://eco-web.com/index/index
EE-Link (USA)	http://www.nceet.snre.umich.edu/index.html
Envirolink	http://www.envirolink.org/envirohome
Environment Agency (UK)	http://www.environment-agency.gov.uk:80/who.html
Environment Protection Agency (Scotland)	http://www.sepa.org.uk/
Environment Protection Agency (USA)	http://www.epa.gov/epahome/index
European Environment Agency	http://www.eea.dk/
Friends of the Earth	http://www.foe.co.uk;80/index.html
Going for Green	http://www.gfg.iclnet.co.uk
Greenpeace	http://www.greenpeace.org/greenpeace.html
Natural History Museum (UK)	http://www.nhm.ac.uk/education/
Planet Ark	http://www.planetark.org/
Sustainable London	http://www.greenchannel.com/slt/index
Worldwide Fund for Nature (WWF)	http://www.panda.org/home.htm
Worldwide Home Environmentalists Network	http://home.vicnet.net.au/-when/

APPENDIX 2
BIBLIOGRAPHY

Ackerman, E. A. (1959) 'Population and Natural Resources' in Hauser, P. M. and Duncan, E. D. (Eds) 'The Study of Population: An Inventory and Appraisal', Chicago, University of Chicago

Allen, T. and Thomas, A. (Eds) (1992) *Poverty and Development in the 1990s*, Oxford, Oxford University Press

Blowers, A. and Glasbergen, P. (Eds) (1995) *Environmental Policy in an International Context 3 – Prospects*, London, Arnold

Commoner, B. (1971) *The Closing Circle, Nature, Man and Technology,* New York, Knopf

Ehrlich, P. (1968) *The Population Bomb,* New York, Ballantine Books

European Environment Agency (1995) *Environment in the European Union 1995*, Brussels, EEA

Ghai, D. (Ed.) (1994) *Development and Environment – Sustaining People and Nature*, Oxford, Blackwell/UNRISD

Glasbergen, P. and Blowers, A. (Eds) (1995) *Environmental Policy in an International Context 1 – Perspectives*, London, Arnold

Goldsmith, F. B. and Warren, A. (Eds) (1993) *Conservation in Progress*, Chichester, John Wiley & Sons

Hannigan, J. A. (1997) *Environmental Sociology*, London, Routledge

Huckle, J. and Sterling, A. (Eds) (1996) *Education for Sustainability*, London, Earthscan

IUCN/UNEP/WWF (1991) *Caring for the Earth: A Strategy for Sustainable Living*, Gland, Earthscan

Meadows, D. H., Meadows, D. L., Randers, J. and Behrens, W. W. (1972) *The Limits to Growth,* New York, New American Library

McCormick, J. (1995) *The Global Environmental Movement* (2nd Edition), Chichester, John Wiley & Sons

Myers, N. (Ed.) (1994) *The Gaia Atlas of Planet Management* (2nd Edition), London, Gaia Books

O'Riordan, T. (Ed.) (1995) *Environmental Science for Environmental Management*, Harlow, Longman

Palmer, J. and Neal, P. (1994) *The Handbook of Environmental Education*, London, Routledge

Peattie, K. (1992) *Green Marketing*, London, ME Handbooks

Pearce, D. (Ed.) (1990) *Blueprint 1 – Blueprint for a Green Economy*, London, Earthscan

Pearce, D. (Ed.) (1991) *Blueprint 2 – Greening the World Economy*, London, Earthscan

Pearce, D. (Ed.) (1993) *Blueprint 3 – Measuring Sustainable Development*, London, Earthscan

Pepper, D. (1996) *Modern Environmentalism*, London, Routledge

Pickering, K. T. and Owen, L. A. (1994) *An Introduction to Global Environmental Issues*, London, Routledge

Sarre, P. and Blunden, J. (Eds) (1995) *An Overcrowded World? Population, Resources and the Environment*, Oxford, Oxford University Press for the Open University

Simmons, I. G. (1993) *Environmental History: A Concise Introduction*, London, Routledge

Sloep, P. and Blowers, A. (Eds) (1995) *Environmental Policy in an International Context 2 – Conflicts*, London, Arnold

UK Government (1994) *Sustainable Development; the UK Strategy* (Cmd 2426), London, HMSO

Ward, B. and Dubois, R. (1971) *Only One Earth,* Harmondsworth, Penguin

Welford, R. (1995) *Environmental Strategy and Sustainable Development: The Corporate Challenge for the 21st Century*, London, Routledge

Welford, R. (1996) *Corporate Environmental Management – Systems and Strategies*, London, Earthscan

INDEX

acid rain 31, 100–1, 169, 210
Agenda 21 17, 20, 203, 204, 205, 218, 219, 229, 235
aid 28, 33, 34
ALARP principle 185
Antarctica 140–1, 146, 152, 170–1, 178
anthropocentrism 18
Apollo space programme 14
Areas of Outstanding Natural Beauty (AONB) 217
Argentina 32
Aswan Dam 68, 143
Audubon Society 198

Bacon, Francis 9
BATNEEC principle 185–6
Belgrade Charter 211
Bentham, Jeremy 10
Bhopal 15, 169, 223–4
biodiversity 6, 37, 64, 105–8, 124, 126, 128, 141, 179, 203, 204, 217, 222, 233, 234
biomes 59, 61, 63, 69, 70, 105
biosphere reserves 115, 116–19
Bonn Convention 128
Botswana 117
BPEO principle 185, 192
Brandt Report 26, 28
Brazil 32, 84, 99, 162
Brent Spar 12, 227
Bretton Woods Agreement 28
Brown, Lancelot (Capability) 10
Brundtland, Gro Harlem 15, 35, 202, 218
Burkino Faso 34, 84, 227

Carlyle, Thomas 9
Carson, Rachel 13
Chernobyl 5, 15, 98, 169
China 76, 78, 80, 89, 91, 178
climax community 59, 60

Chipko Andalan Movement 228
chlorofluorocarbons (CFCs) 17, 172, 206, 224
CITES 128
Club of Rome 14, 200
coal 88, 91, 94
Commoner, Barry 199
Compassion in World Farming 134
competition 57
conservation 5, 6, 8, 10, 11, 62, 66, 90, 106, 116, 119, 124–36
contingent valuation 38
Cornwall 190–2
cost-benefit analysis (CBA) 39
Council for the Protection of Rural England (CPRE) 216, 217
Council on Environmental Quality 221, 222
Countryside Commission 216

DDT 13
debt 32, 33
Debt for Nature Swaps 33
debtor countries 26
deep ecology 18
demographic transition model 74, 75
Department of the Environment 11, 215
desertification 201
deserts, 57, 65, 68–9, 117, 164
developed countries *see* more developed countries
development 23, 62, 90
development indicator 23, 24, 25
Dobris Agreement 209
dose-response 38
drought 110
Dubois, Rene 200
Dust Bowl 67
dynamic equilibrium 59, 140

ecoauditing 18, 44
Ecocentrism 18
ecolabelling 44
ecology 35, 52
 ecological niche 57, 66
 ecological pyramids 56
 ecological succession 58, 59
ecosystem 52, 57, 60, 62, 67, 105, 108, 113
Egypt 68, 143
Ehrlich, Paul 199
electricity 88, 94, 95, 96
El Niño and the Southern Oscillation (ENSO) 161–2
energy 87–103, 111, 141, 153–4, 157
English Nature 11, 114, 216, 217
environmental
 Environmental Action Programme (EAP) 209
 environmental auditing 188
 environmental economics 36
 environmental impact assessment (EIA) 100, 189–90, 192, 206, 223, 234
 environmental impact statement (EIS) 221
 Environmental Protection Agency 11, 221, 222
Environmentally Sensitive Area (ESA) 217
Ethiopia 42
European Environmental Agency 208
European Union 13, 20, 32, 95, 143, 149–50, 175, 186, 187, 188, 189, 191, 197, 206–10, 217–19
eutrophication 114, 148
Exxon Valdez 16, 92

feedback 58
fishing 142–4
Food and Agricultural Organisation (FAO) *see* United Nations Food and Agricultural Organisation
food webs 54, 140
forestry 37, 95, 116
forests 57, 59, 61, 62–5, 105, 108–12, 129, 132, 204
Friends of the Earth 5, 12, 173, 235
fuelwood 88, 89, 93, 95, 99, 109

Gaia hypothesis 51
Gambia, The 32, 96

gas 88
General Agreement on Trade and Tariffs (GATT) 29
globalization 47, 105, 176
grasslands 65, 124–5, 132
Greenham Common 19, 228
greenhouse effect 16, 100, 110, 152, 169, 174–9, 234
Green
 Green Consumerism 42, 43
 Green Movement 17, 19, 41
 Green Party 19, 229
Greenpeace 5, 173, 225, 227, 235
Group of Eight (G8) 29
gross national product (GNP) 23, 25, 32, 33, 78

habitat 52, 66
Hardin, Garrett 200
health 74, 75, 82, 99, 100, 102, 134–6, 169, 170–2, 224
hedonic pricing 38
high yielding varieties (HYVs) 107
Hong Kong 76
hurricane 16, 30, 152, 159–60, 176, 178, 179, 184

India 76, 80–1, 88, 102, 110, 126, 161, 222–4, 228
infant mortality 25
interdependency 28
Intergovernmental Panel on Climatic Change (IPCC) 175–6, 178, 179
international
 International Chamber of Commerce (ICC) 44, 46
 International Monetary Fund (IMF) 29
 International Seabed Authority 146
 International Union for the Conservation of Nature and Natural Resources (IUCN) *see* World Conservation Union
 International Whaling Commission 144

Jersey 118–19

Kenya 66

less developed countries (LDCs) 22, 28, 30, 32, 33, 34, 43, 73, 75, 78, 79, 81, 82, 83, 84, 95, 96, 102, 109, 111, 173, 200, 201, 204, 212, 223, 227, 233, 238

life cycle analysis (LCA) 187–8
life expectancy 25, 74
Limits to Growth 14, 35, 84, 200, 236
literacy 25
Lovelock, James 51

Malaysia 34, 107
Malthus, Thomas 84–5, 199, 232
management 7
marine ecosystems 69–70, 138–51
maximum sustainable yield 61
Mediterranean 64, 67, 143, 146, 149, 164, 178, 210
Mexico 31, 32, 76, 101, 145, 160, 237
mid-latitude depressions 158–9, 165, 178
Mill, John Stuart 10
monetary appraisal 37
Montreal Protocol 13, 172–3, 201, 209, 222, 224
more developed countries (MDCs) 22, 25, 29, 30, 31, 33, 34, 43, 73, 74, 75, 78, 79, 80, 81, 82, 88, 109, 112, 126, 127, 130, 132, 190, 200, 201, 204, 223, 228, 233

Naess, Arne 18
Narita airport 20
national
   National Environment Policy Act 221
   National Nature Reserves (NNRs) 216
   national parks 10, 11, 66, 112, 114, 115, 116–18, 124–6, 132–3, 215, 216
   National Trust 11, 216
nature 8, 9
Nature Conservancy *see* English Nature
Nepal 32, 93, 97
New Forest 60
Newbury bypass 20
Newlands Reclamation Act 11
newly industrialized countries (NICs) 26, 31
Niger 34
nitrates 5
non-governmental organization (NGO) 11–12, 33, 79, 80, 112, 116, 131, 173, 203, 214, 219, 224, 225–7, 230, 235
Norfolk Broads 60, 112, 113–14
nuclear power 88, 98–9
nutrition 74

Office of Coastal Zone Management (OCZM) 149

Official Development Assistance (ODA) 33
oil 68, 69, 88, 91, 92, 94, 101–2, 145
opportunity costs 38
Organisation for Economic Cooperation and Development (OECD) 29, 33
Organisation of Petroleum Exporting Countries (OPEC) 14, 26, 30, 41, 92
ozone depletion 17, 101, 152, 169, 170–3, 224

Pergau Dam 34
pesticides 13
photosynthesis 53, 54, 55
physical quality of life index (PQLI) 25
plagioclimax 60
polluter pays 16, 39, 207
pollution 31, 38, 40, 65, 69, 78, 100, 101, 113, 114, 146–8, 149, 152, 169, 182, 186, 199, 206, 210, 215, 217, 218, 226
population 73–86, 109, 233
poverty 22, 24, 35, 79, 81, 83, 93, 222, 224, 234
precautionary principle 44, 144, 149, 182–3, 219
predation 54, 57, 58
preservation 6
productivity 56, 57, 113, 141

quality of life 23, 34, 41, 230

radical environmentalism 19
Ramsar Convention 113, 128
recycling 43
renewable energy 96–8
reproduction 54
resources 80–4, 88, 113
respiration 53, 54
restoration 7
Rio de Janeiro 15, 205
   Rio Declaration 17
   Rio Summit 15, 17, 36, 106, 179, 203–5
risk assessment 183–6
romanticism 9, 10
Roosevelt, Theodore 11
Royal Society for the Protection of Birds (RSPB) 12, 198, 226

Sahel 34
Saudi Arabia 33, 83
Sea Surface Temperatures 157, 158, 159, 161

Seers, Dudley 24
Sierra Club 5, 12, 227
Sites of Special Scientific Interest (SSSIs) 115, 216, 217
soil erosion 22, 30, 34, 37, 64, 67, 93, 110, 119–22, 132–3
South Africa 78
Southampton 97, 115
South Downs 60
South Korea 31
standard of living 34, 41
stewardship 9, 14, 108
sustainability 18, 34, 39, 82, 85, 182, 229, 234, 236–8
sustainable development 7, 14, 15, 34, 35, 36, 44, 202, 203, 208, 218–20, 233
systems 53

Taiwan 31, 98, 130
Tanzania 66
technocentrism 18, 19
third world 26
tiger economies 25
tornado 160
Torrey Canyon 16
tourism 31, 66, 67, 113, 116, 117, 120, 125, 133, 144, 149, 178
tragedy of the commons *see* Hardin, Garrett
trophic level 55
tundra 69, 165
Turkey 31

United Nations (UN) 12, 29, 33, 35, 75, 198
  UN Commission on Sustainable Development 203
  UN Conference on the Human Environment 15, 200–1
  UN Conference on the Laws of the Sea (UNCLOS) 145, 148
  UN Educational, Scientific and Cultural Organisation (UNESCO) 198, 211
  UN Environment Programme (UNEP) 106, 171, 197, 201, 205
  UN Food and Agricultural Organisation (FAO) 13, 127, 142, 198
  UN Human Development Report 25
  UN Population Fund (UNFPA) 73
  UN World Commission on Environment and Development (WCED) 15, 35, 202–3
USA 83, 84, 91, 95, 97, 98, 101, 112, 117–18, 127, 136, 147, 148–9, 160, 162, 175, 189, 198, 220–2, 226, 230
utilitarianism 10

Ward, Barbara 200
waste 45, 68, 69, 78, 94–5, 146, 148, 185, 191, 206, 218
West Indies 31
wetlands 6, 108, 112–15, 227
wilderness 9, 38, 117
World
  World Bank 29, 32, 226
  World Climatic Research Programme 161
  World Conservation Strategy (WCS) 15, 106, 115, 201–2
  World Conservation Union 13, 15, 130, 131, 198
  World Industry Conference on Environmental Management (WICEM) 36, 44
  World Meteorological Organisation (WMO) 13, 161, 171, 173
  Worldwide Fund for Nature (WWF) 12, 106, 112
  World Wildlife Fund *see* Worldwide Fund for Nature (WWF)

yield 61, 62

Zambia 66, 125
Zimbabwe 132–3
zoos 124, 126, 131